MEETING HOUSE AND
COUNTING HOUSE

MEETING HOUSE

And Counting House

THE QUAKER MERCHANTS
OF COLONIAL PHILADELPHIA

1682-1763

BY

FREDERICK B. TOLLES

W · W · NORTON & COMPANY

New York · London

W. W. Norton & Company, Inc., 500 Fifth Avenue, New York, N.Y. 10110
W. W. Norton & Company Ltd., 37 Great Russell Street, London WC1B 3NU

ISBN 0-393-00211-X

PRINTED IN THE UNITED STATES OF AMERICA
7 8 9

FOR ELIZABETH

THE Society of Friends, as Rufus M. Jones has observed, has always tended to produce two distinct types. There has been, on the one hand, a small body of individuals unreservedly committed to the ideal, to whom compromise has been out of the question. "If obedience to the soul's vision involves eye or hand, houses or lands or life, they must be immediately surrendered." On the other hand, there have been those—a somewhat larger number—"who have held it to be equally imperative to work out their principles of life in the complex affairs of the community and the state, where to gain an end one must yield something; where to get on one must submit to existing conditions; and where to achieve ultimate triumph one must risk his ideals to the tender mercies of a world not yet ripe for them."

The attention and admiration of the world has been focused mainly upon the first group—the prophets, martyrs, and saints of the company of George Fox, Mary Dyer, John Woolman, and the young William Penn imprisoned in the Tower of London for conscience' sake. This study by contrast is devoted to a group of Friends of less heroic and saintly mould, who, following the lead of the older William Penn, chose the second path, casting their lot in the world as they found it and endeavoring by earthly means to make it over into as close a replica of the Kingdom of God as possible. It seeks to understand the mutual interaction of religion and life among the Quaker founders of Philadelphia and their successor generations down to the eve of the Revolution.

An indispensable tool for the building of their New Jerusalem on the banks of the Delaware was the so-called "Protestant ethic" which the Quakers brought in modified form from their Puritan background. With its help they wrought handsome fortunes out of the wilderness to which Penn had led them. Hence the hoary jibe (from which I have drawn my title) that the Philadelphia Quakers had one foot in the meeting house and the other in the counting house. The pleasantry is not without its measure of truth, although it overlooks the correlative truth that these "God-fearing, money-making people" were quick to give of their substance to their less fortunate brothers. It also fails to do justice to the undeniable fact that the members of Philadelphia Meeting hardly spent more time in the counting house than they did in the State House, the Court House, and the cultural and humanitarian centers of the city—the American Philosophical Society, the Library Company, and the Pennsylvania Hospital. It is with all these facets of their lives—one cannot call them secular for the Quakers recognized no dividing-line between the religious and the mundane—that we shall be concerned in this book.

In directing my attention to the relatively unexplored everyday aspects of the economic, social, and intellectual life of the Quaker merchants between 1682 and 1763, I would ascertain what happened to a religious group of predominantly lower-class sectarian origins with a pronounced mystical and perfectionist outlook in the presence of material prosperity, social prestige, and political power. If my conclusions seem pessimistic, I would point out that they but document the sense of failure which many of the more sensitive Friends felt in 1756 when they turned their backs upon the "world" in whose affairs they had played such a prominent role for nearly fourscore years. Nevertheless, despite my preoccupation with the developments which led to the ultimate frustration of the "holy experiment," I would not have anyone conclude that I underestimate for a moment the positive contributions which the Quaker merchants made to the humanizing and enriching of American life. If I have seemed to slight these contributions, it is because they lay outside the province of this book or because they have already been adequately dealt with by other hands.

Thus the experience of the Quakers in provincial politics and in dealing with the Indians has merely been sketched in; there is need for a thoroughgoing reassessment of that experience, but I have not considered it part of my task in the present book to fill this need. The contributions of the Philadelphia Quakers to education and to the movement for the abolition of slavery have been discussed only incidentally in these pages because they have received considerable attention from other writers. My dominant purpose, to repeat, has been to study the interaction of religion and life among the colonial Quakers, and I have chosen to give particular attention to those aspects of life which historians have hitherto slighted.

The writings of William Penn are quoted in my text with what may seem undue frequency in the light of the fact that Penn actually spent less than four years on this side of the Atlantic. My excuse for this is threefold. In the first place, Quaker thinking on most subjects varied relatively little from place to place, so that the ideas of English and American Friends down at least to the Revolution can be regarded as practically interchangeable. In the second place, Penn was by far the most articulate and quotable of all the early Friends on many of the questions of individual and social ethics with which we shall be concerned. Finally, insofar as there were differences of opinion among Friends relative to participation in the affairs of the "world," the Philadelphia Quaker merchants deliberately followed the lead of Pennsylvania's founder. In a real sense, the experience of the merchants represents the working out, for better or worse, of many of the ideas for which William Penn stood.

For permission to quote from manuscripts in their collections I am indebted to the following libraries and depositories: The Historical Society of Pennsylvania, 1300 Locust Street, Philadelphia; The Library Company of Philadelphia, Broad and Christian Streets, Philadelphia; The Department of Records of

Philadelphia Yearly Meeting, 302 Arch Street, Philadelphia; The Harvard University Library, Cambridge, Massachusetts; The Quaker Collection of the Haverford College Library, Haverford, Pennsylvania; and the Friends Historical Library of Swarthmore College, Swarthmore, Pennsylvania.

Here I should like also to acknowledge with gratitude the assistance given me by many fellow librarians, especially E. Virginia Walker and Dorothy G. Harris of the Friends Historical Library of Swarthmore College; Thomas E. Drake and Anna B. Hewitt of the Quaker Collection of the Haverford College Library; J. Harcourt Givens and Catherine Miller of the Historical Society of Pennsylvania; the late J. Henry Bartlett and Eleanor Melson of the Department of Records of Philadelphia Yearly Meeting; May Morris and James W. Phillips of the Dickinson College Library; Barney Chesnick of the Library Company of Philadelphia; and John H. Powell of the Free Library of Philadelphia.

Nor can I omit to mention the heavy debt which I feel to certain of my elders and betters in the historical profession who read part or all of my manuscript and gave me the benefit of their wisdom and scholarship: Arthur M. Schlesinger, Perry Miller, Howard Mumford Jones, I. Bernard Cohen, and Henry J. Cadbury, all of Harvard University.

To the Institute of Early American History and Culture I am beholden not only for making publication possible but also for a grant which enabled me to spend the summer of 1947 revising the manuscript. Carl Bridenbaugh, Director, and Lester J. Cappon, Research Editor, have been particularly sympathetic and helpful.

There is one person to whose help I owe much more than I can say here. She deserves (and has) a whole page in this book to herself.

F. B. T.

CONTENTS

xi

ILLUSTRATIONS

BETWEEN PAGES 62-63

JOHN REYNELL, TYPICAL QUAKER MERCHANT OF PRE-REVOLUTION-ARY PHILADELPHIA. *Silhouette*
Courtesy of the Historical Society of Pennsylvania

JAMES LOGAN. *Portrait by Gustavus Hesselius*
Courtesy of the Historical Society of Pennsylvania

MARY LLOYD NORRIS. *Portrait by Sir Godfrey Kneller* (?)
Courtesy of the Free Library of Philadelphia

ISAAC NORRIS II. *Copy of portrait by an unknown artist*
Courtesy of the Historical Society of Pennsylvania

SARAH LOGAN NORRIS. *Portrait by an unknown artist*
Courtesy of Albert Cook Myers

JOHN SMITH. *Silhouette*
Courtesy of the Historical Society of Pennsylvania

HENRY DRINKER. *Silhouette*
Courtesy of Henry S. Drinker, Esq.

DR. SAMUEL PRESTON MOORE. *Silhouette*
Courtesy of the Historical Society of Pennsylvania

JAMES PEMBERTON. *Silhouette*
Courtesy of the Historical Society of Pennsylvania

MEETING HOUSE AND

COUNTING HOUSE

"There are another sort of persons, not only fit for, but necessary in Plantations, and that is, Men of universal Spirits, that have an eye to the Good of Posterity, and that both understand and delight to promote good Discipline and just Government among a plain and well intending people; such persons may find Room in Colonies for their good Counsel and Contrivance, who are shut out from being of much use or service to great nations under settl'd Customs."

WILLIAM PENN
Some Account of the Province of Pennsilvania

"Where late the Wolves and Bears in plenty b[red]
Now Flocks and Herds of useful Kind are fed.
And on the Banks of Del'ware's Crystal flood,
Where shading Oaks, and lofty Cypress stood,
A Spacious City soon was seen to rise,
That fill'd Beholders with a just Surprize:
Where by the Wharves, or floating in the Tide
A numerous Fleet of Top Sail Vessels ride.
In Space so short, few Cities have been known
That might with her Magnificence have shown,
But now Alas how shall my feeble Quill
In Prose or Verse some slender pages fill
In pointing out, among the many Crimes,
A part so obvious in these latter times.
All Flesh is Grass, an awful Herald cries,
All Flesh is Grass, a solemn Voice replies
Today 'tis fresh, is flourishing and gay,
The Morrow cut and shrivel'd into Hay:
Carnation now the flower, or deck'd with Gold,
Now drop'd in dust and mix'd with common Mould.
So Mortal Man when he aspires too high,
Ere yet he learns to live, is taught that he must die."

JOSEPH WHITE
The Little Looking Glass New Fram'd and Enlarg'd

· *Chapter One* ·

THE TWO PLANTATIONS

A s the first Quaker colonists set sail for Pennsylvania in 1682, they carried with them sober words of advice and caution from George Fox, founder of the Society of Friends: "My friends, that are gone, and are going over to plant, and make outward plantations in America, keep your own plantations in your hearts, with the spirit and power of God, that your own vines and lilies be not hurt."[1] For three-quarters of a century, these Quakers and their sons labored in the outward plantation. Superimposing a gridiron pattern of streets upon the wilderness between the Delaware and the Schuylkill, they created a city of red-brick houses and shops that was eventually to become the capital of a new nation. Building their wharves out into the Delaware and dispatching their ships all over the western world, they developed a commerce that became the envy of the older American ports. Ruling their province with benevolent paternalism and keeping the peace with their Indian neighbors, they enjoyed and enabled others to enjoy a calm and comfortable prosperity such as few regions of the earth have ever known for so long a period.

But amid the unexampled flourishing of the outward plantation, what happened to the delicate plants of the inner life?

---

1. *An Epistle to All Planters, and Such Who Are Transporting Themselves into Foreign Plantations in America, &c.* (1682), in *The Works of George Fox*, VIII, 218.

3

In 1756, as the "holy experiment" was drawing to a close, Samuel Fothergill, a spiritual heir of George Fox, felt obliged to utter this judgment upon the descendants of the Quaker pioneers:

Their fathers came into the country, and bought large tracts of land for a trifle; their sons found large estates come into their possession, and a profession of religion which was partly national, which descended like a patrimony from their fathers, and cost as little. They settled in ease and affluence, and whilst they made the barren wilderness as a fruitful field, suffered the plantation of God to be as a field uncultivated, and a desert. . . . A people who had thus beat their swords into plough-shares, with the bent of their spirits to this world, could not instruct their offspring in those statutes they had themselves forgotten.[2]

The social history of Philadelphia Quakerism in the colonial period is thus a record of two plantations—the inward and the outward; and their interrelationship provides a basis for evaluating the results of the "holy experiment."

THE PLANTATION WITHIN

Intensive cultivation of the inward plantation was the distinguishing feature of seventeenth-century Quakerism. For the early Friends the central truth of religion was the indwelling Spirit of God, the immanent Word of Light and Life in the hearts of men. Many a restless seeker in Commonwealth England found satisfaction and peace, as George Fox did, by turning to the Inner Light. "That which People had been vainly seeking Without, with much Pain and Cost," wrote William Penn, "they by this Ministry, found Within. . . . *For they were directed to the Light of Jesus Christ Within them, as the Seed and Leaven of the Kingdom of God . . . a Faithful and True Witness, and just Monitor in every Bosom.*"[3]

For the Quaker the source of religious authority was not, as it was for the Puritan and most other Protestants, the outward

2. Samuel Fothergill to James Wilson, 9 Nov. 1756, George Crosfield, *Memoirs of the Life and Gospel Labours of Samuel Fothergill*, 281-82.
3. *A Brief Account of the Rise and Progress of the People, Call'd Quakers* (1694), in *A Collection of the Works of William Penn*, I, 865 (italics in original). Hereafter cited as *Works*.

word, revealed in the Scriptures, nor did it reside in the hierarchy of an infallible Church. The Quaker regarded the Scriptures as *"a Declaration of the Fountain, and not the Fountain it self"*; therefore, he concluded, *"they are not to be esteemed the principal Ground of all Truth and Knowledge, nor yet the Adequate Primary Rule of Faith and Manners,"* but rather *"a secondary Rule, subordinate to the Spirit, from which they have all their Excellency and Certainty."* [4] In their testimony against a "hireling clergy" the Friends literally put into practice the Reformation slogan of "the priesthood of all believers," for they recognized no distinction between clergy and laity so far as access to religious truth was concerned. Indeed they may be said to have abolished the laity, making all men bearers of the inward Word. Thus Quakerism, though rising out of the Puritan environment of Commonwealth England and betraying many marks of its origin, was nevertheless in some respects neither Protestant nor Catholic, but a *tertium quid,* suspect in the eyes of Puritan and Anglican alike. In its complete reliance upon the Spirit of God manifested in the soul of every man, Quakerism revealed itself as one of the varieties of mystical religion.

The typical experience of the early Quaker was, however, no Nirvanic contemplation, no *via negativa* leading to ecstatic absorption in the Godhead. The religious temper of primitive Quakerism was not mysticism in the classical sense, but rather what contemporaries in fear and scorn called "enthusiasm." It was activism, not quietism. In their religious experience George Fox and his compeers had more in common with the Hebrew prophets than with the great mystics of the Church. There was a strong prophetic strain in the preaching of the early Quakers. They traveled about England in the power of the Spirit, calling men off from the sins and vanities of the world, exhorting them to be faithful to the Inward Light of Christ. In their insistent

---

4. Robert Barclay, *An Apology for the True Christian Divinity* (1680), Proposition III, in *Truth Triumphant, through the Spiritual Warfare, Christian Labours, and Writings of that Able and Faithful Servant of Jesus Christ, Robert Barclay,* II, 67. Hereafter cited as *Writings.*

dwelling upon the moral demands of the Christian religion, they yielded nothing to Puritan prophets of righteousness.

Indeed the early Friends went beyond their Puritan contemporaries in this respect. They were frankly perfectionist in their ethical teaching. They insisted that the Holy Spirit enabled men to overcome the disabilities of the body of sin and death and to live in accordance with the injunctions of the Sermon on the Mount, not in a future Kingdom of Heaven but here and now in this world of flesh and blood. "Now was I come up in Spirit through the flaming sword into the paradise of God," wrote George Fox. "All things were new; and all the creation gave another smell unto me than before, beyond what words can utter. I knew nothing but pureness, and innocency, and righteousness, being renewed into the image of God by Christ Jesus to the state of Adam, which he was in before he fell."[5]

The possibility of turning to the Light and thereby entering upon a state of sinless perfection was not limited to a small body of the elect. There was "that of God" in every man, Jew or Gentile, bond or free; and Friends often quoted the words of John: "That was the true light which lighteth every man that cometh into the world." The Friends of the first generation took literally the universalistic implications of their faith and set out to bring the whole world to the inward teacher, not overlooking the Pope and the Grand Turk. It was only later, when the pristine evangelical ardor had cooled, that the Society of Friends abandoned its global outreach and concentrated upon perfecting the spiritual life of a "peculiar people."

The religious faith of the Quaker immigrants to Pennsylvania thus represented an equilibrium of four elements—mysticism, prophetism, perfectionism, and universalism. These four strains, each with its peculiar spiritual dynamic, mingled to produce a religious compound of extraordinary potency. By virtue of this equilibrium and of the organizing genius of its founder, Quakerism achieved a stability and survival power not given to most of the other sects of Commonwealth England.

---

5. *Journal of George Fox* (Bi-Centenary Edition: London, 1891), I, 28.

The Quakerism of the immigrants is misconstrued, however, if it is regarded as rampant individualism or anarchism in religion. Since the God from whom each private revelation came was forever *one*, there could be no final disharmony between the light vouchsafed to one individual and that of any other truly enlightened person, including the prophets and apostles who recorded their revelations in the Bible. Moreover, the Spirit of God as experienced in corporate worship was felt as a unifying power, binding the worshippers together in love and unity. When Robert Barclay, the Scotch apologist of Quakerism, first entered one of the "*silent Assemblies* of God's People," he recalled, he felt a secret power among them which touched his heart, and he became "knit and united unto them, hungering more and more after the Increase of this Power and Life."[6] So far did Friends carry their conviction that God revealed himself to groups that in their monthly, quarterly, and yearly meetings for discipline they acted always in accordance with the "sense of the meeting" as gathered by a clerk; the corporate judgment thus reached was regarded as having greater validity than the often imperfect and clouded light of an individual. This strong sense of community, arising in the first instance out of the common experience of the divine presence, and fostered by persecution, which drove Friends in upon themselves, offset the centrifugal tendencies inherent in the doctrine of the Inner Light, and substituted an organic social theory for one that might otherwise have been wholly atomistic. For the Quakers who settled Pennsylvania, the solidarity generated by the intangible but deeply felt presence of the Spirit was as real and as effectual as that represented by the outward covenants of the Puritans. As with the Mennonites and other groups in the Anabaptist tradition, however, there was an exclusive aspect to the "holy community" which presently came to overshadow the sense of world mission.

Certain practical corollaries of the basic Quaker beliefs, manifested in the form of social "testimonies," were integral parts of the way of life which the immigrants transplanted to

---

6. *Apology*, Prop. XI, sec. vii, *Writings*, II, 357.

Pennsylvania. All of these "testimonies" can be understood as practical expressions of three Quaker principles: equality, simplicity, and peace.

Because Friends believed that God imparted a measure of his Spirit to all men, regardless of race, sex, or class, it followed that all men and women were equal in his sight and must be treated as equals by their fellow men. This principle lay behind their use of the "plain language": Friends felt constrained to say *thou* to all persons, whatever their social station, because the pronoun *you* in the seventeenth century connoted social superiority. The same principle led Friends to testify against all flattering titles of address, all bowing and scraping, and uncovering the head in the presence of superiors. It led them to give women a place of equal responsibility and honor in their meetings for worship and business, and to minister tenderly to the needs of the poor and unfortunate both within their own membership and in the world at large. As they came to realize the implications of this basic tenet for their relations with other races, they were to lead the attack upon Negro slavery and to treat the American Indians with the same respect which white men were accustomed to use in their dealings with one another.

The "simplicity of Truth" dictated not only plain dress but plain living and simple integrity in all human relationships. Useless ornaments and ostentatious superfluities that served only to please the "creaturely" mind were banished from Quaker costume, furniture, meeting houses, and dwellings. Since judicial oaths (in addition to being expressly forbidden in the Gospels) implied a double standard of truth-telling, simplicity and integrity demanded that Friends refuse to use them, even at the cost of fines and imprisonment. Quaker merchants appear to have initiated the practice of setting fixed prices on merchandise in order to avoid the insincerities inseparable from the prevailing custom of haggling, in which the buyer offered less than he expected to pay and the seller demanded more than the article was worth.

Music, the fine arts, belles-lettres, and the theater, since they served no immediate practical or edifying purpose but seemed rather to be useless and sometimes dangerous adornments of life, were suspect in Quaker eyes. "*Plays, Parks, Balls, Treats, Romances, Musicks, Love-Sonnets*, and the like," wrote William Penn in *No Cross No Crown*, "will be a very invalid Plea, for any other Purpose than their *Condemnation*, who are taken, and delighted with them, *at the Revelation of the righteous Judgment of God*."[7] In their rigoristic rejection of the arts and graces of life, the early Quakers were more "puritanical" than the Puritans themselves.

From the beginning, Friends recognized the inconsistency of warfare with the perfectionist ethic of the New Testament and the law of love revealed within their hearts. "Dwelling in the light," wrote George Fox, "it takes away the occasion of wars, and gathers our hearts together to God, and unto one another, and brings to the beginning, before wars were."[8] Accordingly, they refused military service and dissociated themselves from all violent methods of social control and social change. In due time, their pacifism was to be extended into the fields of prison reform and the care of the mentally ill, where they were to pioneer in non-violent methods of treatment and rehabilitation. Their own bitter experience of persecution in Restoration England having intensified their conviction that conscience ought not to be coerced, they were thorough and consistent exponents of religious toleration.

In their peace testimony, as in their strong sense of community, the Friends resembled the Mennonites and other sects in the Anabaptist tradition. Identifying divine law primarily with the Sermon on the Mount, they regarded its ethic of love and non-resistance as literally binding upon them as followers of Christ and dwellers in the Light. With this Anabaptist position, however, they combined the essentially Calvinistic conviction that religion must be integrated with life on the natural plane; in other words, they recognized no cleavage between the spheres of

---

7. *Works*, I, 356.
8. *Works*, IV, 43. Note the emphasis upon community and upon a state of perfection like that of Adam before the fall.

divine and natural law.[9] Unwilling at this stage to withdraw, Mennonite-fashion, behind protecting walls thrown up around the *Gemeinschaft*, Quakers participated actively in politics wherever they were not disqualified by law or excluded by popular prejudice. In 1682 William Penn expressed the conviction that government was "a part of religion itself, a thing sacred in its institution and end."[10] For the early Quaker there was but one morality for the individual and for the state, and that was dictated by the uncompromising demands of the Gospel. During seventy-five years of Quaker rule in Pennsylvania this faith in the practical applicability of the Sermon on the Mount to the governing of men was to be subject to severe tensions. Nevertheless in 1757, when the Friends had been driven from the government, Anthony Benezet could still insist that "there is no distinction in Christianity between civil and religious matters; we are to be pure, holy, undefiled in all manner of conversation."[11]

In a Quaker commonwealth, Penn believed, there would be slight need for "coercive or compulsive means."

They weakly err [he wrote in his Frame of Government] that think there is no other use of government than correction, which is the coarsest part of it: daily experience tells us, that the care and regulation of many other affairs more soft and daily necessary, make up much the greatest part of government; and which must have followed the peopling of the world, had Adam never fell, and will continue among men on earth under the highest attainments they may arrive at, by the coming of the blessed second Adam, the Lord from Heaven.[12]

A land peopled largely by Friends, brought by the Spirit into a state of perfection like that of Adam before the fall, would thus become a second Eden. The coercive functions of the state could

9. See Ernst Troeltsch, *The Social Teaching of the Christian Churches,* trans. by Olive Wyon, 780-84; also Guy F. Hershberger, "The Pennsylvania Quaker Experiment in Politics, 1682-1756," *Mennonite Quarterly Review,* 10 (1936), 187-221.
10. Preface to the first Frame of Government, *Charter to William Penn and Laws of the Province of Pennsylvania* (Harrisburg, 1879), 92.
11. Letter to John Smith, 13 Dec. 1757, in George S. Brookes, *Friend Anthony Benezet,* 225.
12. *Charter to William Penn,* 92.

be expected to wither away from disuse, and a "holy community" of love and peace under the sway of God's Spirit would come into being on the banks of the Delaware. The environment indeed was fit to be the seat of the new Eden: "The Country itself," observed William Penn with characteristic Quaker understatement, "in its *Soil, Air, Water, Seasons and Produce*, both Natural and Artificial, is not to be despised."[13] With George Fox's advice—"keep your own plantations in your hearts, with the spirit and power of God"—still sounding in their ears, the Quakers set to work, building up the outward plantation. The lurking danger, as Fox had warned, was that in such a favoring material environment, the rank growth of earthly prosperity and power might choke out the tender vines and lilies of the inner life.

"AN HOLY EXPERIMENT"

The instruments of political power were in Quaker hands from the beginning in Pennsylvania. The manner in which they were wielded was conditioned by three important factors: the Quaker faith, including the testimony for peace; the Founder's Whig philosophy, enshrined in his successive frames of government and perpetuated by the Quaker ruling class; and the geographical situation of Pennsylvania as a principal theater of growing Anglo-French imperial rivalries. The first two factors remained fairly constant throughout the colonial period, suffering only minor modifications; the third became more important as time passed, and finally produced an impasse from which there was no escape except through the liquidation of William Penn's "holy experiment." With these basic factors in mind, we may trace the course of the Quaker experiment in government, dividing it, for convenience's sake, into four equal periods of approximately two decades each.[14]

---

13. *Letter from William Penn to the Committee of the Free Society of Traders* (1683), reprinted in Albert Cook Myers, ed., *Narratives of Early Pennsylvania, West New Jersey, and Delaware*, 225.

14. It is outside the purpose of this book to present a detailed history of Quaker government in Pennsylvania. Only a bare outline is therefore given as a backdrop against which the social and cultural life of the Quaker merchants can be projected.

The first two decades, from the founding of the colony in 1682 to the granting of the Charter of Privileges in 1701, were the only years of undisputed Quaker hegemony in Pennsylvania. The great majority of inhabitants were Friends, and except for the two years of royal control between 1692 and 1694, Quaker rule was not challenged by any substantial non-Quaker interest. It is said that during this period the custom prevailed for the Assemblymen "to sit in silence awhile like solemn worship, before they proceeded to do business."[15] The public business, however, was conducted in anything but the spirit of a Quaker meeting. Hardly had William Penn sailed for England in 1684 after his first visit to the colony when the struggle for power between rival interests began. The Assembly, composed of Quaker merchants and farmers, contended vigorously and vociferously with the Council, likewise composed of Quaker merchants and farmers, for its rights and privileges. If the two legislative bodies acted in concert, it was usually to oppose the Proprietary interest represented by the Deputy-Governor. This incessant wrangling and jockeying for position caused the harassed Proprietor to cry out: "For the love of God, me, and the poor country, be not so *governmentish.*"[16]

If Penn the Proprietor found himself vexed by the strife of parties jealous for their rights and privileges, he could thank Penn the Whig publicist. In 1687, desirous, as he said, that all Pennsylvanians should understand their "inestimable inheritance" as freeborn Englishmen, he caused to be printed in Philadelphia a copy of Magna Charta, Edward I's Confirmation of the Charters, the statute *De tallagio non concedendo*, and other related documents, together with an abstract of his patent from the King and his Frame of Government. He explained in a preface that he was publishing these documents in order that "it may raise up noble resolutions in all the Freeholders . . . not to give away anything of Liberty and Property that at present they do, (or of right as loyal English subjects ought to) enjoy, but take up the

---

15. *An Account of the Gospel Labours, and Christian Experiences of a Faithful Minister of Christ, John Churchman* (Philadelphia, 1780), 94.
16. Samuel M. Janney, *The Life of William Penn*, 277.

good example of our ancestors, and understand that it is easy to part with or give away great privileges, but hard to be gained if once lost."[17] This was the strong meat of Whig doctrine and some of his colonists, as we shall see, were to learn their lesson too well!

There is no doubt of Penn's genuine devotion to the principles of Whiggism. In the critical elections of 1679 he had worked actively on behalf of Algernon Sidney, writing a forceful statement of Whig objectives called *England's Great Interest in the Choice of This New Parliament*, in which he laid stress upon three fundamental rights of Englishmen: property ("that is, Right and Title to your own Lives, Liberties and Estates"), representative government, and trial by jury.[18] A few years later he was instrumental in securing pardons from James II for such prominent Whigs as John Trenchard and John Locke.[19] Although it is not true, as some have tried to maintain, that Penn's political philosophy was derived directly from Sidney and Locke, it cannot be denied that in the main his views harmonized with the most advanced political thought of his day. It was as a Whig and a Dissenter, who had felt the heavy hand of royal absolutism, that he laid down the basic principles upon which Pennsylvania was founded: "as my understanding and inclination," he wrote in 1681, "have been much directed to observe and reprove mischiefs in government, so it is now put into my power to settle one. For the matters of liberty and privilege, I propose that which is extraordinary, and to leave myself and successors no power of doing mischief, that the will of one man may not hinder the good of the whole country."[20] The next two decades were to bring into bold relief the inevitable conflict between the principles of a sincere Whig and the interests and responsibilities of the Proprietor of a vast semi-feudal barony.

---

17. "To the Reader," *The Excellent Privilege of Liberty and Property Being the Birth-right of the Free-born Subjects of England* (reprinted, Philadelphia, 1897), 5-6.
18. *Works*, II, 679. This pamphlet has been called "one of the first clear statements of party doctrine ever put before the English electorate."—David Ogg, *England in the Reign of Charles II* (Oxford, 1934), II, 586.
19. Janney, 300-7; William I. Hull, *William Penn: A Topical Biography*, 246.
20. Letter to Robert Turner *et al.*, 12 Apr. 1681, in Janney, 172.

That the Quaker settlers of Pennsylvania were imbued with the Whig philosophy of government and were ready to turn it against the Proprietor and his deputies soon became clear. Their attitude was effectively dramatized by Samuel Richardson, a wealthy merchant and member of the Council, who upon the arrival of Governor John Blackwell in 1688 heatedly denied Penn's power to appoint a governor and on being ordered out of the room, stood his ground, protesting, "I will not withdraw, I was not brought hether by Thee, and I will not goe out by thy order; I was sent by the people, and thou hast no power to put me out."[21] In 1693, during the interlude of royal control, the man who was to be the most persistent and jealous guardian of the people's prerogatives first entered the legislature. David Lloyd (ca. 1656-1731), who was to serve for many years as Speaker of the Assembly, led a united Quaker bloc against Governor Fletcher, who represented the authority of the crown. No sooner had the province been returned to the Quaker Proprietor than the Assembly was demanding a new frame of government, which Penn's Deputy-Governor, William Markham, was forced to grant. Under this new constitution the Assembly was given the right, for which it had long contended, of initiating legislation; it was also accorded the privilege of sitting on its own adjournment. In thus successfully asserting their control over the government, the Quaker legislators were simply carrying forward at the Proprietor's expense the Whig principles of liberty and representative government which they had brought from England and which the Proprietor himself had been at pains to keep alive in their breasts.

From the day of Penn's second departure in 1701 until his death in 1718, Pennsylvania politics continued to be characterized by turmoil and party strife. At the very beginning of the period, the Yearly Meeting, speaking as the official voice of the Society of Friends in Pennsylvania and New Jersey, was obliged to reprove this spirit of faction as a scandal to the profession of Truth: some Friends, it declared disapprovingly, "have by their

---

21. *Minutes of the Provincial Council,* I, 244.

Seditious Words, Insinuations, and Practices, disquieted the Minds of others, to the making of Parties and Disturbances: and some under the Fair Colours of Law and Priviledges, have promoted their Sinister Ends, when indeed it was but to take Vengeance, against those whom they had taken disgust against. . . ."[22] As two major parties assumed definite form, their social basis became clearly apparent. Both were Quaker parties and both sincerely professed allegiance to the principles of Whiggism, but the familiar political process of fission was taking place. Friends were dividing into a radical "country party," led by the brilliant and somewhat unscrupulous lawyer David Lloyd, and a conservative party dominated by city merchants under the leadership of the Proprietor's secretary, James Logan (1674-1751). A third party, composed chiefly of Anglicans, was beginning to emerge, but it was overshadowed by the two Quaker factions and was not to figure importantly in Pennsylvania politics for several decades to come.

The key to the political struggles of this period lies in the contrasting personalities and philosophies of the two major protagonists. Unfortunately the character and motives of David Lloyd present something of a puzzle. He has been hailed as a pioneer proponent of radical democracy and reviled as a demagogue and party boss. But whatever his deficiencies in character, there is no question that he and those Quaker farmers who rallied behind him represented the more extreme wing of the movement which in England had culminated in the Glorious Revolution of 1688. In a "Vindication of the Legislative Power," submitted to the Assembly of which he was Speaker, Lloyd gave expression to his faith in the common man and his distrust of the mercantile aristocrats with whom we shall be concerned in this book: "according to my Experience," he wrote, "a mean Man of small Interest, devoted to the faithful Discharge of his Trust and Duty to the Government, may do more Good to the State

22. Manuscript Minutes of Philadelphia Yearly Meeting, I, 87, Department of Records, Philadelphia Yearly Meeting, 302 Arch Street, Philadelphia. Hereafter cited as MS Minutes of Phila. YM.

than a richer or more learned Man, who, by his ill Temper, and aspiring Mind, becomes an Opposer of the Constitution by which he should act."[23]

The Logan party, on the other hand, which dominated the Council and sometimes controlled a majority in the Assembly, was composed largely of substantial Quaker merchants and landed proprietors; and Logan, its chief spokesman, frequently complained with ill-concealed petulance of the "mobbish" people who "think privileges their due and all that can be grasped to be their native right."[24] Isaac Norris (1671-1735), Logan's principal adjutant, found it prudent never to say anything which the popular party might construe as an attempt "to abridge Libertys and priviledges," but being at a safe distance in London, he ventured the revealing observation that the policies of that faction were obnoxious because they might prove "pernicious to the growth and freedom of trade."[25] In Isaac Norris spoke the voice of the Quaker merchant class of Philadelphia. One can say, then, without undue oversimplification that in the first two decades of the eighteenth century, two Quaker parties arose in Pennsylvania, drawing their strength respectively from the country and the city, and that between them they divided the Whig heritage, the one cherishing liberty above all things, and the other, property.

The major issue of the period arose over the nature of the judiciary. The Assembly, controlled by Lloyd, preferred a decentralized system in which the county courts would be vested with virtually independent jurisdiction, and the Governor and Council insisted that *they* should constitute the court of equity for the whole province and that the Supreme Court should have full common-law jurisdiction throughout the colony. In the

---

23. *Votes and Proceedings of the House of Representatives of the Province of Pennsylvania*, in *Pennsylvania Archives*, 8th Ser., II, 1687.
24. Letter to William Penn, 14 July 1704, Edward Armstrong, ed., *Correspondence between William Penn and James Logan . . . 1700-1750* (2 vols.), in Historical Society of Pennsylvania, *Memoirs*, 9 (1870), 299. Hereafter cited as *Penn and Logan Correspondence*, I.
25. Norris to Richard Hill, 17 May 1707, *Penn and Logan Correspondence*, II, 223-24.

course of the debate the right of the Council to participate in the legislative process was called in question and an effort was made to impeach James Logan on charges of having endeavored to deprive the Queen's subjects of "the Priviledges and benefitts which they ought to enjoy by the fundamental Laws of England and Established Constitutions of this Govmt" and to introduce "an arbitrary Govmt" into Pennsylvania.[26] The impeachment failed, and a strong revulsion of feeling, helped along by subtle pressure from the Yearly Meeting, swept the Lloyd party out of power in 1710 and gave control of the Assembly to the conservative faction.[27]

Richard Hill (d. 1729), a prominent Philadelphia merchant, was Speaker of the new Assembly. One of its principal acts was to render tribute unto Caesar by appropriating two thousand pounds "for the Queen's use" in the War of the Spanish Succession. Although this was the largest sum which Quaker legislators had ever granted for such a purpose, it was not the first (or the last) occasion on which the momentous subject of military appropriations was to arise in colonial Pennsylvania. In 1689, at the outbreak of King William's War, the Council had been ordered to place the province in a posture of defense. One skeptical Quaker had asserted that he saw no danger "but from the Bears and Wolves," adding in a more consistent pacifist vein: "I know not but a peaceable spirit, and that will do well." Another feared that arming might provoke an Indian rising and a third opined that the country could not afford military expenditures. Samuel Carpenter, Philadelphia's wealthiest merchant, declared that those who put their trust in carnal weapons were free to arm

---

26. *Minutes of the Provincial Council*, II, 344. The Charter of Privileges had stripped the Council of its legislative functions but, as H. L. Osgood remarks, "nothing is clearer than the fact that the council virtually legislated" during this period.—*The American Colonies in the Eighteenth Century*, II, 272.

27. In a folio entitled *Friendly Advice to the Inhabitants of Pennsylvania*, written by Isaac Norris and published by order of the Yearly Meeting on the eve of the election, Friends were urged to turn out the Lloydeans, who were charged with having done little for the commonwealth except to raise "that popular and plausible Cry, of Standing for *Liberties* and *Privileges*." The piece closed with a frank appeal to Friends to return an Assembly which would support the Proprietor's policies.

themselves, but added: "it being contrary to the judgmt of a great part of the people, and my own to[o], I cannot advise to the thing, nor Express my liking it." The King was aware, he continued, of the Quakers' well-known testimony against war, but "if we must be forced to it," he concluded, "I suppose we shall rather choose to suffer than to do it, as we have done formerly."[28]

In 1693, when the province was under the crown, Governor Fletcher had presented a royal order for military aid to the neighboring colony of New York. Under the threat of dissolution, the Assembly made a grant, stipulating, however, that it should not be "dipt in blood" but used to "feed the hungry and clothe the naked" Indians.[29] When a similar order came at the onset of Queen Anne's War, the Assembly evaded the issue by maintaining that Pennsylvania had to look to her own frontiers. The basic objection, however, clearly sprang from the peace testimony; even James Logan, who was far from a consistent pacifist, adduced this as a justification for the colony's refusal to contribute to the defense of New York.[30] In appropriating five hundred pounds "for the Queen's use" in 1709, the Assembly made it clear to the Governor that the money was not designed for the projected military expedition to Canada "but to be a Part of the Queen's Revenue, and to be safely lodged here till the Queen shall be pleased to order the Disposal of it."[31] No such restriction appears to have been placed upon the grant of two

28. *Minutes of the Provincial Council*, I, 306-7. Carpenter's position was consistent with Robert Barclay's argument that "*war*, undertaken upon a just occasion" was not unlawful for those who were still "in the mixture, and not in the patient suffering spirit," but that "for such whom Christ has brought hither, it is not lawful to defend themselves by *arms*."—*Apology*, Prop. XV, sec. xv, *Writings*, II, 568.

29. *Minutes of the Provincial Council*, I, 400, 492.

30. See his letter to William Penn, 2 Sept. 1703, *Penn and Logan Correspondence*, I, 228, in which he seems for once to affirm his own adherence to the Quaker position, though recognizing that "this will not answer in English government, nor the methods of this reign."

31. *Votes and Proceedings*, II, 871. Governor Gookin, who refused to accept this proffer, later stated that the Assembly had required "that the money should be put into a safe hand, till they were satisfied from England it should not be employed to the use of the war."—Gookin to the Secretary of the Venerable Society, 27 Aug. 1709, William S. Perry, ed., *Papers Relating to the History of the Church in Pennsylvania* (n.p., 1871), 51.

thousand pounds by the conservative Assembly of 1711; in fact we have it on the authority of Isaac Norris, a prominent member, that the house did not consider it inconsistent with Quaker principles "to give the Queen money, notwithstanding any use she might put it to, *that* being not our part, but hers."[32]

The years between Penn's death in 1718 and the end of Governor Gordon's administration in 1736 were years of peace, and no serious problem of reconciling the Quaker testimonies with the requirements of government arose to perplex the legislators. During this period, however, the back country was beginning to fill up with German and Scotch-Irish immigrants whose unrelenting pressure against the Indian frontier would eventually raise the problem again in more insistent terms. The first decade of this peaceful interim was marked by severe economic depression, which had immediate repercussions in politics; the second decade was economically one of unexampled prosperity and politically an "era of good feelings," in which parties virtually disappeared only to form again on new lines in the succeeding years.

Upon the death of the Quaker founder, the province passed into the hands of his sons, whose attachment to the Quaker faith was feeble.[33] Governor William Keith, who had come to Pennsylvania with the confidence of the Proprietary family and the Council, soon manifested a disposition to flout the interests of both and to patronize the popular party in the Assembly. Thus he came presently to find most of the great merchants arrayed against him. This situation was dramatized early in his administration when four weighty Quaker merchants stalked out of the Council chamber in protest against his disregard of their prerogatives;[34] actually, Keith was merely following the Charter of Privileges, which had deprived the Council of its legislative functions. With this balance-wheel eliminated, the government of

---

32. Letter to James Logan, 28 Aug. 1711, *Penn and Logan Correspondence*, II, 436.

33. Richard became a communicant of the Church of England at an early age. Thomas openly avowed his lack of sympathy with Friends, although he delayed joining the Church until the 1750's. John attended Quaker meeting only infrequently.

34. *Minutes of the Provincial Council*, III, 39.

Pennsylvania assumed in the eyes of the great merchants a frighteningly democratic aspect. Their apprehensions were heightened by the elections of 1721 and 1722, which were, in the words of one of them, "very mobbish and carried by a levelling spirit." The Governor's speeches, in which he drew invidious distinctions between the common people and "those he was pleased to term the great, rich, or knowing," revealed the degree to which he had accommodated himself to the prevailing current of radicalism.[35] David Lloyd, now Chief Justice, was no longer the active leader of the "country party," but his place was ably supplied by two Philadelphia merchants of democratic leanings, Francis Rawle and Anthony Morris. With the Governor's encouragement and against the protests of the leading businessmen, the Assembly enacted bills for the emission of paper money and took other measures to relieve the poorer classes, who were suffering from the province's worst depression.[36] Keith overreached himself, however, when he removed Logan from the Secretaryship of the province, and even though the aged David Lloyd re-entered the legislative battle to defend him, Keith was dismissed from office in 1726 by William Penn's widow. Thereafter he made a futile effort to create an opposition party, but his prospect of success vanished when Lloyd went over to the support of the new Governor, Patrick Gordon. For the next ten years political peace and commercial prosperity reigned in Pennsylvania and the political issues which had divided Friends disappeared from view. The way was thus paved for the emergence of a united Quaker party.

The two troubled decades from 1736 to 1756 witnessed the rise of a strong anti-Proprietary feeling among the Friends. Increasingly alienated by the Tory and Anglican sympathies of the Proprietors, radical and conservative Quakers, their differences buried, joined forces to fashion a united and well-disciplined political party, led by such prominent Friends as John Kinsey (1693-1750) and the younger Isaac Norris (1701-1766), and faithfully supported by the votes of the Germans in the

---

35. The quoted phrases are from a letter of James Logan to Henry Gouldney, 8 April 1723, in Osgood, II, 547.
36. See below, pp. 100-6, for a discussion of the paper-money movement.

hinterland. The major plank in its platform was opposition to the encroachments of the Proprietors upon the constitutional rights of the people. This "Quaker party," embodying the traditional Whig devotion to liberty and property, was to maintain its principles and its name down to the Revolution, although after 1756 its leadership fell into the hands of men who were not members of the Society of Friends.

James Logan, after governing the province for two years as President of the Council, gradually withdrew from public life to the well-stocked library at his country estate of Stenton. The office of Secretary of the province passed to the Reverend Richard Peters, a priest of the Church of England, and the Anglican group which had been steadily growing since the turn of the century, strengthened now by the adherence of certain prominent former Quakers, rallied to the support of the Proprietors. Large numbers of Presbyterians, German Reformed, and Lutherans in the back country, concerned about security against Indian attack, also joined the ranks of the Proprietary party. By 1740 the new alignment was quite evident. Robert Proud, the Quaker historian, apparently forgetful of the earlier strife between rival Quaker interests, speaks of the "formation and increase of party" at this period among some of the "later inhabitants, joined and instigated by divers others"; these dissidents, he says, fomented a spirit of opposition against "the *old interest*, and the defenders of the established constitution of the province, and the descendants of the early settlers, who were principally concerned for its preservation, being chiefly *Quakers. . . .*"[37]

Historians have persisted in regarding the Quakers' refusal to appropriate money for the defense of the frontiers as the paramount issue of this period. The fact is, however, that the Quaker Assembly did vote considerable sums which were used for military purposes. The more important underlying issues of the period arose out of differing attitudes towards the authority of the Proprietors and the best means of achieving a *modus vivendi* with the Indians. The struggles over these issues took

---

37. *The History of Pennsylvania*, II, 228-29.

place against a background of imperial rivalries whose grand strategy was being worked out thousands of miles away from Philadelphia at Versailles and Whitehall. Since these rivalries were focused upon the Ohio Valley, Pennsylvania, its principal gateway, came to occupy a position of pivotal importance in eighteenth-century power politics.

James Logan, watchdog of the Proprietary interests and a frank critic of Quaker pacifism, foreseeing the importance of the Ohio Valley in the British imperial scheme, had been an early advocate of direct negotiations with the Iroquois, who controlled the tribes of that region, in order to keep them out of the hands of the French.[38] The majority of Quakers, however, unconcerned with the grand strategy of imperialism, and conscious that their peculiar genius lay in face-to-face relationships, in which mutual trust and good will could flower, preferred to deal with the nearby tribes, particularly the Delawares. Logan, however, persuaded Thomas Penn to adopt the broader policy.

In 1732 the first great conference with the Iroquois was held in Philadelphia, and the Six Nations ceremoniously pledged fidelity to the English. A second council fire was kindled in 1736, the conference opening at Logan's country estate and concluding in the Great Meeting House in Philadelphia. After a treaty had been signed, releasing all lands on either side of the Susquehanna to which the Six Nations had ever laid claim, a few chiefs gathered at the home of Conrad Weiser, the interpreter, at Tulpehocken, and made a further declaration to the effect that their tributaries the Delawares, having signed away their tribal hunting grounds, had no title to any lands which the English were bound to respect.[39] Many years before, in 1686, the Delawares had ceded to

---

38. See his memorandum "Of the State of the British Plantations in America," ed. by Joseph E. Johnson, *Pennsylvania Magazine of History and Biography*, 60 (1936), 97-130.

39. This highly controversial incident is discussed by Julian P. Boyd, "Indian Affairs in Pennsylvania, 1736-1762," in *Indian Treaties Printed by Benjamin Franklin, 1736-1762*, xxvi-xxviii; and Paul A. W. Wallace, *Conrad Weiser: Friend of Colonist and Mohawk* (Philadelphia, 1945), 71-75. See also Charles Thomson, *An Inquiry into the Causes of the Alienation of the Delaware and Shawanese Indians from the British Interest* (London, 1759), 32 ff.

William Penn some lands lying northwestward from the Delaware River as far as a man could walk in a day and a half. The Proprietors, although armed with the statement that the Delawares had no claim to these lands, nevertheless caused them to be "walked off" in 1737, taking care to employ the fleetest runners and to clear the underbrush away from their path. This "Walking Purchase" was certainly not without a taint of dishonor, although its obliquity was undoubtedly magnified by Quakers and Indians when it became a *casus belli* in 1756. The alienation of the Delawares was completed at the conference of 1742, when they were publicly humiliated at the hands of the Onondaga orator Canasatego.

While the indignation of the Delawares smoldered, the long interval of peace came to an end with the outbreak of the War of Jenkins's Ear in 1739. The Assembly refused to raise troops for an expedition to the West Indies, whereupon the Governor recruited them upon his own authority, enlisting a number of indentured servants who had not yet served out their terms. The Quaker legislators, more concerned about the sanctity of contracts than about the siege of Cartagena, declined to appropriate any funds for provisions and transports unless the servants were returned to their masters. The controversy between the Assembly and Governor Thomas raged for months, the Assembly using its control of the purse as a weapon, and the Governor retaliating by holding up approval of bills and finally appealing to the home government for a law disqualifying Friends from holding public office. Party feeling reached a climax in the "bloody election" of 1742 in which the "Gentlemen's" or Proprietary party sent sailors armed with clubs to the polls to intimidate the voters; several Quakers were knocked down and the heads of some of their German supporters were broken, but the Quaker party returned all its candidates to office. After this show of voting strength, relations with the Governor gradually improved. The Assembly still balked at raising troops, but in 1744 it voted four thousand pounds for "the purchase of Bread, Beef, Pork, Flour, Wheat or other Grain" to be sent to Louis-burg, which had just fallen to the forces of New England.[40] The Governor proceeded to construe "other Grain" to mean gunpowder, insisting to Benjamin Franklin, no doubt with a wink, that he understood this to be the intent of the Assembly.[41]

When a summons came in the next year for a contribution towards an expedition for the reduction of Canada, the Assembly issued its usual demurrer and then appropriated five thousand pounds "for the king's use." Thereafter, although the war was carried to the very shores of Pennsylvania, when Spanish and French privateers appeared at the mouth of the Delaware the Assembly refused to take defensive measures. At this point Benjamin Franklin wrote his *Plain Truth*, in which he depicted the horrors of invasion and gently castigated the Quakers (with whom on most political matters he was in sympathy) for failing to defend the province. Under his leadership a voluntary "Association" for defense was formed. Except for a few renegades, the Friends kept aloof from this movement. John Smith, a young Quaker merchant, was moved to write an apology for Quaker pacifism in answer to a defense of the Association by the redoubtable Reverend Gilbert Tennent, and Franklin, with his customary broadmindedness, and care not to alienate the Quakers, published it.[42]

The expected attack failed to materialize, and the next few years passed without untoward or important happening. Fateful events were in the making, however. Settlers were constantly pushing westward, and the sullen Delaware Indians were coming under the influence of the French. The stage was being set for the last act of the "holy experiment." Although the *dénouement* was to be precipitated by the unwillingness of certain Friends to serve in a government at war, the issue of popular rights

---

40. *Votes and Proceedings*, IV, 3042.
41. *Autobiography* in A. H. Smyth, ed., *The Writings of Benjamin Franklin*, I, 367-68. It is true, as Franklin observed, that the Assembly never repudiated this reading of its act, but the argument from silence alone is not sufficient to prove that the Assembly actually intended the money to be used for the purchase of munitions.
42. Smith's pamphlet was called *The Doctrine of Christianity, as Held by the People Called Quakers, Vindicated: In Answer to Gilbert Tennent's Sermon on the Lawfulness of War.*

versus Proprietary prerogatives was never far in the background. The importance of this issue can be judged from the tone of an epistle which Philadelphia Quarterly Meeting addressed to the Meeting for Sufferings (the executive body of the parent Yearly Meeting in London) in May, 1755, as the crisis was drawing on. It refers to the difficulty of maintaining the peace testimony unimpaired and suggests the possibility that under certain circumstances Friends may have to abdicate their offices, but its major emphasis is upon the political issues of the moment, a fact which is significant in itself, since communications between official bodies of Friends seldom touched upon such matters. "We have abundant cause to complain," the epistle declares, "that the most unwearied endeavours are and have some time past been used, and various artifices attempted, to wrest from us our most valuable privileges, and the conduct and language of those whose duty it is to protect us in the enjoyment thereof, fully convince us of the pernicious tendency of their designs."[43] At the same time, Isaac Norris II, Speaker of the Assembly and acknowledged leader of the Quaker party, was saying in a letter to England: "We have very much Thrown our Disputes from being a Quaker Cause, to a Cause of Liberty, and the Rights derived to us by our Charter and our Laws."[44]

Early in 1755, Pennsylvania was asked to contribute its share towards the expense of Braddock's ill-fated expedition to Fort Duquesne. The Assembly promptly responded with a supply bill, but insisted upon raising the funds in its own way (by an issue of paper money) and upon retaining control of expenditures in its own hands. The bill was hedged about with so many restrictions that Governor Morris felt obliged to veto it. Such aid as the British general received was largely owing to

---

43. Quoted in Isaac Sharpless, *A Quaker Experiment in Government*, 238.
44. Letter to Robert Charles, 18 May 1755, Norris Letter Book, 1719-56, 73, Norris Papers, Hist. Soc. Pa. Norris himself, like his father-in-law James Logan, was not a strict pacifist. Only a few months earlier he had written to the same correspondent: "I am satisfied the Law of Nature, and perhaps the Christian system leaves us a right to defend ourselves as well against the Enemies who are within the reach of our Laws, as those who owe no subjection to them." As Speaker of the House, however, he felt obliged to voice its sentiments rather than his own.—Letter dated 7 Oct. 1754, *ibid.*, 56.

the ingenuity and initiative of Benjamin Franklin. Braddock's disastrous defeat in July turned the Delawares (now wholly in the French interest) loose upon the frontiers of Pennsylvania. The Governor summoned the Assembly and begged it to pass a militia law and to vote funds for the purchase of arms and ammunition. The house quickly appropriated fifty thousand pounds "for the King's use," the money to be raised by a tax on real and personal estates. Governor Morris refused his assent because the bill contemplated taxing the estates of the Proprietors. The Assembly was adamant and the deadlock continued until the Proprietors agreed to a contribution of five thousand pounds in lieu of taxes, whereupon a supply bill was passed, granting sixty thousand pounds "for the King's use." A militia bill was also passed, but it fell short of the Governor's desires by providing only for voluntary enlistment and exempting Quakers and other conscientious objectors from service.

Meanwhile by gifts and concessions the Quakers were actively seeking to win back the confidence and friendship of the Delawares. Effective as this policy had proved in the past, it was no longer adequate because the vital decisions which governed Indian-white relations in the Pennsylvania forests were being made in the chancelleries of Europe. "The issues at stake," as Julian P. Boyd has put it, "were such that mere altruism was ineffectual as a policy; the balance of power in Europe was of the utmost concern to the French and at the root of their determined advance. . . . Aggression could not be stopped at this stage by mere generosity or friendliness to the Indians."[45]

As conditions steadily deteriorated on the frontier, the clamor for retaliation upon the Delawares rose higher and higher. In April 1756 Governor Morris and his Council prepared a declaration of war in which bounties were offered for Indian scalps—$130 for that of a male over twelve years of age and $50 for that of a female. A last-minute protest against this descent into barbarism and a plea for the resumption of negotiations, signed by six of the weightiest Quakers in Philadelphia, was

---

45. "Indian Affairs in Pennsylvania," lv.

brushed aside, and the Council shrewdly advised the Governor to consult the Assembly only *after* issuing the declaration of war.[46] On April 14th the proclamation was published at the Court House, and Pennsylvania, after three-quarters of a century of unbroken peace, found itself at war.

The Proprietors blamed the Quaker Assembly and the Friends countered with charges of fraud and injustice on the part of the Proprietors, but the real cause of the war, as we have seen, lay deeper than either party realized. Wherever the onus might lie, however, it was clear to certain Friends that they could no longer remain in public office and preserve any shadow of consistency. Accordingly, within a few weeks, six Quaker members of the Assembly, led by James Pemberton, requested leave to resign their seats, giving as their reason that many of their constituents felt "that the present Situation of Public Affairs call[s] upon us for Services in a military Way, which, from a Conviction of Judgment, after mature Deliberation, we cannot comply with."[47] Perhaps their decision to resign was precipitated by the rumor that the Board of Trade, in response to a petition from Pennsylvania, had recommended to Parliament the imposition of a test oath upon all members of colonial legislatures, a provision which would have effectually disqualified from office-holding, all Friends not only in Pennsylvania but in other colonies as well. The Meeting for Sufferings in London had agreed to use its influence to persuade the Pennsylvania Quakers to withdraw voluntarily from office, and had dispatched two emissaries across the Atlantic to make the recommendation more forcible. Before the two ambassadors arrived, however, the fall elections had been held and it was apparent that the Friends had decided to renounce political power, for many Quaker Assemblymen declined to stand

---

46. The signers of the address were men whose names we shall meet frequently in the succeeding pages: Samuel Powel, Anthony Morris, John Reynell, Dr. Samuel Preston Moore, Israel Pemberton, and John Smith. The only voice raised in the Council against the declaration of war was that of William Logan, son of the late Secretary, but a more consistent Friend than his father. The other Councilors with one exception were non-Quakers or men who had been disowned from the Society of Friends.

47. *Votes and Proceedings*, V, 4245-46.

for re-election, and four who were elected against their wishes refused to claim their seats.

The Quaker majority in the Assembly thus evaporated, and although the anti-Proprietary party was to remain strong, its leadership was assumed by members of other denominations. A few Friends continued to serve in the legislature, especially after the cessation of hostilities, but henceforth the Quakers were to make their influence felt chiefly through their activities as private individuals. As such they labored through the Friendly Association for Regaining and Preserving Peace with the Indians by Pacific Measures to bring an end to the war and to restore amicable relations with the Delawares. The "Quaker party" under new leadership kept up the fight against Proprietary encroachments which Quakers had waged unremittingly since the founding of the province. Through these separate channels were perpetuated the Whig and pacifist principles to which the merchants had always been committed. The Anglo-French imperial conflict, which had precipitated their withdrawal from political life, presently gave way to a struggle within the British Empire which was to culminate in American independence. Quaker merchants participated in the early non-violent phases of that struggle, but when it eventuated in a clash of arms, their pacifism took precedence over their Whiggism, and most of them adopted a position of neutrality which caused them to be generally regarded as Tories. Although our story stops short of the Revolution, it is clear at least from our outline of the story up to this point that, far from being Tories in the usual sense, the Quaker merchants had stood for years as outspoken exponents of the Whig ideals of liberty and property.

Chapter Two

A DOOR OF MERCY

I N 1682, when the settlement of Philadelphia began, Friends had been "publishing the Truth" with apostolic zeal for thirty years on both sides of the Atlantic. Between forty and fifty thousand men and women had been "convinced" and had accepted the evangel of the Inner Light.[1] Abundant human material for the "holy experiment" lay at hand in every shire of England, in Scotland, Ireland, and Wales, on the continent of Europe, and in the American colonies.

GEOGRAPHICAL PROVENANCE

The greatest stronghold of Quakerism was in the north of England—Westmoreland, Cumberland, York, and Lancaster—where it had first been given to George Fox to see "a great people in white raiment . . . coming to the Lord."[2] The southeastern counties held another large concentration of Friends; in the city of London alone, it is estimated, there were ten thousand Quakers in 1678.[3] And Bristol, second largest city in the kingdom, was a veritable hotbed of Quakerism; in 1660 it had been reported that "these monsters are more numerous in Bristol than in all the West of England."[4] Quakerism had made some slight

---

1. William C. Braithwaite, *The Second Period of Quakerism*, 459.
2. *Journal*, I, 110.
3. A. R. Barclay, ed., *Letters of the Early Friends* (London, 1841), 156.
4. John Latimer, *The Annals of Bristol in the Seventeenth Century* (Bristol, 1900), 300.

headway in East Anglia, the Puritan preserve, and was a far from negligible factor in the north Midlands and the south-western shires. The district least affected by Quakerism was the tier of counties forming the south Midlands.[5]

The significance of this geographical distribution becomes apparent when one realizes that throughout the seventeenth century the north and west, where Quakerism flourished most vigorously, were the poorest sections of England, and that, *per contra*, the south Midlands, where Quakerism never took firm root, was the wealthiest region.[6] The correlation cannot be carried out in detail because the evidence is inadequate, but it is clear that in general the areas in which Quakerism prospered most were those in which the standard of living was relatively low. To be sure, Middlesex, which included the city of London, was the richest county in the realm, but in the years before the settlement of Philadelphia it is probable that most of the Quakers in the metropolis were found among the poorer classes.

"Children of the Light" were also scattered in considerable numbers among the small farmers and unpretentious gentry of Wales. There were six or seven hundred Quaker families in Ireland, divided among the yeoman farmers of English stock in Leinster and Munster provinces and the tradesmen and manual workers of Dublin. Quakerism made relatively few converts in Scotland, where it ran counter to a long and tenacious tradition of Presbyterianism. In the towns of Holland and northern Germany were a few groups of Quakers, largely composed of weavers and other craftsmen. And by the time Pennsylvania was founded there were large numbers of Friends in the New World, in the West Indies, North Carolina, Virginia, Maryland, New Jersey, New York, Rhode Island, and Massachusetts Bay.

When a Quaker left his home, he normally took with him to his new abode a certificate from his Monthly Meeting, attest-

---

5. Statements regarding the geographical distribution of Quakers in England are based on the episcopal returns of 1669, collected and analyzed in G. Lyon Turner, *Original Records of Early Nonconformity under Persecution and Indulgence,* especially III, 125-26. 136-39.
6. H. D. Traill and J. S. Mann, *Social England* (London, 1903), IV, 384-85.

ing that his "walk and conversation" had been orderly and according to the dictates of Truth. This certificate was received and recorded by the Monthly Meeting within whose bounds he settled. From an analysis of the certificates recorded by Philadelphia Monthly Meeting it is therefore possible to determine with some degree of accuracy the geographical provenance of the Quaker settlers of Philadelphia.[7]

It is not without significance that the greatest number of certificates—a total of seventy-nine between 1682 and 1750—were from meetings in the city of London. With due allowances for the fact that many Friends may have removed there temporarily to await transportation to Pennsylvania, and may have exchanged their original credentials for certificates issued by the meeting which they attended while sojourning in London, it is nevertheless beyond question that that city supplied a large proportion of the Quaker settlers of Philadelphia. Bristol, the second great seaport, likewise dispatched a significant number of Quaker colonists to Philadelphia: sixteen certificates were recorded as from Bristol Monthly Meeting. Thus nearly a third of the Quaker immigrants to Philadelphia came from these two places alone. This fact, together with the number of certificates from the smaller cities in the British Isles—Dublin, Rochester, Worcester, and others—suggests (as indeed one might expect) that Friends with urban backgrounds tended to gravitate to Philadelphia where they would find a more or less familiar environment, whereas country Friends preferred to take up farm lands outside the city or in Chester or Bucks county.

---

7. The list of certificates received has been published by Albert Cook Myers in *Quaker Arrivals at Philadelphia, 1682-1750.* A few cautions must be observed in interpreting this list: (1) The certificates recorded here represent only a portion of the total number of Quakers who settled in Philadelphia; some families may have neglected to bring a certificate and some certificates may not have been recorded. There is no reason to doubt, however, that the recorded certificates represent a rough cross-section of the settlers so far as geographical origin is concerned. (2) Not all families whose certificates were recorded by Philadelphia Monthly Meeting remained in Philadelphia. (3) The meeting which granted the certificate was not in all cases the family's home meeting; in some instances, indeed, the document states that the family has been under the meeting's care for only a brief period, having recently removed from some other locality.

Most numerous among the immigrants aside from the London Friends were dalesmen from the poverty-stricken north of England and farmers and artisans from the economically depressed shires of Chester, Stafford, Worcester, Gloucester, Wilts, and Somerset in the west. Only a handful hailed from the prosperous region just north of the Thames. From the provinces of Munster and Leinster in Ireland, predominantly from the urban centers of Dublin and Cork, came many Friends, chiefly of English stock.[8] Quaker immigrants from the West Indies and the continental American colonies were few in number, but formed a highly important element in the mercantile society of Philadelphia; like the Irish Friends, they too were essentially transplanted Englishmen.

The Philadelphia Quakers were thus predominantly English in origin, but there were Quaker groups of non-English descent on the periphery of the town who were to play some part in its life. Most of the Welsh Friends settled as a body in the so-called Welsh Tract northwest of Philadelphia, hoping there to maintain political autonomy and to preserve their racial and cultural integrity. A few Welsh Quakers took up lots in Philadelphia and others drifted into the city later as the dream of an autonomous Welsh Barony faded away. Most of the Quaker immigrants from the Dutch-German towns of Krefeld and Krisheim made their homes in the first instance in Germantown, whence in the course of years, having lost much of their linguistic and cultural distinctiveness, a few moved into Philadelphia. Finally (to complete the roll of non-English stocks), a few French Huguenots took refuge in Philadelphia and became Quakers.[9]

---

8. Albert Cook Myers in his exhaustive study of Irish Quaker immigration finds that 26 per cent of the Irish Quaker immigrants presented their certificates to Philadelphia Monthly Meeting.— *Immigration of the Irish Quakers into Pennsylvania, 1682-1750*, 117.
9. Wayland F. Dunaway, "The French Racial Strain in Colonial Pennsylvania," *Pa. Mag. of Hist.*, 53 (1929), 339. At least fifteen French names appear in the records of Philadelphia Monthly Meeting before 1763. See William Wade Hinshaw, *Encyclopedia of American Quaker Genealogy*, II, *passim*.

MOTIVES FOR EMIGRATION

Why did the Quakers flock in such multitudes to William Penn's colony? The usual explanation is simply that Pennsylvania provided a timely haven for harassed victims of persecution. In large measure this is correct, but unless one inquires into the special character of the persecution, one can hardly do justice to the complex nature of the motivation which led Friends to forsake their homes and cast their lot in a new and distant land. The economic motive which commonly figures in colonial migrations also played its part, but it is not enough simply to say that Friends came to Pennsylvania in search of opportunities for material advancement. The fact is that the religious and economic motives were inextricably intermingled and that each determined the nature of the other.

Something of the mixture of motives is conveyed by the anonymous *Planter's Speech to His Neighbours and Countrymen of Pennsylvania, East and West-Jersey, and to All Such As Have Transported Themselves into New Colonies, for the Sake of a Quiet and Retired Life*, published in 1684 by the London Quaker printer Andrew Sowle. First among the inducements which brought the author and his fellow Quakers to Penn's colony was the promise of "a *peaceable life*," where they might worship God and obey His law as revealed by the Light within, unobstructed by the "mouldy errors" and "fierce invasions" of religious traditionalists, crafty politicians, or cruel and covetous persecutors. The second reason is a variation on the first: "That we might here, as on a *virgin elysian shore*, commence, or improve such an innocent course of life, as might unload us of those outward cares, vexations and turmoils, which before we were always subject unto, from the hands of self designing and unreasonable men." In the third place, like Lot fleeing from Sodom, they sought to escape from the corrupt atmosphere of Restoration England. They did not overlook the opportunities for economic advancement, which Penn had stressed in his promotional literature; indeed they frankly anticipated that "as *trees* are transplanted from one soil to another, to render them

more thriving and better bearers, so . . . in peace and secure retirement, under the bountiful protection of God, and in the lap
of the least adulterated nature, might everyone the better improve his talent, and bring forth more plenteous fruits, to the
glory of God, and public welfare of the whole creation." Finally
(and this was a common theme in seventeenth-century Quaker
writing), they hoped to bring the Indians out of heathenism into
a saving awareness of the divine principle within them.[10]

In the early 1680's the persecution of Quakers, which had
been carried on intermittently in England for a quarter of a
century, was intensified. Charles II, having dissolved the last of
the Whig Parliaments, and having received assurance of a sub-
sidy from France, unleashed a savage campaign against the
Dissenters, and as usual the brunt of it was borne by the Quakers.
By the end of three years of Charles's personal rule, nearly
fourteen hundred Friends were in prison. The persecution was
especially severe in the regions from which Philadelphia was to
draw most of its first settlers. In 1682 some five hundred Bristol
Quakers were indicted under the statutes against Recusancy,
and warrants were sworn out for fines or distresses amounting
to more than sixteen thousand pounds. The sufferings at London
were scarcely less severe, and by the end of the King's reign,
there were more Quaker prisoners in Yorkshire than in any
other county.[11]

This vindictive and sanguinary persecution might be
thought a sufficient cause in itself for the flight of the Quakers
to their New-World refuge, but it should be borne in mind that
Friends were not easily cowed and that for a quarter of a
century of almost constant persecution, they had stood their
ground with quiet but heroic tenacity. Indeed, if a meeting suspected that a member was fleeing to America to escape suffering,
it was unlikely to give its sanction to his emigration. One meeting in Ireland, for example, reluctantly granted a certificate to
an intending emigrant but frankly expressed its dissatisfaction

---

10. *The Planter's Speech* is reprinted in part in Proud, *History*, I, 226-227n.
11. Braithwaite, 99-115.

with his plans, stating that "he hath given us no satisfactory reason for his removing, but our godly jealousy is that his chief ground is fearfulness of sufferings here for the testimony of Jesus, or courting worldly liberty."[12] Friends in Pennsylvania, equally jealous of the good name of Truth, were prepared to admit that in some instances the suspicions of the home meetings were justified, for, wrote one early settler, "here cam som peopel that had not a right end in their removals[,] som for fere of persecution[,] some that were discontented with their brethren where they were, and others that promised to themselves to be great in the world."[13] So strong in some quarters was the opposition to emigration that in 1682 an English Quaker, William Loddington, was moved to write an apologetic tract directed to "such who ignorantly Brow-beat or Tongue-beat the *American* Plantations," and comprehensively entitled *Plantation Work the Work of This Generation. Written in True-Love to All Such as Are Weightily Inclined to Transplant Themselves and Families to Any of the English Plantations in America. The Most Material Doubts and Objections Against It Being Removed, They May More Cheerfully Proceed to the Glory and Renown of the God of the Whole Earth, Who in All Undertakings Is to Be Looked Unto, Praised, and Feared for Ever.*

The significant fact is that persecution entailed more than mere personal inconvenience and suffering. Under the second Conventicle Act, accurately described by Andrew Marvell as "the quintessence of arbitrary malice," heavy fines were levied for attendance at Friends meetings; and under the statutes against Recusancy which, in Braithwaite's words, were "perverted into a scourge for the Quakers," even heavier fines were levied for the correlative crime of non-attendance at services of the Church of England. What bore with special harshness upon Friends, subject as they were to repeated indictments, was the provision that the fines could be recovered by distress, i.e.,

12. Certificate from Mountmellick Monthly Meeting for Nicholas Newland, *Pa. Mag. of Hist.*, 6 (1882), 174.
13. Hugh Roberts to William Penn, *ca.* 1695, *Pa. Mag. of Hist.*, 18 (1894), 206.

seizure of goods in default of a money payment. The intent of the acts was clearly to ruin the offenders economically. The conduct of the enforcement officers is graphically described in a paper called "The Devouring Informers of Bristol," written in 1682:

Their manner of levying this Distress is as follows, *viz.* When they enter a Shop, albeit there is Abundance of Goods in View, yet they break open Chests, Counters, &c. and thence take away the Money; if no Money to be had, then they take either Shop or Household Goods, and of them generally to double their Value: If any durst speak to them by way of Reproof for these unreasonable Proceedings, then they huff and threaten to send them to Prison....[14]

Craftmen's implements and farmers' livestock and tools were frequently seized; looms were wantonly destroyed and work-benches smashed when they proved too heavy to be carried away.[15] The hapless victims were thereby prevented from work-ing steadily at their callings. Imprisonment had the same effect except when the prisoners were allowed, as they sometimes were, to carry on their trade within prison walls. The weapons of religious persecution were thus economic in nature, and con-temporary Friends suspected that the measures were partly motivated by a desire to eliminate the Quakers as business com-petitors. The severity of the anti-Quaker campaign in Cork, observed William Penn, "without doubt was at least as much from envy about trade as zeal for religion."[16]

Thus we find Benjamin Chambers of Rochester suffering distraint of goods in 1681 for being present at a Quaker meet-ing, and John Gardner of Purton, Wiltshire, being fined £10 in 1684 and relieved of goods to the value of £11/10. In 1676 Charles Lee of Clitheroe in Lancashire, a laborer, "had taken from him four Horses with their Accoutrements, one Heifer, a Cow, and four Calves" worth £26/11/8; no doubt this repre-

---

14. Joseph Besse, *A Collection of the Sufferings of the People Called Quakers*, I, 62.
15. See, for example, Besse, I, 10, 96, 674.
16. Janney, *Life of Penn*, 63. Compare George Fox's similar comment in his *Journal*, I, 186.

sented the greater part of his worldly goods, but the vindictive informers were not through with him, for not long afterwards he was imprisoned two years for non-payment of tithes amounting to three shillings sixpence. John Simcock, a substantial farmer, had eight cows and eleven heifers, worth ninety pounds, taken from him in 1678; in the next year he lost goods to the value of one hundred pounds, and two years later he was further distrained upon to the amount of forty pounds.[17] When William Penn threw open the doors to Pennsylvania in 1681, these Friends and many others similarly circumstanced accepted his invitation with joy.

We can now begin to appreciate how inextricably intermingled were economic and religious considerations in the complex of motives which impelled the Quakers to seek new homes. Physical hardships they could endure for the glory of the Truth, although the prospect of leaving behind the noisome jails and bloodthirsty informers of their native land could hardly have been displeasing. But the persecuting measures were cunningly contrived so that one who bore his testimony to the Truth by suffering was effectively estopped from working in his calling, which, as we shall see, Friends regarded in the light of a religious duty.[18] The Children of the Light felt that they were called to suffer for the vindication of the Truth, but they knew that an equally binding injunction was laid upon them to labor diligently in their callings for the honor of God and the welfare of their fellow men. The protracted persecutions of the Restoration period thus placed them in a dilemma from which emigration provided a means of escape. The nuances of human motivation are difficult to interpret, and no doubt some of the Friends who came to Philadelphia were animated by simple fear of persecution or love of gain. For the majority, however, the considerations just outlined were probably determinative.[19]

---

17. Besse, I, 107-8, 296, 321, 323; II, 47.
18. See below, pp. 51-62.
19. Within less than a decade of the founding of the colony, of course, religious persecution came virtually to an end in England. Thereafter, particularly during the lean years from 1693 to 1699, purely economic motives were no doubt responsible for the continued migration.

Herein lies the real meaning of the simile quoted above of the tree transplanted to more favorable soil: by coming to Pennsylvania, where conditions were favorable to uninterrupted economic activity, the harassed Quaker "might . . . the better improve his talent, and bring forth more plenteous fruits, to the glory of God, and public welfare of the whole creation."

SOCIAL ORIGINS

This survey of the geographical provenance of the settlers and their motives for emigration has prepared the way for a closer analysis of their social backgrounds. By indicating that they came, by and large, from the towns and depressed rural areas of their homelands, it has suggested a conclusion regarding their social status for which we must now seek further evidence. This is the more necessary since misconceptions on this subject, given currency in the first instance by Philadelphia Friends themselves, have long prevailed. As early as 1739, William Fishbourne, a wealthy Quaker merchant, declared that "most of those who had first come over, were not people of low circumstances, but substantial livers." Sixteen years later, Philadelphia Quarterly Meeting, in an epistle to the Meeting for Sufferings in London, asserted that "the first Settlers of this Province were men of Interest and Reputation in their native Country." And at the end of the eighteenth century, Deborah Morris, an elderly Quakeress who had known some of the original colonists, wrote that "few of our first settlers were of the laborious class."[20]

It is fairly well established that at its origin Quakerism took root chiefly in the lower strata of English society. Ephraim

---

20. William Fishbourne, "Some Few and Short Hints of the Settlement of the Province of Pennsylvania to the Year 1739," Miscellaneous MSS, Etting Collection, I, 56, Hist. Soc. Pa.; MS Minutes of Phila. YM, II, 59; John F. Watson, *Annals of Philadelphia and Pennsylvania*, I, 48. Recent historians have perpetuated this view: see, for example, Sidney G. Fisher, *The Quaker Colonies* (New Haven, 1919), 22, 37. Illustrative of the confusion existing on this subject are the statements of Scharf and Westcott: on the one hand they state that the first settlers of Philadelphia were "well-to-do people at home" and on the other hand that they were "chiefly of the plebian classes, the true English democracy, yeomen, tinkers, tradesmen, mechanics, retail shopmen of the cities and towns."—*History of Philadelphia*, I, 101, 141.

Pagitt, the heresiographer of the Commonwealth period, declared that the Quakers were "made up of the dregs of the common people," and a modern writer has called them "a typical church of the disinherited."[21] In the episcopal returns regarding conventicles made in 1669 by order of Archbishop Sheldon, Quakers were consistently described as "of meane condition," "of the inferior Gang," "poorer sort," "Meanest Mechanicks," "Very mean, the best scarce worth the title of Yeomen."[22] If one is inclined to discount the findings of avowed heresy-hunters or of a sociologist bent on proving a thesis, further evidence of an unimpeachable sort is abundant. Analysis of the social status of the early ministers of the Society of Friends reveals that the majority were connected with the land, the largest single group being husbandmen, a class which at this period was suffering severely from the exactions of rack-renting landlords.[23] In the cities, whence, as we have seen, the majority of Philadelphia's first settlers came, the Quakers were found predominantly among the working classes. This conclusion emerges from a study of 250 Quaker marriages recorded in London and Middlesex Quarterly Meeting around the year 1680, just before the tide of emigration to Pennsylvania set in. More than three-fifths of the bridegrooms can be classified as manual workers—smiths, sawyers, coopers, bricklayers, weavers, shoemakers, and the like—while most of the remainder were tradesmen and shopkeepers. Evidence on this point from Bristol is even more decisive: a total of 178 Quakers were fined there in 1683 for non-attendance at church, of which number only six were not identified as either artisans or shopkeepers.[24]

---

21. Pagitt, *Heresiography* (London, 1661), 244; H. Richard Niebuhr, *The Social Sources of Denominationalism*, 52.

22. Turner, I, *passim*.

23. Ernest E. Taylor, "The First Publishers of Truth," Friends Historical Society, *Journal*, 19 (1922), 66. On the economic condition of the husbandmen see R. H. Tawney, ed., *Studies in Economic History: The Collected Papers of George Unwin* (London, 1927), 345-51. A recent historian observes, "While all other classes generally showed a balance, however small, of income over expenditure, this class shows a deficit; and neither contemporaries nor modern economists can explain how they lived."—Ogg, *England*, I, 85.

24. William Beck and T. Frederick Ball, *The London Friends Meetings*, 90; Besse, I, 68-70.

The general conclusion is inescapable that the majority of Quakers in England from whom the first settlers of Philadelphia were drawn (and similar evidence could be produced for Ireland) were persons in moderate or humble circumstances, some of them on the edge of destitution. If we use Gregory King's table of social classes for the year 1688, it is apparent that most Friends fell within those groups—"freeholders of the lesser sort," "farmers," "shopkeepers and tradesmen," "artisans and handicrafts"—which stood lowest on the list of those "increasing the wealth of the kingdom" (i.e., those whose incomes covered their expenditures with something to spare), and that a sizable proportion came from those classes—laborers, servants, and cottagers—who were "decreasing the wealth of the kingdom."[25]

There is little reason to suppose that the selective process involved in emigration would result in the peopling of Philadelphia with the more prosperous and fortunate of the European Friends. Indeed the presumption would be quite the opposite: one would expect that on the whole the opportunity to start life anew in a favoring environment would appeal chiefly to those most hard-pressed in their outward circumstances at home, especially since their meetings stood ready to advance the necessary five or six pounds passage money at a low rate of interest.[26] The certificates of removal do not yield much information on this point, but those which mention the bearer's occupation or social status tend on the whole to bear out this expectation. Among the sixty-four immigrants for whom evidence of this kind exists were four carpenters, four shoemakers, three seamen, two each in the following occupations: weaver, cooper, cutler, brazier, smith, shopkeeper, and husbandman; and one each of the following: fisherman, baker, leather-dresser, comber, grocer, last-maker, maltster, linen-draper, parchment- and glue-maker, glazier, saddletree-maker, chandler, stay-maker, and wheelwright. Below these in the social scale were eighteen indentured

25. King's table is conveniently reproduced in George N. Clark, *The Later Stuarts* (Oxford, 1934), 25.
26. Auguste Jorns, *The Quakers as Pioneers in Social Work*, trans. by T. K. Brown, 70.

servants; above them were four schoolmasters (although it is questionable whether a schoolmaster enjoyed more economic security than an artisan or tradesman), a merchant's wife, a "Cittizen and Skinner of London," and another Londoner identified as "ye great Mercer" of Bartholomew Close.[27]

The records of marriages under the care of Philadelphia Monthly Meeting provide a rough index of the social status of the early Quakers in Philadelphia. There are ninety marriages of record during the twenty-five-year period from 1683 to 1708 in which the calling of the bridegroom is known. The list of occupations is of sufficient interest to be given in full:

Merchants	16	Clothier	1
Cordwainers	8	Sadler	1
Tailors	7	Glassmaker	1
Carpenters	5	Tanner	1
Bricklayers	4	Glover	1
Bakers	4	Winedresser	1
Weavers	4	Worsted comber	1
Coopers	3	Combmaker	1
Joiners	3	Blacksmith	1
Shipwrights	3	Bodice maker	1
Mariners	2	Vintner	1
Chandlers	2	Locksmith	1
Turners	2	Tobacco pipe	
Brickmakers	2	maker	1
Sawyers	2	Laborer	1
Wheelwrights	2	Clerk	1
Husbandmen	2	Physician	1
Yeomen	2	Gentleman	1 [28]

This list discloses several significant facts. It reveals, in the first place, that the great majority of the first settlers were men who worked with their hands for a living. No doubt many of them

27. Myers, *Quaker Arrivals, passim.* An imperfect registry of arrivals at the port of Philadelphia between 1682 and 1687 tells the same story. Almost one-third of the arrivals were servants under indentures. There were in addition 22 craftsmen and tradesmen, 11 husbandmen and one yeoman, two merchants, and one schoolmaster.—"A Partial List of the Families Who Arrived at Philadelphia between 1682 and 1687," *Pa. Mag. of Hist.,* 8 (1884), 328-40.
28. MS Records of Marriages, Philadelphia Monthly Meeting, I (1672-1759), *passim.*

were or soon became master craftsmen, for in the expanding economy of early Philadelphia an industrious artisan was normally able within a few years to employ journeymen or indentured servants. The social mobility characteristic of a frontier society was to enable the children of some of these craftsmen to become merchants and thus to enter the ranks of the upper class. It is important to bear in mind, however, that the typical Philadelphia Quaker of the immigrant generation was a man of lowly origins and humble circumstances. One of these immigrants, writing to George Fox in 1685, expressed what was no doubt in the minds of many of his fellows (and incidentally implied that it had been the less prosperous Quakers who had emigrated): "I wish that those that have estates of their own and to leave fullness to their posterity, may not be offended at the Lord's opening a door of mercy to thousands in England, Especially in Wales and other nations who had no estates either for themselves or children."[29]

One may note, in the second place, the extraordinary variety of crafts represented in the infant community. William Penn, who in 1681 had issued a special invitation to "Laborious Handicrafts" to settle in his province, was able, four years later, to write with satisfaction of Philadelphia: "There inhabits most sorts of useful Tradesmen, As Carpenters, Joyners, Bricklayers, Masons, Plasterers, Plumers, Smiths, Glasiers, Taylers, Shoemakers, Butchers, Bakers, Brewers, Glovers, Tanners, Felmongers, Wheelwrights, Millwrights, Shipwrights, Boatwrights, Ropenakers, Saylmakers, Blockmakers, Turners, etc." In 1690 John Goodson reported twenty-nine shopkeepers, great and small, in Philadelphia, in addition to more than a hundred artisans engaged in over thirty different crafts. Seven years later Gabriel Thomas was able to enumerate sixty different trades being practiced in the town. An astonished visitor in 1710 observed that "There is hardly any Trade in *England*, but the same may be met with in Philadelphia."[30] The number and variety of em-

29. Thomas Ellis to G[eorge] ff[ox], 13 June 1685, Friends Hist. Soc., *Jour.*, 6 (1909), 174.
30. William Penn, *Some Account of the Province of Pennsylvania*, in Myers,

ployments represented by the Quaker settlers no doubt contributed in large measure to the rapidity with which Philadelphia, last of the major colonial towns to be founded, took its place as one of the principal seaports and market towns, challenging within a few years the leadership of Boston.

Finally, in this roster of Quaker callings one can observe the origin of the merchant class which is the subject of this book. From the outset there was in Philadelphia, as in the other colonial towns, a small nucleus of wealthy merchants who dominated the economic and social life of the community and played an important role in its religious and political life. One striking fact about the geographical provenance of these early Quaker merchants in Philadelphia is worth noting: most of them came not directly from England, but from the other American colonies, where for a period of years they had had an opportunity to exercise their talents in mercantile pursuits with somewhat less hindrance from persecuting authorities than in Great Britain.[31] From Barbados came Samuel Carpenter, the richest man in early Philadelphia; from Jamaica, Samuel Richardson, reputedly second only to Carpenter in the amount of his worldly goods. Isaac Norris and Jonathan Dickinson (1663-1722), great merchants and active figures in early Pennsylvania politics, also hailed from Jamaica. From Boston came Edward Shippen (1639-1712), who was reputed to be worth at least ten thousand pounds sterling, and who was known as the owner of the biggest house and the biggest coach in Philadelphia; from New York, Humphrey Morrey (d.

---

ed., *Narratives*, 209; Penn, *A Further Account of the Province of Pennsylvania, ibid*, 261; John Goodson to John and S. Dew, 24 Aug. 1690, "Some Letters and an Abstract of Letters from Pennsylvania," *Pa. Mag. of Hist.*, 4 (1880), 194-95; Thomas, *An Historical and Geographical Account of Pensilvania and West-New-Jersey*, in Myers, ed., *Narratives*, 326-28; *The Voyage, Shipwrack, and Miraculous Escape of Richard Castelman, Gent., With a Description of Pensilvania and the City of Philadelphia* in *The Voyages and Adventures of Captain Robert Boyle* (London, 1726), 365.

31. The General Court of Massachusetts (where the persecution of Quakers had been sharpest) was commanded by the Crown in 1665 to allow Friends to attend to their secular business without molestation.—Rufus M. Jones *et al.*, *The Quakers in the American Colonies*, 110n. Sporadic persecution continued (for example, Edward Shippen, who later removed to Philadelphia, was publicly whipped in Boston for attending Friends meeting in 1671), but it was neither as intense nor as systematic as in the mother country under Charles II.

1715/16), Philadelphia's first mayor, and William Frampton (d. 1686), owner of one of the first wharves on the Delaware river front. William Fishbourne (d. 1742), Samuel Preston (1665-1743), and Richard Hill, all substantial traders, removed to Philadelphia from Maryland; and Anthony Morris (1654-1721), a wealthy brewer, mayor of Philadelphia, and provincial councillor, crossed over from Burlington, New Jersey, when he saw that the commercial future lay on the other side of the Delaware.

These were men of ability, both in the older sense of financial power and in the more usual sense of intellectual and practical capacity. They were men who answered William Penn's description of the type of persons "not only fit for, but necessary in Plantations . . . that is, Men of universal Spirits, that have an eye to the Good of Posterity, and that both understand and delight to promote good Discipline and just Government among a plain and well intending people."[32] Here was the beginning of an aristocracy not merely of wealth, certainly not of birth, but of virtue and talents, whose ranks were to be constantly recruited from among the "Laborious Handicrafts" who formed the bulk of early Quaker Philadelphia's population.

---

32. *Some Account*, Myers, ed., *Narratives*, 210.

Chapter Three

THE WAY TO WEALTH

DILIGENCE is [a] Virtue useful and laudable among Men: It is a discreet and understanding Application of one's Self to Business; and avoids the Extreams of Idleness and Drudgery. It gives great Advantages to Men: It loses no Time, it conquers Difficulties, recovers Disappointments, gives Dispatch, supplies Want of Parts; and is that to them, which a Pond is to a Spring; tho' it has no Water of it self, it will keep what it gets, and is never dry.... Shun Diversions: think only of the present Business, till that be done.... *Solomon* praises Diligence very highly, First, it is the Way to Wealth: *The diligent Hand makes Rich....* Secondly, it prefers Men ... *Seest thou a Man diligent in his Business he shall stand before Kings. Thirdly, it preserves an Estate....* There is no living upon the Principal, you must be diligent to preserve what you have, whether it be Acquisition or Inheritance; else it will consume.

Frugality is a Virtue too, and not of little Use in Life, the better Way to be Rich, for it has less Toil and Temptation. It is proverbial, *A Penny sav'd is a Penny got;* It has a significant Moral; for this Way of getting is more in your own Power and less subject to Hazard, as well as Snares, free of Envy, void of Suits, and is before-hand with Calamities. For many get that cannot keep, and for Want of Frugality spend what they get, and so come to want what they have spent.

Trust no Man with the main Chance, and avoid to be trusted.

This little essay on the economic virtues was written, not

by Benjamin Franklin, but by William Penn,[1] a third of a century before Poor Richard was introduced to the world and almost sixty years before Father Abraham delivered himself of that classic summary of the bourgeois philosophy to which Franklin, using the phrase which Penn had used, gave the title "The Way to Wealth." It is no mere coincidence that Franklin, whom modern sociologists have regarded as the arch-exemplar of the capitalist spirit, received his early business training and developed his economic philosophy in Quaker Philadelphia. The pattern of Franklin's life in Philadelphia—his rise from journeyman printer to wealthy and respected bourgeois—was a familiar one in the Quaker town, where from its founding "Laborious Handicrafts" had been rising by dint of industry and thrift into the ranks of the respectable and the well-to-do. Franklin was a model of those "Men of Universal Spirits" whom Penn considered indispensable in colonial society, but it should be remembered that Franklin was preceded and surrounded by a group of Quaker merchants who had risen by the same route and who lacked only Franklin's brilliant versatility and his talent for self-advertisement.

THE LEGEND OF THE QUAKER
AS BUSINESSMAN

The popular conception of the Quaker as a shrewd businessman has a long history and cannot be lightly dismissed. Early in the history of the Society, George Fox himself observed that "Friends had more trade than many of their neighbours, and if there was any trading, they had a great part of it," and towards the end of his life, as he saw his followers steadily rising from poverty to wealth, he grew increasingly concerned lest material prosperity clog the spiritual life of the Society of Friends. William Edmundson, the apostle of Quakerism in Ireland, felt the same concern. At the end of the seventeenth century, looking back over the first fifty years of the Society of Friends, he noted a lamentable declension from the spirit of the early years

---

1. *The Advice of William Penn to His Children,* in *Works,* I, 908-9, 898.

when, as he put it, "the things of this World were of small Value with us" and "Great Trading was a Burthen." As the Society had grown, he observed, "it happen'd that such a Spirit came in amongst us, as was amongst the *Jews*, when they came up out of *Egypt*, this began to look back into the World, and *traded* with the *Credit* which was not of it's own purchasing, striving to be great in the Riches and Possessions of this World."[2]

Opponents of the Quakers delighted to call attention to their acquisitive talents. The following character of the Quakers, for example, appeared in an enormously popular book first published in 1684:

As to these modern Seducers, they are not Men of *Arms* but a herd of silly insignificant People, aiming rather to heap up Riches in Obscurity, than to acquire a Fame by an heroick Undertaking. They are generally Merchants and Mechanicks, and are observ'd to be very punctual in their Dealings, Men of few Words in a Bargain, modest and compos'd in their Deportment, temperate in their Lives and using great Frugality in all Things. In a Word, they are singularly Industrious, sparing no Labour or Pains to increase their Wealth; and so subtle and inventive, that they would, if possible, extract Gold out of Ashes. I know none that excel them in these Characters but the *Jews* and the *Banians*: The former being the craftiest of all Men, and the latter so superlatively cunning that they will over-reach the Devil.[3]

Sixteen years later another mordant portrait was etched with even stronger acid: the Quakers, wrote an anonymous critic, "are a People that mistake their Interest as seldom as any, being Men of Industry, and Experience, such as are intent upon their Business, Cunning in their Bargains, and Crafty upon all Occasions for their own Ends. And some we find of these *Children of Light* have been so much Wiser than the *Children of this World*, that 'tis now good Advice to look to your Pockets when

2. Fox, *Journal*, I, 186; Braithwaite, *Second Period*, 436-37; *A Journal of the Life, Travels, Sufferings, and Labour of Love in the Work of the Ministry of ... William Edmundson* (Dublin, 1715), 324-25.
3. Giovanni Paolo Marana, *Letters Writ by a Turkish Spy* (10th edn.: London, 1734), VI, 17.

you have any dealing with the Quakers."[4] The imputation of trickery and deceit can perhaps be discounted as the product of pique or jealousy, although these traits are persistent elements in the popular stereotype; in any event, it is difficult either to prove or disprove the charge. The statement of another anti-Quaker writer, however, to the effect that Gracechurch Street Meeting in London at the end of the seventeenth century was composed of "the *Richest* Trading Men in London" must simply be accepted as a statement of historical fact.[5]

Quakers in Philadelphia soon acquired the same reputation as shrewd and successful businessmen. As early as 1701, the Pennsylvania Assembly, composed largely of Quakers, spoke of "the cultivation . . . of the articles of trade and commerce, in which the *Quakers* were known to excel."[6] Dr. Alexander Hamilton, stopping at a tavern in Philadelphia in 1744, sketched a revealing picture of a varied company including Presbyterians, Anglicans, Roman Catholics, Methodists, Moravians, and Anabaptists, vigorously discussing politics and religion while "a knot of Quakers there talked only about selling of flour and the low price it bore."[7] That the less complimentary reputation for slyness and hypocrisy was also popularly attached to Philadelphia Quakers at this period is clear by implication from the comment of a Virginian who, meeting a merchant in Philadelphia in 1744, noted that although he was a Friend, he "seem'd not much Affected to their underhand way of Dealing and Cloak of Religion."[8] Towards the end of the colonial period, a New York merchant, outstripped in the race for foreign orders, sighed that "the Quakers and the Jews are the men nowadays."[9]

---

4. *Remarks upon the Quakers: Wherein the Plain-Dealers Are Plainly Dealt with* (London, 1700), 9.

5. Charles Leslie, *The Snake in the Grass* (London, 1698), 362. The list of attenders at this meeting, situated in the heart of the trading and financial district, reads like a bead-roll of the most important banking and commercial families of England; it includes the Barclays, Gurneys, Hanburys, Lloyds, Osgoods, Hoares, Dimsdales, and Christys, to name only some of the most famous. See Beck and Ball, *London Friends Meetings*, 150, for a fuller list.

6. "Address to the Proprietary," quoted in Proud, *History*, I, 427.

7. Carl Bridenbaugh, ed., *Gentleman's Progress*, 20.

8. R. Alonzo Brock, ed., "Journal of William Black," *Pa. Mag. of Hist.*, 1 (1877), 408.

9. Gerard Beekman to Samuel Fowler, 7 Dec. 1761, quoted in Virginia D.

The strongest proof that this reputation for commercial sagacity and success was justified can be found in the Philadelphia tax list for 1769. Although at this period the Quakers probably constituted no more than one-seventh of Philadelphia's population,[10] they accounted for more than half of those who paid taxes in excess of one hundred pounds. Even more striking is the fact that of the wealthiest seventeen persons in Philadelphia eight were Quakers in good standing and four were men who had been reared in the faith. Only five were non-Quakers, and one of these—William Shippen—owed the basis of his fortune to his Quaker grandfather.[11]

INCIDENTAL FACTORS IN QUAKER BUSINESS SUCCESS

The simplest explanation of this striking circumstance is that it merely reflects the early arrival of the Quakers on the Philadelphia scene and the consequent economic advantage which they enjoyed over all subsequent rivals. This view obviously has some validity, but is hardly adequate to account for the overwhelming commercial pre-eminence of the Quakers in Philadelphia, and it is wholly inapplicable to the situation of Friends in England, who achieved equal economic success in spite of being subject to persecutions and therefore at a strong initial disadvantage in relation to businessmen of other religious persuasions.

Dismissing this accidental circumstance, then, as insufficient by itself to explain the commercial success of the Philadelphia Quakers, we may turn to certain factors common to Friends on both sides of the Atlantic and incidental to their status as a peculiar religious minority. The argument has often been advanced (by Voltaire among others) that since Friends were excluded by statute or conscientious scruple from government office and from all the professions except medicine, their best tal-

Harrington, *The New York Merchant on the Eve of the Revolution* (New York, 1935), 229.
10. Proud, *History*, II, 339.
11. The Proprietary Tax List for 1769 is printed in *Pennsylvania Archives*, 3d Ser., XIV, 151-220. I have defined as "wealthiest" those who paid a tax of more than £500. The tax rate was six pence in the pound.

ents were channeled perforce into trade and commerce.[12] This position too is not without considerable validity, but unlike the first, it relates with peculiar force to the English Quakers and is subject to a number of qualifications when applied to Friends in Pennsylvania.

The testimony against oaths effectually barred Friends from active participation in English politics. The usual avenue to professional life there led through the universities, but even without the barrier of the matriculation oath, the traditional Quaker hostility to universities as nurseries of error and training-grounds for a "hireling priesthood" would have stood in the way of university education for Friends. Unwillingness to take or tender judicial oaths excluded them from the practice of law or service as justices of the peace in the mother country. Law-courts and lawyers, moreover, were in bad odor among Friends; unpleasant experience had led many to join with George Fox in crying out: "away with those lawyers, twenty shilling Councellors, thirty shilling Sergents, ten groat Attourneys, that will throw men into Prison for a thing of nought."[13] The professional ministry, the Army, and the Navy were of course closed to Friends in America as in England by reason of specific Quaker testimonies. Medicine was left as the one profession which was completely eligible for Quakers on both sides of the Atlantic.[14]

In Pennsylvania, on the other hand, the case was altered. No oaths of allegiance were required for officeholding, and for three-

---

12. Voltaire's views are found at the end of the fourth of his *Lettres philosophiques*. See also, for example, Werner Sombart, *The Quintessence of Capitalism*, trans. by M. Epstein (London, 1915), 287; and Amelia M. Gummere, *The Quaker in the Forum* (Philadelphia, 1910), 41.

13. *To the Parliament of the Comon-wealth of England* (London, 1659), 5.

14. See below, pp. 222-28. Another factor which would appear to deserve mention in this connection is the cityward trend of the English Quaker population in the eighteenth century. This phenomenon was observed by Thomas Clarkson who pointed out in 1806 that the Quakers were "flocking into the towns, and . . . abandoning agricultural pursuits." Clarkson attributed this migration to the Quaker objection to the payment of tithes, but added that "the large and rapid profits frequently made in trade, compared with the generally small and slow returns from agricultural concerns, may probably have operated with many, as an inducement to such a change."— *A Portraiture of Quakerism* (New York, 1806), II, 42. No attempt has been made, so far as I know, to verify Clarkson's hypothesis, but in any case it does not apply to Friends in Pennsylvania.

quarters of a century, the important posts in the provincial government were occupied at one time or another by Quakers, most of the Quaker merchants serving for longer or shorter periods in the Assembly or the Governor's Council. By the same token, the substitution of affirmation for the oath enabled Quakers to exercise judicial functions, and throughout the colonial period, Friends served as justices of the peace, presiding justices of county courts, and even as Chief Justice of the provincial Supreme Court. In spite of a residual prejudice against the legal profession and the fact that most differences among Friends were settled out of court by the Monthly Meeting,[15] a few Quakers like David Lloyd, John Kinsey, and Nicholas Waln (1742-1813) became outstanding lawyers. Thus, whatever may have been the case in the mother country, it is clear that in Philadelphia commerce was not the only available livelihood, although it may be granted that it held out the greatest promise of material reward.

THE QUAKER ECONOMIC ETHIC

Although some weight must obviously be given to the incidental factors just mentioned, it should be plain that by themselves they are not adequate to explain the extraordinary absorption and success of the Friends in commercial undertakings. Given the identical phenomenon of unusual economic success under markedly different outward conditions in England and Pennsylvania, it becomes apparent that the fundamental explanation must be sought in something inherently characteristic of Quakerism and thus common to Friends on both sides of the Atlantic. Where shall we find it except in their religious and social philosophy?

It is a commonplace of recent historical writing that an intimate relationship existed between certain of the distinctive ideas of Protestantism and the rise of modern capitalism. Fortunately it is unnecessary here to venture into the disputed realm of priority or to take a position on the moot question of whether the

---

15. See below, pp. 75-80.

Protestant ethic in some way generated modern capitalism or whether it represented merely an accommodation to or rationalization of a pre-existing capitalist spirit. It is sufficient to admit with Troeltsch that "both possessed a certain affinity for each other, that [the] Calvinistic ethic of the 'calling' and of work, which declares that the earning of money with certain precautions is allowable, was able to give [capitalism] an intellectual and ethical backbone, and that, therefore, thus organized and inwardly supported, it vigorously developed, even though within the limits of anti-mammon."[16] Discussion of this problem has been carried on primarily with reference to the Calvinist wing of Protestantism. It would seem desirable to determine how far this line of investigation may be carried with respect to Quakerism.

Quakerism as it arose in the middle of the seventeenth century cannot be understood unless it is seen as one of the variant expressions of the dominant and all-pervasive Puritanism of the age. Atypical in many respects, it yet shared with Puritanism a common substratum of religious and social ideas and habits of mind, some of which were not wholly compatible with the peculiar doctrines which differentiated Quakerism from Puritan orthodoxy. Although Friends believed that the substance of their ethical ideas was the product in each instance of immediate revelation, it is undeniable that in many respects the form and framework in which these ideas were expressed were those of Puritanism. This is not surprising since most converts to Quakerism came from backgrounds which were Puritan in either the specific or the general sense, and, as a recent writer puts it, "Puritans who turned Quaker did not shed their puritanism."[17]

It is this Puritan-Calvinist background which explains the significant difference between the social outlook of the Quakers and that of the Anabaptist groups with which they shared many of their peculiar doctrines and testimonies. It will be remembered that Anabaptism, coming into being almost simultaneously with the Protestant Reformation, arose, like Lutheranism, out of a

16. *Social Teaching*, II, 915.
17. Richard B. Schlatter, *The Social Ideas of Religious Leaders, 1660-1688*, 235.

Roman Catholic background, and that its affinities were with the medieval and earlier sectarian movements—Montanism, Donatism, Waldensianism—and with certain aspects of monasticism as the ecclesiastical counterpart of the sectarian ethos. From these sources it derived a philosophy of separation from the unregenerate world. Regarding the world as hopelessly lost in wickedness, the Anabaptists, like the medieval sects, withdrew from it into their own communities which were regarded as oases in the midst of the wilderness of sin. The Quakers adopted the New-Testament ethic of the Anabaptists, but instead of rejecting the gross world of human appetites and passions, insisted that it was the material out of which the Kingdom of God was to be fashioned. This combination of the ethical position of the Anabaptists with the Calvinist attitude towards the material world was the distinctive feature of Quaker social thought.

With the Puritans, then, Friends looked upon the material world of daily toil and daily bread as God's world in which men were called to do His will. There are few more vigorous expressions of the Protestant attitude towards monastic rejection of the world than William Penn's attack upon "Religious Bedlams" in which monks practiced "a *lazy, rusty, unprofitable Self-Denial,* burdensome to others to feed their Idleness."

The Christian Convent and Monastery [he insisted] are within, where the Soul is encloistered from Sin. And this Religious House the True Followers of Christ carry about with them, who exempt not themselves from the Conversation of the World, though they keep themselves from the Evil of the World in their Conversation. . . . True Godliness don't turn Men out of the World, but enables them to live better in it, and excites their Endeavours to mend it.[18]

God's will, in other words, could be carried out more faithfully on the wharves and in the warehouses and counting rooms of Philadelphia than in the monastic cell or the hermit's cave.

Friends were adjured to remember, however, that this world was transitory and that their hearts should be set not upon its

18. *No Cross No Crown* (1669), in *Works*, I, 295-96.

evanescent goods but upon eternal treasures. "So every one strive to be rich in the life, and in the kingdom and things of the world that hath no end. . ." wrote George Fox to the merchants in 1661. "And therefore, let him that buys, or sells, or possesses, or uses this world, be as if he did not."[19] This was, of course, no other than the doctrine of loving the world with "weaned affections" which, we are told, was "a staple moral of Puritan discourse."[20] William Penn was no less insistent on this theme. "Have a care of cumber, and the love and care of the world . . ." he wrote to Friends in Pennsylvania in 1684; "truly blessed is that man and woman who, in the invisible power, rule their affections about the visible things, and who use the world as true travellers and pilgrims, whose home is not here below."[21]

This *innerweltliche Askese* was an integral part of the way of life which the Quakers brought over to Philadelphia. Let the two Israel Pembertons, father and son, both wealthy and prominent Quaker merchants, speak on this point. "Therefore, Dear Son," wrote the elder Israel Pemberton in 1748 to his son James who was setting off on a business trip to England, "let not the Cares, Profitts or Pleasures of this Transitory life divert thee from the pursuit of a holy self-denying life in which thou wilt find more Solid Satisfaction and Peace of mind, than can be enjoyed in any thing short of it."[22] The younger Israel, writing in the next year about a severe financial loss occasioned by the sinking of one of his ships, summed up this aspect of the economic philosophy of the Quaker merchants in classic form. Experiences of this sort, he declared,

tend to wean the Mind from delighting in transitories and if rightly improv'd—dispose us to look after Enjoyments more certain and permanent. . . . I am sensible there's a Satisfaction and I believe Something of a duty, in doing for ourselves: the Principle of True Religion being Active and never disposes the Mind to Indolence and Sloth, but it likewise Leads us to Consider, I

19. *The Line of Righteousness and Justice Stretched Forth over All Merchants, &c.* (1661), in *Works*, VII, 197.
20. Perry Miller, *The New England Mind* (New York, 1939), 42.
21. Janney, *Life of Penn*, 255.
22. 17 Nov. 1748, Pemberton Papers, IV, 155, Hist. Soc. Pa.

may say often reminds us of the End and Purpose of our Views and Pursuits, and Reproves us for them, if not Consistent with the one Point to which they ought Solely to tend, the Honour of God and Good of Mankind.[23]

Here are the "weaned affections," the "active principle" of true religion, the "duty" of economic activity, and the end thereof conceived in terms of "the Honour of God and Good of Mankind." Neither Richard Baxter nor John Cotton could have quarreled with any of this pious Quaker's sentiments. Even the phrase about "the Good of Mankind" can be duplicated in Puritan sermons, although the overtones of humanitarianism which the phrase carried for the Quaker were largely alien to Puritan thought and practice.[24] In the Quaker's mind, the "Good of Mankind" represented a positive claim upon his material wealth,[25] and no doubt the prospect of being able to help those in need operated as an incentive to further acquisition.

The Puritan concept of the "calling" as the task in life to which each individual was summoned by God was taken for granted by the Quakers.

All Friends [wrote George Fox] in the wisdom of God train up your children in the fear of God . . . and as they are capable, they may be instructed and kept employed in some lawful calling, that they may be diligent, serving the Lord in the things that are good; that none may live idle, and be destroyers of the creation. . . .[26]

No lawful occupation was too gross or too menial to be included among those appointed by God for his service: "the Perfection of Christian Life," declared William Penn, "extends to every honest Labour or Traffic used among Men."[27] Every Quaker minister or "public Friend" followed a mundane calling, although the frequent absences occasioned by their travels in the ministry prevented them from pursuing their temporal vo-

---

23. Letter to John Pemberton, 7 June 1749, Pemberton Papers, V, 107.
24. John Cotton, for instance, declared that in the choice of a calling one must aim at "the publike good."—Quoted in Edmund S. Morgan, *The Puritan Family* (Boston, 1944), 32.
25. See below, Chapter IV.
26. "An Additional Extract from Other of G. F.'s Epistles," *Works*, VII, 345.
27. *No Cross No Crown*, in *Works*, I, 295.

cations with the same assiduity as the full-time merchant, shop-keeper, or farmer. We owe to Thomas Chalkley (1675-1741), minister, sea-captain, and merchant, our most representative Quaker rationale of the calling:

We have Liberty from God, and his dear Son, lawfully, and for Accommodation's Sake, to work or seek for Food or Raiment; tho' that ought to be a Work of Indifferency, compar'd to the great Work of Salvation. Our Saviour saith, *Labour not for the Meat which perisheth, but for that which endureth for ever, or to eternal Life:* By which we do not understand, that Christians must neglect their necessary Occasions and their outward Trades and Callings; but that their chief Labour, and greatest Concern ought to be for their future Well-being in his glorious Kingdom; else why did our Lord say to his Disciples, *Children, have you any Meat?* They answered, *No;* and he bid them *cast their Nets into the Sea, and they drew to Land a Net full of great Fishes;* and Fishing being their Trade, no doubt but they sold them, for it was not likely they could eat 'em all themselves. . . . By this, and much more, which might be noted, it appears that we not only have Liberty to labour in Moderation, but we are given to understand that it is our Duty so to do. The Farmer, the Trades-man, and the Merchant, do not understand by our Lord's Doc-trine, that they must neglect their Calling, or grow idle in their Business, but must certainly work, and be industrious in their Callings.[28]

If one kept one's inner eye single to the Lord and labored diligently in one's calling, one could expect that God would show His favor by adding His blessing in the form of material pros-perity. And conversely business success could be regarded as a visible sign that one was indeed living "in the Light." Thomas Chalkley's *Journal* contains many entries like the following: "After these several Journeys were over . . . I was some Time at Home, and followed my Business with Diligence and Industry, and throve in the Things of the World, the Lord adding a Bless-ing to my Labour."[29] Subject to qualifications implicit in the

---

28. *A Journal, or Historical Account, of the Life, Travels, and Christian Experiences, of that Antient, Faithful Servant of Jesus Christ, Thomas Chalkley,* in *A Collection of the Works of Thomas Chalkley* (Philadelphia, 1749), 97-98.
29. *Ibid.,* 52.

doctrine of stewardship (which, as we shall see, Friends took more seriously than their Puritan contemporaries), property rights were regarded as absolute. In this respect most of the Quaker merchants were in unity with Penn's Whig philosophy which held property, along with liberty, to be the birthright of every Englishman. They agreed with Penn's definition of property as "an Ownership and undisturbed Possession: That which [men] have, is rightly theirs, and no Body's else."[30]

Thus by God's blessing the faithful and diligent Friend, living austerely in accordance with "the simplicity of Truth," almost inevitably accumulated wealth for "the Honour of God and Good of Mankind." James Logan, Penn's erstwhile secretary and a great dealer in furs and skins, confided to an English correspondent that he looked upon it as a particular Providence that he had entered the Indian trade; "should I with open eyes," he added, "give away those advantages that by God's Blessing my own Industry and management have . . . thrown on me to others who have had no part in that Management . . . I could never account for it to my Self and family. . . ."[31]

The virtues of industry and frugality were held in high repute among Quakers. Idleness was looked upon with horror as the breeder of vice and a vain conversation and Friends regarded diligence in a warrantable calling as a religious duty. A striking example of this conception is found in an observation of William Penn when he visited Cork in 1669: he found most of the Friends in prison, but busily engaged, when not gathered in silent worship, in pursuing such crafts and trades as could be carried on under those circumstances. "The jail by that means," he commented, "became a meeting-house and a work-house, for they would not be idle any where."[32] Thomas Chalkley, the sea-

---

30. *England's Present Interest Discovered* (1675), in *Works*, I, 675. "If anything," says a recent student of economic ideas in America, "Penn was more insistent on the sanctity of property rights than were the Puritans."—Joseph Dorfman, *The Economic Mind in American Civilization, 1606-1865* (New York, 1946), I, 91-92.
31. Letter to J. Askew, 9 July 1717, Letter Books, IV, 37, Logan Papers, Hist. Soc. Pa.
32. From a fragment of autobiography printed in Janney, 63.

going Quaker minister quoted earlier, likewise linked the religious with the secular life and associated the virtue of diligence with both: "I followed my Calling; and kept to Meetings diligently; for I was not easy to be idle; either in my spiritual or temporal Callings."[33]

Frugality was most often recommended on religious grounds as essential to that austere simplicity of life which Truth demanded. Occasionally, however, it was justified on more "practical" grounds as tending to increase one's capital and credit. Isaac Norris, a great merchant who had prospered exceedingly in Philadelphia, revealed something of this motivation when he advised his son, just starting out on his first business trip to London: "thou must remember that the more frugall thou art the more will by thy Stock. . . . Come back plain[.] this will be a reputation to thee and recommend thee to the best and most Sensible people—I always suspect the furniture of the Inside Where too much application is Shewn for a Gay or fantasticall outside."[34] Benjamin Franklin, who was soon to open a shop in Philadelphia after a period of training under the Quaker merchant Thomas Denham (d. 1728), was to recall, years later, the methods by which he had established his reputation: "In order to secure my credit and character as a tradesman," he was to write, "I took care not only to be in *reality* industrious and frugal, but to avoid all appearances to the contrary. I drest plainly. . . ."[35] He does not expressly avow it, but he may well have learned this lesson from his Quaker preceptor.

Prudence, honesty, and a strong sense of order were other virtues which contributed to Quaker business success. Friends became known for their extreme caution in business undertakings. Their book of discipline contained a standing advice against buying, bargaining, or contracting beyond one's abilities, and in meetings for discipline Friends were constantly warned against imprudent ventures by the Query: "Are Friends careful to live

33. *Journal*, in *Works*, 37.
34. Isaac Norris I to Joseph (?) Norris, April (?), 1719, Norris Letter Book, 1716-30, 183-84.
35. *Autobiography*, in *Writings*, I, 307.

within the Bounds of their Circumstances, and to avoid launching into Trade or Business beyond their ability to manage?" [36] If a Friend were so imprudent as to be forced into bankruptcy without prospect of meeting his obligations, he stood in danger of disownment by the meeting. Thus prudence had its spiritual as well as its temporal sanctions.

Because Quaker businessmen were known to be scrupulously honest, people were glad to deal with them. From almost the very beginning, as George Fox records, "when people came to have experience of Friends' honesty and faithfulness, and found that their yea was yea and their nay was nay; that they kept to a word in their dealings, and that they would not cozen and cheat them," customers flocked to do business with them.[37] An incident during the Seven Years' War may be cited as illustrative of the honesty for which American Quaker merchants were known. The brigantine *Hannah*, owned by James Pemberton and Peter Reeve of Philadelphia, sailed from Jamaica in 1758, laden with molasses, coffee, and sugar. She was captured, being unarmed, by a French privateer from New Orleans. The captain of the *Hannah*, knowing that the cargo was worth more than four thousand pounds, treated with the privateer for ransom, and an agreement was reached that the owners should pay eight thousand dollars. Two of the crew were left on board the privateer as hostages. The *Hannah* put in at Boston, and a message was dispatched to Philadelphia. Merchants in Boston meanwhile informed the French officer on the *Hannah* that he could not expect legally to collect the ransom money, the bond having been given without the consent of the owners. The French officer told them: "Me no fraid; me got Quaker to deal with." Upon arrival at Philadelphia, he was informed of the same illegality by merchants at the coffee-house who also tried to persuade Pemberton not to pay the bond. Pemberton nevertheless agreed to pay the ransom as soon as he should learn that the hostages had arrived safely in a French

36. "The Book of Discipline as Revised by the Yearly Meeting for Pennsylvania and New Jersey in the Year 1719," MS in Friends Historical Library of Swarthmore College, 15, 76.
37. *Journal*, I, 186.

port. When the privateer made land in the French West Indies, the hostages escaped and met an English privateer which brought them to Philadelphia. They said that their primary inducement for running away had been their expectation that the *Hannah's* owners would have been discharged from payment of the ransom. Although the Attorney-General disallowed the claim and in spite of criticism from his fellow merchants, James Pemberton paid the ransom in full.[38]

Paradoxically, it was probably an aspect of this very virtue of strict truthfulness that gave Friends the opposite reputation for slyness and dishonesty. Cherishing such a respect for the truth in its stark simplicity, Quakers were characteristically taciturn: "they recommended *Silence* by their Example," reported William Penn, "having few Words upon all Occasions."[39] One recalls Franklin's precept concerning silence: "Speak not but what may benefit others or yourself; avoid trifling conversation."[40] The advice of Friend John Reynell to young Elias Bland, just completing his mercantile apprenticeship, shows how taciturnity could be an asset in the conduct of business:

In doing business be a little on the Reserve, and Observe well the Person thou has to do with. . . . Keep thy Business to thy self, and don't let it be known, who thou dost Business for, or what Sorts of Goods thou Ships off. Some will want to know both, perhaps with a Design to Circumvent thee. Endeavour to know what Prices other People give for Goods, but Say nothing of what thou gives thy self,—or where thou Buys, its very Probable some will tell thee, they give more for a thing than they did, on Purpose to make thee buy dear, in Order to do thee an Injury in thy Business. If thou finds out a Place where they Sell cheap, keep it to thy Self, for if thou Ships off Goods cheaper than others, it will increase Business.[41]

---

38. This story is told without documentation in John and Isaac Comly, eds., *Friends Miscellany* (Byberry, Pa., 1837), VII, 53-56. The main outlines, however, agree with a "State of the Case" signed by James Pemberton in the Letters and Papers of William Penn, 87, Dreer Collection, Hist. Soc. Pa.
39. *The Rise and Progress of the People Called Quakers*, in *Works*, I, 869.
40. *Autobiography*, in *Writings*, I, 327.
41. Letter dated 22 June 1743, Reynell Letter Book, 1741-44, Coates-Reynell Papers, Hist. Soc. Pa.

It is not difficult to understand how the uncommunicative Quaker, who found that it "paid" to be close-mouthed, could come to seem secretive and subtle, and how consequently the traits of slyness and dishonesty could be build into the legend of the Quaker businessman.

A sympathetic French visitor to Philadelphia shortly after the American Revolution was to call especial attention to "the order which the Quakers are accustomed from childhood to apply to the distribution of their tasks, their thoughts, and every moment of their lives. They carry this spirit of order everywhere," he went on; "it economizes time, activity, and money." [42] This virtue was essential for success in a "rationalized" capitalist economy in which the pursuit of gain was regarded as a continuous and intensive activity based upon the expectation of regular production, markets, and profits. William Penn had advised his children to cultivate this habit of order, suggesting that they set apart a definite part of each day for meditation and worship of God, a definite part for business ("in which remember to ply that first which is first to be done"), and a definite part for themselves. [43] Again one cannot help recalling Benjamin Franklin, who listed "order" as third in his catalogue of virtues, adding this precept: "Let all your things have their places; let each part of your business have its time." [44]

When the unfinished manuscript of Franklin's autobiography happened to fall into the hands of a Quaker merchant of Philadelphia after the Revolution, he at once recognized how consummately it inculcated virtues which Friends held in high regard. He therefore urged Franklin to complete and publish it, adding that "the influence writings under that class have on the minds of youth is very great, and has nowhere appeared to me so plain as in our public friends [i.e., Quaker ministers'] journals." He expressed confidence that Franklin's account of his early life

---

42. Jean Pierre Brissot de Warville, *Nouveau voyage dans les Etats-unis de l'Amérique septentrionale*, II, 187. Brissot adds that this is quite opposite to the training and habits customary in Catholic France.
43. *Advice to His Children*, in *Works*, I, 899.
44. *Autobiography*, in *Writings*, I, 328.

would lead the post-Revolutionary generation to emulate the diligence and temperance which the young Franklin had so notably exhibited. "I know of no character living," concluded the good Quaker, ". . . who has so much in his power as thyself to promote a greater spirit of industry and early attention to business, frugality, and temperance with the American youth."[45]

---

45. Abel James to Benjamin Franklin, *ibid.*, I, 313-14. See Appendix A: "Benjamin Franklin and the Quakers."

JOHN REYNELL
*Typical Quaker Merchant of pre-Revolutionary Philadelphia
Courtesy of the Historical Society of Pennsylvania*

JAMES LOGAN

Scientist, philosopher, humanist, chief justice, successful fur merchant

The Historical Society of Pennsylvania

Free Library of Philadelphia

MARY LLOYD
NORRIS

Wife of the first Isaac Norris, daughter of Deputy-Governor Thomas Lloyd

ISAAC NORRIS II

Speaker of the Provincial Assembly, opulent merchant, son-in-law of James Logan

The Historical Society of Pennsylvania

Albert Cook Myers

SARAH LOGAN NORRIS

Daughter of James Logan, wife of Isaac Norris II and mistress of Fairhill

JOHN SMITH

Success in business and marriage to Hannah Logan enabled him to retire early and devote himself to the service of the Meeting

The Historical Society of Pennsylvania

HENRY DRINKER

Partner in the firm of James and Drinker, investor in western lands and pioneer in manufacturing enterprises. Courtesy of Henry S. Drinker, Esq.

DR. SAMUEL
PRESTON MOORE

*One of a notable group of
Quaker physicians who parti-
cipated fully in the life of the
Quaker mercantile aristocracy*

The Historical Society of Pennsylvania

JAMES PEMBERTON

*Member of a leading Quaker
family, who divided his attention between the counting
house, the state house, and the
meeting house*

EDWARD SHIPPEN'S HOUSE,
SOUTH SECOND STREET

The Historical Society of Pennsylvania

CHARLES NORRIS'S MANSION,
CHESTNUT STREET

FAIRHILL, BUILT BY ISAAC NORRIS I
ABOUT 1716

The Historical Society of Pennsylvania

PEMBERTON'S PLANTATION,
BUILT ABOUT 1735

THE "GREAT MEETING HOUSE"
AND THE COURT HOUSE

The Historical Society of Pennsylvania

THE FOURTH STREET MEETING HOUSE
AND THE FRIENDS PUBLIC SCHOOL

Chapter Four

THE HOLY COMMUNITY

I F one phase of the Quaker ethic promoted economic individualism and the accumulation of wealth, there were strong countervailing tendencies in the direction of corporate responsibility and criticism of the acquisitive spirit. The aim of the Quaker settlers in coming to Pennsylvania was not primarily the improvement of individual fortunes but the establishment of a society penetrated by religious values and firmly controlled in the interests of the community. "Our business . . . here, in this *new land*," wrote one of them, "is not so much to *build houses*, and *establish factories*, and promote *trade* and *manufactories*, that may enrich ourselves, (though all these things, in their due place, are not to be neglected) as to erect temples of *holiness* and *righteousness*, which God may delight in; to lay such lasting frames and foundations of *temperance* and *virtue*, as may support the superstructures of our future happiness, both in this, and the other world."[1] All the affairs of life in the Quaker colony were to be ordered for the greater glory of God, and the secular government was looked upon, especially in the early years, as an appropriate agency for promoting distinctive Quaker ideas of the social order.

Although in the first chapter of the "Great Law" it was specifically provided that Church and State should be separated,

---

1. "The Planter's Speech to His Neighbours," quoted in Proud, *History*, I, 227*n*.

nevertheless, in the earliest days of the colony, when almost all the inhabitants were Friends, Monthly Meetings often exercised the functions of civil administration. Philadelphia Monthly Meeting, for example, appointed committees to lay out roads.[2] As the civil government became more competent, there was a separation of functions, but since Friends dominated the legislature long after they had become a minority in the population at large, the laws of Pennsylvania for many years were shot through with their moral and religious concepts. Penn's first Frame of Government required the Provincial Council to appoint "a committee of manners, education, and arts, that all wicked and scandalous living may be prevented, and that youth may be successively trained up in virtue and useful knowledge and arts";[3] and the Proprietor openly expressed approval of sumptuary legislation.[4] Medieval ideas of regulating economic life were taken for granted by Philadelphians of the first generation, as, for example, when the Provincial Council, composed of Quakers, passed laws controlling prices and empowering justices of the county courts to fix wages.[5] In his *Further Account of Pennsylvania*, published in 1685, Penn made a point of stating that "the hours for Work and Meals to Labourers are fixt, and known by Ring of Bell."[6] In these respects, the ideal of early Quaker Philadelphia was, as Troeltsch has pointed out, "the same ideal as that of Geneva in the days of early Calvinism."[7]

It was the Monthly Meeting, however, which, more than anything else, was the outward embodiment of the "holy com-

2. Gummere, *The Quaker in the Forum*, 183.

3. *Charter to William Penn and Laws of the Province of Pennsylvania*, 96.

4. "Our Noble *English Patriarchs* as well as Patriots . . . made several excellent Laws, commonly called *Sumptuary*, to *Forbid*, at least *Limit* the *Pride* of the People, which because the Execution of them would be our *Interest* and *Honour*, their Neglect must be our just Reproach and Loss."—*Some Fruits of Solitude* (1693), in *Works*, I, 854.

5. *Minutes of the Provincial Council*, I, 91, 98.

6. Myers, ed., *Narratives*, 262.

7. *Social Teaching*, II, 782. Robert K. Merton, referring to R. H. Tawney's suggestion that "Calvinist theology was accepted where Calvinist discipline was repudiated," has cogently observed that "the converse may likewise be maintained."—"Science, Technology, and Society in Seventeenth-Century England," *Osiris*, 4 (1938), 416.

munity." In addition to nourishing the religious life and guarding the morals of its members, it functioned as a dispenser of poor relief, a loan office, a court of arbitration in economic matters, an employment agency, and a source of advice to new arrivals on the management of their affairs.

"THE LORD'S POOR"

One phase of the economic role of the Monthly Meeting was closely akin to the long-standing Anabaptist-Mennonite custom of "mutual aid," and represented a similar implementation of the concept of the "holy community" as a voluntary association of believers united in common commitment to the highest end— the *Nachfolge Christi*.[8] Within the bonds of this fellowship, the absolute theory of property was qualified, and the existence of material need anywhere in the fellowship represented a moral claim upon the wealth of the other members. It can be argued that the sensitivity of the Quakers to the needs of the poor arose from the fact that the memory of their own lean years was still fresh. The more compelling explanation lies, however, in their conviction that every man was a vehicle of the Seed of God and therefore deserved the love and, in the event of misfortune, the sympathetic help of all his fellow men. Nothing could have been further removed from the Puritan view of poverty as a crime and a disgrace, a visible sign of God's displeasure and a punishment for the sins of laziness and improvidence. The obligation of charity was a corollary of the venerable doctrine of stewardship (and as such will be discussed later); it was also a function of the basic Quaker conception of community and of the belief that all men were brothers and children of the one Father of Lights.

At the first session of Philadelphia Monthly Meeting in 1682 it was agreed that "because some may through sickness, weakness, or Death of Relations be reduced to want or distress . . . care shall be taken to administer present supplies."[9] For this purpose collec-

8. See J. Winfield Fretz, "Mutual Aid among Mennonites," *Mennonite Quarterly Review*, 13 (1939), 28-58, 187-209.
9. Manuscript Minutes of Philadelphia Monthly Meeting, I, 1 (9 Feb. 1682)

tions were regularly taken towards the monthly meeting's "stock," from which funds were disbursed to those in need. As the principal port of entry for Pennsylvania, Philadelphia was disproportionately burdened with the care of poor and sick immigrants. In 1685 this problem had become so great that it was laid before the Quarterly Meeting, which comprised meetings held at the nearby settlements of Oxford, Byberry, Cheltenham, Haverford, Merion, and Radnor; the Quarterly Meeting made provision for the collection of a stock to be applied to the necessities of "poor friends in general." "This is proposed," read the minute, "that we may continue to have a true feeling sence of such among us as are the Lord's true poor, who may cry to the Lord for relief, that as children of one father there may be such provision made amongst us . . . that there may not be a beggar amongst us, nor any justly to complain in our streets, but that our Bowels may be open to them for their Relief." [10]

Since contributions to the meeting's stock by common agreement were proportioned to the individual Friend's ability, the wealthier merchants from the beginning bore the major part of the burden of poor relief. Moreover, it usually fell to them as "weighty Friends" to serve as Overseers charged with the administration of relief. For example, in 1712 Anthony Morris, wealthy merchant and brewer, and William Hudson, owner of several tanneries in Philadelphia, were asked by the Monthly Meeting to inquire into the condition of "a poor friend that came lately from England . . . and help him out of the monthly meetings Stock." Being hard-headed if soft-hearted men of business, the Overseers usually preferred to see the meeting's funds appropriated for specific purposes, as when the meeting in 1696 gave the necessitous family of John Gardner the amount of five pounds towards the expense of building a house, or when a sum was raised in 1691 to buy a cow for a poor widow, "her former cow being dead." [11]

Department of Records, Philadelphia Yearly Meeting. Hereafter cited as MS Minutes of Phila. MM.

10. MS Minutes of Phila. MM, I, 21 (7 Dec. 1685).

11. *Ibid.*, I, 306 (26 Sept. 1712); I, 98 (27 March 1696); I, 67 (27 March 1691).

The Overseers, acting on behalf of the meeting, frequently underwrote the medical expenses of needy members: a minute of 1689, for example, states that "Samuel Carpenter and Alexr Beardsley having promised to John Goodson to see him satisfied for the curing of Thomas Smith, the meeting are willing to repay them again."[12] Upon occasion, the meeting even provided a form of workmen's compensation, ordering in 1687 "that William Vidler shall have 3/. a week allowed him towards his maintenance, as not being able to work." In the earliest years, before the appropriate secular agencies existed in Philadelphia, the meeting performed a wide range of additional services for its poor. The early minutes contain references to providing "Corn in store for poor friends before the river be frozen up," supplying employment for those who needed it, and "counselling such as come over from England at their first arrival, what course to take to manage what they bring and also relating to their settlement."[13]

By 1713 the problem of Philadelphia's poor had reached a point where it could only be handled on a systematic institutional basis. In that year the meeting opened an Alms House on Walnut Street on a property bequeathed to it by one John Martin, a poor tailor who had been cared for by the meeting. In 1729 a larger and more adequate Alms House was erected by the meeting. An almost unique feature (for this period) of the Friends Alms House was that it was so arranged as to allow a degree of privacy to the families lodged there. Those who were able were expected to practice their callings so as to contribute to their own support and to their mental health.[14]

The Monthly Meeting stock also served as a loan fund. Sometimes the loan was made in order to enable a Friend to

---

12. *Ibid.,* I, 56 (30 Aug. 1689). John Goodson (d. 1727) was one of the first practicing physicians in Philadelphia. See below, pp. 224-25.
13. MS Minutes of Phila. MM, I, 34 (29 April 1687); I, 21 (2 Nov. 1685); I, 15 (9 Feb. 1684); I, 22 (4 Jan. 1685).
14. Carl Bridenbaugh, *Cities in the Wilderness,* 235-36; Davis H. Forsythe, "Friends Almshouse in Philadelphia," Friends Historical Association, *Bulletin,* 16 (1927), 16-25.

discharge a debt incurred in connection with his passage to Pennsylvania, as when Thomas Speakman in 1712 was advanced seven pounds "to clear the Shipmaster from what he is indebted to him." When, as in the case of Robert Burrows in 1713, the application was for a larger amount ("Twenty two pounds to answer his necessity for the paying some debts, which the people are very urgent upon him for"), two or three Friends of sound financial judgment were appointed to advise the borrower on the management of his affairs.[15] Loans from the Monthly Meeting, which generally carried no interest, were most often made for specific projects—for building a house or setting a young man up in trade.[16]

With the steady increase of prosperity among Friends, there were fewer calls on the Monthly Meeting's funds for the relief of needy members. From the beginning, however, special subscriptions had from time to time been raised to meet emergencies that arose among the membership, particularly as a result of natural catastrophes. In 1695, for example, Friends collected more than twenty two pounds for Joseph Phips, whose house had burned down, and in 1701 a collection was taken for Richard Townsend "who hath lost great part of what he had, lately by a great Flood."[17] The principal donors were naturally the more substantial merchants. Frequently individual merchants took the responsibility for raising the money. When Friend Preserve Brown's brewhouse burned to the ground in 1749, John Smith carried a subscription paper about among his fellow merchants, finding some "very free to give," and others to his sorrow "very skillful in distinctions to Excuse themselves." Israel Pemberton the elder headed the list of contributors with thirty pounds and his son Israel followed with twenty-five; twenty-nine other

---

15. MS Minutes of Phila. MM, I, 308 (29 Nov. 1712); I, 312-13 (27 March 1713).
16. For example, the Meeting in 1713 lent one Friend a sum of money "in order for carrying on his trade of Candle making"; and in 1744 it lent another Friend £10 (to be repaid in twelve months) to buy a stocking weaver's loom.—*Ibid.*, I, 319 (28 Aug. 1713); II, 371 (29 June 1744).
17. *Ibid.*, I, 91 (31 May 1695); I, 153 (31 Oct. 1701).

Quaker merchants made contributions of varying amounts, bringing the total to more than two hundred pounds.[18]

The sense of community which underlay the Quaker practice of mutual aid was not restricted to members of the local meeting. By the opening of the eighteenth century, as Rufus M. Jones has observed, "the Friends were *one* people throughout the world, though there was absolutely no *bond* but love and fellowship. . . . Wherever any Friend was in trouble the world over, all Friends, however remote, were concerned, and were ready to help share the trouble if it could be shared."[19] Philadelphians were quick to go to the aid of fellow-Quakers in distress, whether in a nearby town or on the other side of the globe. As early as 1684, one finds this minute: "Derrick Isaacs a Dutch friend of German Town acquainting this meeting of the wants of some of the Dutch there, The meeting ordered Samuel Carpenter and Griffith Jones to pay their subscriptions unto one, or some of them, that are in most need of a present supply."[20] Since Samuel Carpenter and Griffith Jones were two of the wealthiest Friends in Philadelphia, their proportion of the meeting's subscription no doubt constituted a considerable sum. In 1692 Friends in Philadelphia and Chester County contributed more than eighty pounds towards the redemption and relief of a number of Quakers (including one George Palmer, son of a "first purchaser" of land in Pennsylvania) who were held captive by pirates at "Masquenes" (Mequinez, now Meknès).[21]

When reports reached Philadelphia in 1697 of a great calamity which had overtaken "friends and other people . . . to

---

18. MS Diary of John Smith, IX (entries for 13, 15, 17 Jan. 1749), Library Company of Philadelphia.
19. *Quakers in the American Colonies*, 314-15. Compare the statement of John Bellers: "It is not he that dwells nearest that is only our Neighbour, but he that wants our Help also claims that Name and our Love."—*Epistle to the Quarterly Meeting of London and Middlesex* (1718), reprinted in A. Ruth Fry, ed., *John Bellers, 1654-1725: Quaker, Economist, and Social Reformer*, 152.
20. MS Minutes of Phila. MM, I, 14 (3 Feb. 1684). Derrick Isaacs op den Graeff was one of the leaders among the early Germantown Friends. See Hull, *William Penn and the Dutch Quaker Migration*, 211-15.
21. MS Minutes of Phila. MM, I, 75 (24 June 1692); see also [Samuel Tuke,] *Account of the Slavery of Friends in the Barbary States* (London, 1848), 17-22.

the Eastward of Salem in New England," a general subscription was raised among Friends and sent for their relief.[22] Twenty-eight years later, a sum of more than £40 was raised in Philadelphia for the benefit of one John Hanson, a New England Friend, whose wife and children had been taken captive by Indians; this money, increased to more than £180 by contributions from other meetings in Pennsylvania and New Jersey, enabled Hanson to redeem his family from captivity without plunging himself into debt.[23] These collections were precedents for the great effort which Philadelphia Quakers made in 1775 for the relief of Friends and others who were suffering by reason of the British siege of Boston. Philadelphia merchants like the Pembertons were at the forefront of this undertaking, in which more than two thousand pounds was collected and transmitted to the Meeting for Sufferings in New England for relief purposes. Arising in the first instance as a concern for the welfare of Friends, the impulse to alleviate suffering broadened until it embraced all the victims to whom aid could be brought "without distinction of sects or parties."[24]

As the last instance shows, Quaker charity was not limited to members of the Society of Friends. Convinced that all men were equally children of God, the Quakers allowed their compassion to flow forth towards all who were in distress, whether their suffering were the result of an act of God or of the equally desolating acts of their fellow men. In Monthly Meeting on 9 February 1684 "it was proposed whether friends as a people are to take care for any poor but their own, to say, such as walk

22. MS Minutes of Phila. MM., I, 106 (30 July 1697). It is not clear whether the disaster was an epidemic (James Bowden, *A History of the Society of Friends in America*, II, 36) or a series of Indian raids (Jones et al., *Quakers in the American Colonies*, 553).
23. MS Minutes of Phila. MM, II, 129 (31 Dec. 1725). The list of Philadelphia contributors is among the records of Philadelphia Monthly Meeting (Book C26, p. 248).
24. On this signal incident in the long history of nonpartisan Quaker relief in wartime, see Henry J. Cadbury, "Quaker Relief during the Siege of Boston," Colonial Society of Massachusetts, *Transactions*, 34 (1943), 39-179. For other examples see Frederick B. Tolles, "Heralds of the Red and Black Star: Episodes from the Earlier History of Quaker War Relief," *Friends Intelligencer*, 100 (1943), 535-36, 557-58, 574-75.

according to Truth, and will receive their admonition"; and it was the sense of the meeting that regular contributions should be made to the magistrates "for the relief of all poor people." The meeting often anticipated the action of the civil authorities, however, as when in 1699 a committee of Friends was named "to assist the Sick and weak passengers arrived from Liverpool with money and conveniences . . . to be repaid out of this meeting's Stock."[25] The purses of individual Friends were always open to the needy. John Smith recorded in his diary in 1747 that in spite of a great increase in the number of beggars, he had "not yet sent any away Empty handed," adding that " a fellow feeling of the Infirmities and wants of our Brethren—as all mankind are— is a duty, and not sufficiently practiced, without Administering Relief when in our power."[26]

The Friends Alms House was open to the indigent of all faiths; indeed until pressure from individual Friends led the Corporation of Philadelphia in 1732 to erect a public alms house, it was the only such institution in the city. The public alms house, once established, soon became inadequate, and individual Quakers again took the lead in providing better facilities, organizing "The Contributors to the Relief and Employment of the Poor of the City of Philadelphia" to build a new structure. Friend Joseph Wharton contributed eighty pounds to this undertaking and many other Quaker merchants made similar contributions. The new "Bettering House" under a succession of Quaker stewards was a model institution, favorably commented upon by every visitor to Philadelphia.[27]

In 1741 Philadelphia Monthly Meeting extended the hand of Christian charity across colonial boundaries to aid sufferers from a great conflagration which had swept Charleston, South Carolina, in the previous year, destroying over three hundred dwellings and other property amounting to two hundred thou-

25. MS Minutes of Phila. MM, I, 14-15, 124.
26. MS Diary, Vol. III (20 Feb. 1747).
27. Bridenbaugh, *Cities*, 235-36, 394-95; Carl and Jessica Bridenbaugh, *Rebels and Gentlemen: Philadelphia in the Age of Franklin*, 232-35.

sand pounds.[28] When the Shawanese Indians fell upon the peaceful Moravian village of Gnadenhütten in 1755, causing panic-stricken German farmers to seek shelter in Bethlehem and Nazareth, Bishop Spangenberg at once appealed to Philadelphia Friends for food, clothing, and money. Joseph Norris, John Pemberton, and Anthony Benezet quickly raised two hundred pounds and sent wagonloads of blankets, shoes, and other supplies off to the distressed refugees.[29] It is clear that the plight of the refugee from war or other forms of violence made a special appeal to the humanitarian sympathies of the Friends. In the same year as the Gnadenhütten disaster, three boatloads of hapless Acadian exiles, driven from their homes in Nova Scotia by the British government, arrived in the Delaware River. In the face of their obvious destitution the Provincial Assembly provided a trickle of money for their relief, but as control of the Assembly passed from Quaker hands, the main burden of their care fell upon Anthony Benezet who for more than five years trudged regularly from door to door among the Quaker merchants with subscription papers. One Friend provided ground for the construction of homes for the exiles, and others contributed money. Benezet voiced the Quaker theory of personal obligation to suffering humanity when he wrote to his friend John Smith: "Did the good Samaritan hold himself excused from relieving the wounded traveller because there were laws in Judea and persons to whom the duty of taking care of the distressed stranger belonged?" [30] This sense of private obligation, apart from or in addition to public provision for the relief of the distressed, has been a continuing force in Quakerism, most notably manifested in recent years through the work of the American Friends Service Committee.

Such, then, were some of the implications and ramifications of the Quaker concept of the "holy community" in the realm of philanthropy. It is clear that the merchants, who bore the leading

---

28. MS Minutes of Phila. MM, II, 326 (27 Jan. 1741); Bridenbaugh, *Cities*, 372.
29. Letters of Anthony Benezet to Joseph and August Gottlieb Spangenberg, reprinted in Brookes, *Benezet*, 212-19.
30. Letter dated 1 Oct. 1760, Brookes, 241.

parts in the meeting's activities, felt the needs of "the Lord's poor" and of all victims of natural or man-made catastrophes as insistent and irresistible calls to religious duty.

THE ECONOMIC ROLE OF THE MEETING

The meeting's control of the individual Friend's economic life did not cease, however, with this gentle enforcement of the obligation of charity. The whole range of his private affairs was subject to supervision and, at times, interference by the meeting. Final determination of moral questions arising in the conduct of business was by no means left in the hands of the individual, following his own Inner Light. All such problems were considered in their relationship to the good name of Truth, wherein all members of the meeting had an equal stake; any conduct, therefore, which was likely to bring reproach upon the Truth was a matter for discipline by the whole group, acting in the power and wisdom of the divine Spirit.

Since all secular affairs, according to Quaker conviction, came within the purview of religion, there was nothing unusual in Philadelphia Yearly Meeting's expressed concern in 1713 "that all Friends be very careful in making and vending all provisions and other Commodities for Transportation, taking care that the same be good and of due fineness, measure and weight." Nor was the Yearly Meeting in any way overstepping the bounds of its competence when it cautioned Friends against running into debt and courting bankruptcy. Indeed Quarterly Meetings were advised to appoint "Substantial Friends . . . to visit every Family amongst us, where they think there is Occasion to suspect they are going backward in their Worldly Estate, and to Enquire and See how things are with them."[31]

The Queries which, especially after 1743, were regularly read and answered in Monthly Meeting, contained pertinent reminders of the standard of economic morality expected of members. At least four times a year, merchants and all others engaged in business were confronted with these insistent interrogatories:

31. MS Minutes of Phila. YM, I, 152, 128.

Are there any who launch into business beyond what they are able to manage, and so break their promises, in not paying their just debts in due time? And where differences happen, are endeavours used to have them speedily ended?

Are Friends clear of depriving the King of his duties? Do Friends observe the former advices of the Yearly Meeting, not to encourage the importation of negroes, nor to buy them after imported?

Are Friends careful to settle their affairs and make their wills in time of health?[32]

Each Friend answered the Queries silently to himself, conscious that the ultimate sanction for enforcement of the rules of discipline was disownment from the Society. The Overseers prepared responses covering the general state of the meeting and forwarded them to the Quarterly Meeting.

The Epistle of Philadelphia Yearly Meeting in 1695 warned members in strong terms against trading "beyond their Abilities," and further advised that "if any are Indebted abroad or at Home, and Answer not the same in due Time, That such be admonished thereof, that Truth may not be Reproached, and People whether Rich or Poor kept out of their Just Debts."[33] If the circumstances of the bankruptcy reflected neither imprudence nor dishonesty but unavoidable accidents or circumstances beyond the individual's control, the meeting's severity was tempered with mercy and Christian love. Such a person was instructed to offer all his assets to his creditors, and if that fell short, to place his person also at their disposal. Thereafter he might receive the compassion and assistance of the other members of the meeting: "he hath done what he can," read the Epistle of 1710, "and we can expect no further from him."[34] In 1707 the meeting assisted Arnold Cassel, one of the early emigrants from Krisheim in the Palatinate, in dividing his belongings among his creditors, and later proceeded to raise a subscription for his benefit.[35] On the other hand,

---

32. Ezra Michener, *A Retrospect of Early Quakerism*, 255-56.
33. MS Minutes of Phila. YM, I, 54. This concern lest Friends trade "beyond their Abilities" can be traced back to Fox's great *pronunciamento* on commercial ethics in 1661, *The Line of Righteousness*, in *Works*, VII, 196.
34. MS Minutes of Phila. YM, I, 134.
35. MS Minutes of Phila. MM, I, 236, 274 (26 Sept. 1707; 26 May 1710).

if after careful investigation and loving counsel by the Overseers it appeared that the bankrupt did not intend to try to pay his debts, he was forthwith disowned. Herein perhaps lies one of the reasons for so high a proportion of successful businessmen among Friends: those who were notably unsuccessful were disowned and disavowed.

Disputes of many kinds came before the Monthly Meeting for arbitration. For solving such problems without resort to law courts the Discipline laid down an elaborate procedure based upon Matthew XVIII: 15-17, and known as "Gospel Order." This consisted of five or six distinct steps including personal negotiations, hearings, and arbitration by disinterested Friends.[36] If after all these measures had been taken in patience and Christian love, one of the parties still refused to comply, he was disowned by the meeting. Only then, after the offender had been cast out of the fellowship, was it permissible for the aggrieved Friend to commence legal proceedings. The ingrained Quaker dislike of law courts and the desire to keep the Truth free from public reproach combined to render this method of settling grievances remarkably effective. So successfully did it operate that ocasionally one finds record of non-Friends applying to the meeting for the settlement of disputes with Friends: in 1714, for example, Andrew Hamilton, later Attorney-General of the province, submitted to the Monthly Meeting's arbitration a dispute between himself and a Friend named Pentecost Teague.[37] Friends were officially discouraged from going to law with "the world's people," although since the Monthly Meeting could claim no jurisdiction over non-members, legal recourse was permitted when other means of settling differences failed. On the whole, however, it is probable that most disputes to which Quakers were parties were settled out of court.[38]

---

36. See Appendix B for details.
37. MS Minutes of Phila. MM, I, 338 (31 Dec. 1714). Teague was an early antislavery Friend who wrote a paper in 1698 against the selling of Negroes at public auction.—See Henry J. Cadbury, "Another Early Quaker Anti-Slavery Document," *Journal of Negro History*, 27 (1942), 211.
38. Unfortunately it is impossible to test this generalization since most of the Philadelphia County court records for our period have disappeared. Fairly conclusive collateral evidence, however, emerges from a study of the court

Differences brought to the Monthly Meeting for settlement involved such matters as property rights, payment of wages, interpretation of contracts, settlement of estates, and collection of debts. At a very early session of Philadelphia Monthly Meeting, Friends were asked to require one of their number to turn over a "plantation" which another member had contracted for. Two Friends were authorized in 1684 to set a price upon some cattle which one member had promised to another in payment for an indentured servant. In the next year, a glazier in the employ of the Free Society of Traders complained to the meeting that he had not received his wages, and a committee was appointed to speak to officials of the Society about it. In 1698, the meeting was called upon to establish a boundary line between properties owned by two Friends, and to settle a dispute over a party wall. On another occasion, one Nathaniel Lamplugh complained of Samuel Carpenter, who had agreed with him for a vessel to be built for a Maryland Friend; when the specifications came, Lamplugh alleged, they were for a vessel only about half the size originally stipulated so that the lumber which he had prepared was too heavy. The aggrieved Friend demanded satisfaction. Carpenter acknowledged that his complaint was just, but the Maryland Friend refused to pay damages. The meeting therefore appointed a committee to inquire into the matter and effect a settlement.[39] Problems of this sort, together with the oversight of marriages and discipline for immoral conduct, formed the main business of the Monthly Meeting.

The meeting was frequently called upon to serve as an agency for the collection of debts; in this capacity it fulfilled an important function in the business life of colonial Philadelphia.

---

book of the near-by Quaker town of Burlington, New Jersey. Commenting on the Quaker principle of avoiding litigation with one another, H. Clay Reed writes: "That this rule was strictly observed is apparent from the Burlington records; after the first few years, Quakers rarely let their disagreements get as far as the courtroom." He notes, however, that there were a number of suits to which one of the parties was a Friend.—H. Clay Reed and George J. Miller, eds., *The Burlington Court Book: A Record of Quaker Jurisprudence in West New Jersey, 1680-1709* (Washington, D.C., 1944), xi-xii.

39. MS Minutes of Phila. MM, I, 1 (3 April 1683); 10 (1 July 1684); 16 (4 May 1685); 113-14, 116 (24 June, 28 Oct. 1698); 117 (30 Dec. 1698).

The following is a typical entry taken from the minutes of the Monthly Meeting held on 25 April 1729:

Mary Lisle complains against John Heart, that he doth not pay her a just debt due upon bond, and it appearing he hath been dealt with as our Discipline directs, Jonathan Cockshaw and Henry Clifton are desired to acquaint him that unless he satisfies or makes her easy before next Meeting she will be left to her liberty to take such Legal Measures as she may think proper.[40]

Sometimes the meeting was asked to communicate with Friends' meetings on the other side of the Atlantic in order to collect debts owed to its members.[41] Insistent that its members be obedient to the higher powers in the State in all matters where conscience was not involved, the Monthly Meeting, acting upon recommendation of the Quarterly Meeting, took pains to encourage its members to pay up all arrears of quitrents due to the Proprietors.[42]

Occasionally, in the opinion of some Friends, the meeting moved too rapidly. In 1690 Robert Turner, a merchant who had made his fortune as a linen-draper in Dublin, requested Friends to help him collect money which was due from the estate of Christopher Taylor, a Quaker schoolmaster. The two men appointed for this service, finding the sum of forty-eight pounds owed to Turner, caused title to eighty acres of land, formerly the property of Taylor, to be made over to Turner. Two months later, Robert Turner expressed dissatisfaction with the meeting's action "by reason, as he says, he gave no such liberty to the meeting, but only [asked] for their assistance." The meeting left him at liberty "to take what course he can consistent to the order of Truth."[43]

At times the Monthly Meeting in its capacity of guardian of the good name of Truth became an important cog in the machinery of international commerce. For example, Samuel Car-

---

40. *Ibid.*, II, 170.
41. For example, *ibid.*, I, 104 (26 Feb. 1696/7).
42. *Ibid.*, II, 305 (23 Feb. 1738/9). The Monthly Meeting itself, however, was dilatory in paying its quitrents, sometimes putting it off from month to month for almost a year!—*Ibid.*, II, 324.
43. *Ibid.*, I, 65, 68, 69 (30 Jan. 1690/1; 29 May, 31 July 1691).

penter in 1687, acting as attorney for Daniel Wharley, a London Quaker, brought a complaint against Griffith Jones for not making good a protested bill of exchange. The meeting decreed that Jones should give Carpenter the money due to Daniel Wharley, together with lawful charges for damages and protest and interest at 6 per cent. At the same meeting Jones was required to pay Carpenter, acting on behalf of another London merchant, £21/2/6 for a consignment of hats which Jones had not paid for. It was suggestive of the seriousness with which the meeting regarded offenses of this sort that Griffith Jones was ordered "to give satisfaction to Friends for his conduct in these affairs," and furthermore to "forbear putting himself forth in words in . . . quarterly or monthly meetings upon the concerns of Truth until they are better satisfied concerning him." [44]

The Monthly Meeting intervened in mercantile affairs in still other ways. One of the Queries specifically asked whether Friends were clear of depriving the King of his duties, and so effective was the corporate discipline that for the entire colonial period there is little evidence that Quaker merchants or shipowners were guilty of smuggling. [45] During the French and Indian War, when several prominent Quakers were suspected of carrying on illicit trade with the French West Indies and neutral Dutch ports, some of the leading merchants, including the Pemberton brothers, quickly brought pressure to bear through the Monthly Meeting on these offenders. Anxious to keep their skirts spotless, Friends in 1759 warned all their members against carrying on *any* trade in sugar or molasses, even though they intended to pay the duty, in order that they might not "run into snares

---

44. *Ibid.*, I, 39-40 (3 Oct. 1687).
45. The most recent biographer of James Logan has discovered, however, that Logan occasionally evaded the Navigation Acts. In 1723, for example, he shipped to Newfoundland three tierces of tobacco which went "under the Notion of Bread." Logan explained that the "Streightness" of the customs officials in collecting duties forced him and others to resort to this subterfuge, but his Quaker conscience led him to confess that "these methods . . . are not very justifiable tho common."—Joseph E. Johnson, A Statesman of Colonial Pennsylvania: A Study of the Private Life and Public Career of James Logan to the Year 1726 (Doctoral Thesis, Harvard University, 1943), 466.

and inconveniencies, by which we may be likely to bring trouble and uneasiness on ourselves and the Church, or give the least Encouragement or connivance to the promoting a trade to the benefitt of the Enemies to the Crown."[46] These were the years of a thriving illegal trade with the French through the Spanish port of Monte Christi on the northern shore of Santo Domingo. Many non-Quaker merchants in Philadelphia were engaging in this profitable traffic, but according to John Reynell, a Quaker and a great overseas trader, "the Substantial part" of the Society

decline having any thing to do with the Monto Christi Trade for tho' it be a Neutral Port, its well enough known, that the Principal Trade is Carryed on with the French and they do not choose to Trade with the King's Enemies in time of Warr not to be concern'd in importing Sugars whereby he may be defrauded of his Duties. I cannot be concern'd in the Trade, tho' I believe at present it is a Very profitable One and many from here have made great Voyages.[47]

Friends had a testimony against all games of chance, which led the same John Reynell in 1761 to beg to be excused from having anything to do with lottery tickets, explaining that "it has too much of Gaming in it for me to have any thing to do with it."[48] The problem of counterfeiting came up early in Philadelphia's history, and the Monthly Meeting took a forthright stand on it.[49] Nevertheless it cropped up now and again, and in 1751 the meeting was forced to disown several Friends for "making and uttering Counterfeit Gold Coin." Christopher Marshall, a pharmacist, famous during the Revolution as a "Free Quaker," was also dealt with for "having spent much time and pains in attempting the Transmutation of Metals and thereby been lead into an intimacy with dishonest base Men pretenders to that Mistery, by some of whom he is now charged with Assisting and encouraging them in making recieving [sic] and passing Counterfeit Money."

46. MS Minutes of Phila. MM, VI, 171-72 (3 July 1759).
47. Letter to John Sherburne, 12 Mar. 1760, Reynell Letter Book, 1760-62.
48. Letter to John Wendell, 9 April 1761, ibid.
49. See MS Minutes of Phila. MM, I, 6 (6 Nov. 1685).

He was found to be not guilty of the "grosser parts of the accusation," but was nevertheless disowned for having given occasion for reproach to be cast upon the profession of Friends.[50]

THE CRITIQUE OF ACQUISITIVENESS

In their conceptions of the role of mutual aid and corporate discipline, the Quakers thus possessed principles which counteracted those elements in their thinking that promoted economic individualism. These principles by their remarkable persistence prevented the Quaker economic philosophy from developing into the typical bourgeois capitalist pattern. In the midst of great material prosperity, the Quaker merchants retained a measure of the radical equalitarianism and social concern which had characterized the teachings of Friends in the days of their lowly origins.

Although this residual strain of social radicalism tended to be sublimated increasingly into individual philanthropy, it was always posited upon a solidaristic conception of society. Springing out of a genuine sense of human brotherhood, charity was always regarded by the Friends as a religious duty, never as a mere benevolent gesture on the part of the rich. The medieval idea of charity as simple justice, an idea which had carried over into early Protestantism, was on the decline in the second half of the seventeenth century; the Quakers were almost alone in Restoration England in reversing the trend and infusing new life into the time-worn doctrine of stewardship.[51] "Hardly any Thing is given us for our selves," wrote William Penn, "but the Publick may claim a Share with us. But of all we call ours, we are most accountable to God and the Publick for our Estates: In this we are but Stewards, and to hoard up all to our selves is great injustice as well as ingratitude." In discussing the duty of almsgiving, Penn even hinted at a doctrine of justification by good works: "I will not say these Works are *Meritorious* but dare

---

50. MS Minutes of Phila. MM, III, 173, 177 (26 April, 31 May 1751). The reason for Marshall's disownment was thus not, as is usually supposed, his later Revolutionary activities.
51. R. H. Tawney, *Religion and the Rise of Capitalism*, 253–73.

say they are *Acceptable;* and go not without their Reward." [52]

Attacks on the sin of avarice are regularly found in seventeenth- and eighteenth-century Quaker discussions of the conduct of life. It was the object of some of William Penn's most vigorous verbal onslaughts in *No Cross No Crown,* where he described it as "an Epidemical and a Raging Distemper in the World, attended with all the Mischiefs that can make Men miserable in themselves, and in Society." Money was lawful, but the love of it was the root of all evil "if the Man of God say True."

And truly it is a Reproach to a Man [he went on], especially the Religious Man, that *He knows not when he hath enough; when to leave off, when to be satisfied:* That notwithstanding God sends him one Plentiful Season of *Gain* after another, he is so far from making that the Cause of withdrawing from the *Trafficks* of the World, that he makes it a Reason of Launching farther into it; *As if the more he hath the more he may.* He therefore reneweth his *Appetite,* bestirs himself more than ever, that he may have his share in the *Scramble,* while any thing is to be got: This is as if *Cumber,* not *Retirement;* and *Gain,* not *Content,* were the Duty and Comfort of a Christian. [53]

This note was echoed again and again in the Epistles of Philadelphia Yearly Meeting, particularly after the middle of the 1730's when the colony, having weathered two difficult depressions, was reaping the profits of a growing trade in a peaceful world, and Quaker coffers in Philadelphia were becoming filled to overflowing. [54] The burden was taken up by certain individual Friends whose ultra-sensitive consciences made them in economic matters the gadflies of Philadelphia Quakerism. John Woolman of Mount Holly, visiting his wealthy friends in the city, could not refrain from taking them gently but firmly to task for the luxury and "cumber" which marked their manner of living. Anthony Benezet, Quaker son of a Huguenot immigrant, was

---

52. *Some Fruits of Solitude,* in *Works,* I, 854, 857.
53. *Works,* I, 339, 341.
54. See, for example, the Epistles for 1734 and 1737, MS Minutes of Phila. YM, I, 380-81, 406. This emphasis may have reflected primarily the sentiments of the country Friends who dominated the Yearly Meeting numerically.

more caustic: "there are some," he wrote, having in mind certain Quaker merchants whom he saw every First Day in meeting,

who, though they have already a large affluence of wealth, yet are toiling hard to add thereto, without knowing wherefore they thus toil. . . . Why do so many suffer the God of this world so to blind their eyes, and vitiate their reasonable as well as religious senses, as to suffer them to toil after gain, and think it a mighty thing, and themselves notably employed, if they can add £1,000 to £1,000 or £10,000 to £10,000. . . . That a man should labour to be rich, and amass wealth, a state which our Saviour declares to be accompanied with snares and lusts, which tend to destroy the soul . . . is this keeping clear from defilement, and washing our hands in innocency? Now, that such a person shall esteem himself, and be esteemed, a religious man, and perhaps be the more regarded, even by religious people, because he is rich and great, is a mere paradox; yet it is too often the case.[55]

The truth is that there was a conflict implicit in the Quaker ethic insofar as it applied to economic life. On the one hand, Friends were encouraged to be industrious in their callings by the promise that God would add his blessing in the form of prosperity; on the other hand, they were warned against allowing the fruits of their honest labors to accumulate lest they be tempted into luxury and pride. A John Woolman, who found that a steadfast attention to the pure Light could wean the heart away from desires of outward greatness and open the way "to cease from that Spirit that craves riches," could resolve the conflict by curtailing the volume of his outward business when it became too cumbersome.[56] It was more difficult, however, for a great trader like Israel Pemberton, whose ships were seen in most of the major Atlantic ports. In a rather poignant passage in one of his letters,

---

55. Letter to Samuel Fothergill, 27 Nov. 1758, Brookes, 230-31.
56. Woolman himself did not reach this decision without inner conflict, as this passage from his *Journal* reveals: "The increase of business became my burthen, for though my natural inclination was towards merchandize, yet I believed Truth required me to live more free from outward cumbers. There was now a strife in my mind betwixt the two, and in this exercise my prayers were put up to the Lord, who Graciously heard me, and gave me a heart resigned to his Holy will; I then lessened my outward business. . . ."—Amelia M. Gummere, ed., *The Journal and Essays of John Woolman* (New York, 1922), 183.

he acknowledges Woolman's ideal and commends it to his younger brother John, but confesses his own inability to attain it:

thou art at present [he wrote] disengag'd from incumbrances of many kinds, which it is safer to avoid entering into, but hard to quit afterwards; thou knows how long I have been aiming at it, and having Labour'd under the difficulty am heartily desirous thou may be preserv'd in a situation of Life and a Disposition of Mind to render thee ready and capable of improving the Gifts and Talents given thee to thy own eternal advantage. . . . Thou art sensible that by the Blessing of Providence a very moderate Care and industry will be sufficient, little more being necessary than to Keep from wasting what is already provided for us.[57]

John Woolman might almost have had Israel Pemberton in mind when he wrote with sympathy of those rich men who "have at times been affected with a sense of their difficulties, and appeared desirous . . . to be helped out of them," yet, for want of abiding under the humbling power of Truth, continued to be entangled in outward cumber.[58]

Anthony Benezet, owing perhaps to his Gallic temperament, was more caustic on the frailties of the wealthy Friends than the serene and patient Woolman. He felt that the Quakers of his generation in their affluence had become callous to the needs of the poor and weak. "It is much to be wished," he wrote to his friend John Smith, retired from mercantile pursuits and living at Burlington, New Jersey, "that a greater concern prevailed in the Society for the promotion of practical Christianity, as it would be the most likely way to remove that selfishness which is the parent of obduracy of heart and of most other vital evils. I do not mean barely the act of giving to the poor, but I mean true charity, i.e., the love which was in Christ, which is the root of everything that is good." The doctrines of the Sermon on the Mount were often declared in the galleries of the Philadelphia meeting houses, he pointed out, but too often contradicted in practice.

The appellation of *Steward* [he continued] is what we often take

---

57. Letter to John Pemberton, 7 June 1749, Pemberton Papers, V, 107.
58. *Considerations on the True Harmony of Mankind* (1770), in *Journal and Essays*, 443.

upon ourselves, but indeed, in the mouth of many it is but a cant, unmeaning expression. What a paradox it is, that people should imagine themselves to act as such, or that they are indeed fulfilling the second command of loving their neighbour as themselves ... and at the same time live in the utmost ease and plenty, by the possession, perhaps of many thousands, which they esteem so valuable a blessing that they cannot, but with difficulty, think of parting with a small part to their brother, who not only is deprived of this care and plenty, but struggles under difficulties of which he might often be in a great measure relieved by the partaking of as many pounds, as the other has hundreds, if not thousands.[59]

Therein spoke the voice of the primitive Friends for whom the injunctions of the Sermon on the Mount were commands to be literally obeyed by those who through the power of the Spirit had come into perfection of life. This same Friend, the Good Samaritan of the Acadian refugee and friend of the Negro slave, wrote unequivocally of "the necessity for the followers of Christ absolutely to refuse the accumulation of wealth," and, from the vantage point of the radical perfectionist position, observed that "one would think, by the general conduct of even the better sort of Friends in matters of *property*, that some of our Saviour's positive injunctions to his followers had no meaning."[60] Benezet's statements bore witness to the persistent power of the radical social ethics implicit in the Quaker faith.

---

59. Letter dated 1 Aug. 1760, Brookes, 241-42.
60. Letter to John Smith, 13 Dec. 1757, *ibid.*, 224.

· *Chapter Five* ·

IN THE COUNTING HOUSE

I N Philadelphia's rapid rise to unchallenged commercial supremacy in colonial America—a position surpassed in the whole British Empire only by London and Bristol—the Quaker merchants played no inconsiderable part. Singleminded devotion to mercantile pursuits and exceptional business acumen were added, as we have seen, to the advantage of an early start to give the Quakers a disproportionate share in the economic life and prosperity of the teeming Delaware River port. No effort will be made here to treat every aspect of that life; the purpose will rather be to outline the part which the Quakers played in it and to emphasize the distinctive features of their business theory and practice.

THE CONDUCT OF BUSINESS

We make our Remittances a great many different ways sometimes to the West Indies in Bread, Flour, Pork, Indian Corn, and hogshead Staves, sometimes to Carrolina and Newfoundland in Bread and Flour sometimes to Portugall in Wheat, Flour and Pipe Staves sometimes to Ireland in Flax Seed Flour, Oak and Walnut Planks and Barrel Staves and to England in Skinns, Tobacco, Beeswax, staves of all Kinds, Oak and Walnut Planks, Boat Boards, Pigg Iron, Tarr, Pitch, Turpentine, Ships, and Bills of Exchange.[1]

---

1. Letter to Thomas Smith, 4 Sept. 1741, Reynell Letter Book, 1738-41.

Thus did Friend John Reynell summarize the solutions which ingenuity had devised to the persistent problem of obtaining credit in England for the purchase of manufactured goods needed in Pennsylvania. The problem arose from the fact that there was no market in Great Britain for the natural products of the Philadelphia region; hence it was necessary to work out schemes of triangular or polygonal trade whereby local exports could be exchanged for commodities marketable in the mother country.

For a brief period in the early eighteenth century, there was a thriving direct trade with England in which tobacco, raised chiefly in the three "Lower Counties," was the principal commodity; between 1698 and 1704 almost a million and a half pounds were shipped out the mouth of the Delaware.[2] Local tobacco was inferior in quality, however, to that of the southern provinces, and Quaker merchants found the trade troublesome and precarious. "The commodity in general, as ordered among us, is certainly the greatest cheat as well as slavery in trade," complained James Logan; and William Penn, pouring out his vexation to his secretary, impatiently exclaimed: "O that we had a fur-trade instead of a tobacco one, and that thou wouldst do all that is possible to master furs and skins for me."[3] Logan did presently enter the fur trade, at first on behalf of the Penn family and later on his own account, becoming the chief Philadelphia merchant engaged in the Indian trade and amassing a considerable fortune. This fur trade, becoming increasingly important towards the middle of the century, provided virtually the only major channel of direct commerce with Great Britain.

A good deal of experimentation was required before Philadelphia's trade settled into paths yielding steady profits. The West Indies market was eventually found to be the most satisfactory. In the second year of Philadelphia's existence, two ships had been sent to Barbados laden with horses and pipe staves; by 1689 ten vessels were clearing for the Caribbean annually, and

---

2. Curtis Nettels, "The Economic Relations of Boston, Philadelphia, and New York, 1680-1715," *Journal of Economic and Business History*, 3 (1930·31), 210.
3. *Penn and Logan Correspondence*, I, 133n; Penn to Logan, 24 Feb. 1703, *ibid.*, 170.

with the failure of the direct tobacco trade to England, shipments of provisions and lumber to the West Indies became the mainstay of Philadelphia's maritime commerce. Jamaica and Barbados were the principal markets. Philadelphia shared the Jamaica market with New York, but far outdid her Middle-Colony rival in competing with merchants from the mother country for the rich returns of trade with Barbados, Britain's prize sugar colony.[4] The Quaker merchants also carried on a considerable volume of business with Antigua, Dominica, St. Kitts, Curaçao, and the other smaller Caribbean islands.

The chief commodities shipped to the West Indies were grain, flour, and bread, pork and beef, barrel staves, hoops and shingles. These same products, together with New England fish, were frequently sent from the Quaker city to Lisbon and the Wine Islands.[5] Usually the vessels proceeded thence to Great Britain either in ballast or laden with sugar, molasses, rum, or wine. From the British ports the brigs, snows, and sloops of the Philadelphia merchants, if not sold in Europe, turned their prows homeward, loaded with manufactured articles, chiefly hardware and dry goods.

Some typical cargoes carried in Quaker bottoms may be enumerated. In October, 1709, the sloop *Rachel*, owned in shares by Isaac Norris I, Richard Hill, Samuel Preston, James Logan, and Thomas Masters, dropped down the Delaware, laden with two thousand bushels of wheat and about ten tons of bread and flour, consigned to John and Thomas Batts of Lisbon. The master of the vessel was under instructions to proceed to London with a cargo of wine to be delivered to one Thomas Lloyd. Either of

4. Penn, *Letter to the Free Society of Traders*, in Myers, ed., *Narratives*, 229; Scharf and Westcott, *History of Philadelphia*, I, 152; Harrington, *New York Merchant*, 191.

5. Isaac Norris ascribed much of Philadelphia's prosperity in the first decade of the eighteenth century to the Lisbon trade: "I am Apt to think the country has within 10 or 12 years Encreast to near Ten times its . . . produce of Corne [,] wheat Especially [,] and the Markett of Lisbon hath been of great advantage to us."—Letter to Joseph Pike, [?] June 1711, Norris Letter Book, 1709-16, 265. The prohibition of grain exports from England during the War of the Spanish Succession was responsible for the temporary flourishing of this trade.

the consignees was authorized to sell the sloop if a good price should be offered.[6] Elias Bland, an American-trained London businessman who served as factor for several Philadelphia Quakers, kept his correspondents posted on the prices current of the commodities which they might profitably send to the London market from the southern colonies or the Atlantic islands. The variety of exotic products which he listed for them reveals the chief sources of Quaker wealth: rice, logwood, fustic, pitch, tar, turpentine, tobacco, cotton, Madeira, muscovado sugar, lime juice, cocoa, indigo, ginger, and pimentos. None of the commodities mentioned in his letters except flour, pig iron, and rum originated in significant volume in the northern colonies; they were all products of tropical or sub-tropical areas.[7] A cargo which Daniel Flexney shipped to John Reynell in 1741 may stand as representative of those which filled homeward-bound Quaker ships: it consisted of twelve crates of earthenware, twenty casks of nails, six dozen scythes, twenty reams of paper, three gross of ink powder, and bolts of buckram, linen, fustian, oznabrig, garlix, calico, Persian and Chinese taffeta, and other stuffs.[8] Most merchants carried on a business in indentured servants, especially Palatines taken on at Rotterdam. Owing to the conditions of the passage and the danger of sickness, however, this trade was troublesome and disagreeable, and, whether for humanitarian or practical reasons, Quakers preferred when possible to avoid it.[9]

When the merchandise was unloaded on the wharf, a number of courses were open to the merchant. He might, like John Smith, sell the articles at retail at his own store, or he might put them up at public vendue or auction. Quaker merchants presently came to look with disfavor upon vendues, however, because they felt that unscrupulous auctioneers too often fleeced the people unmercifully, gathering them into crowds, plying them with

6. Norris Letter Book, 1709-16, 92-95.
7. Pemberton Papers, III, *passim.*
8. Daniel Flexney to John Reynell, 14 Feb. 1740/41, Coates-Reynell Papers, 1740-41.
9. James Pemberton to John Pemberton, 5 June 1749, Pemberton Papers, V, 102. The importation of slaves, it may be noted, was officially discouraged by the Yearly Meeting after 1696 and from 1715 on was a disownable offense.

liquor, and thus exciting them to a spirit of rash bidding. In 1726 the Yearly Meeting protested against these abuses and three years later the Quaker-dominated Assembly enacted a statute providing for officially appointed vendue masters duly bonded for the faithful performance of their duties. The other merchants joined the Quakers in opposition to the vendue and the system was increasingly restricted down to the Revolution.[10] Some merchants disposed of their goods at wholesale to Philadelphia shopkeepers or back-country traders. If they wanted to take advantage of favorable prices elsewhere, they might re-export them. A flourishing coastwise traffic passed in and out of the Delaware, linking Philadelphia in bonds of trade with New England, New York, Maryland, Virginia, and the Carolinas. Quaker merchants were active in every phase of Philadelphia's multifarious commerce.

Quakers were accused of prospering by virtue of "keeping their Trade within themselves and maintaining a strict Correspondence and Intelligence over all parts where they are."[11] In large measure the charge was correct, although there was nothing either unnatural or discreditable about the practice. Already, in connection with the Quaker custom of mutual aid, we have noticed the existence of a strong sense of community among Friends, transcending colonial and national boundaries. This sense of fellowship, coupled with the conviction that Friends were a "peculiar people" called to be different from "the world's people," caused Philadelphia Friends often to feel that they had more in common with fellow Quakers in England, Jamaica, or Virginia than they had with Presbyterians and Anglicans in their own city. Friends kept up a constant correspondence with their co-religionists in other places, and "public Friends," constantly

---

10. Thompson Westcott, *History of Philadelphia* in the *Philadelphia Sunday Dispatch* (bound copy at Hist. Soc. Pa.), ch. 132. The curtailment of public auctions (which had provided an excitement otherwise lacking in the staid life of the Quaker town) was one of the grievances of the mechanics and artisans against the upper class which came to the surface in the revolutionary movement.—See Charles H. Lincoln, *The Revolutionary Movement in Pennsylvania*, 81-85.

11. George Keith *et al.*, "An Account of the State of the Church in North America," Protestant Episcopal Historical Society, *Collections*, I (1851), xix.

circulating from meeting to meeting, provided the cement which made the larger community of the Society of Friends a reality.[12]

It was not uncommon for ministering Friends to combine religious visits with trading voyages. Thus Thomas Chalkley, touching at Bermuda on business in 1716, seized the opportunity to preach Quakerism to the inhabitants; on another visit in the same year, he recorded in his *Journal* that he "had some Meetings and did some Business on the Island," taking care, however, that his worldly affairs did not obstruct him in carrying out his religious concern.[13] John Pemberton, traveling through England "in the love of the Gospel," carefully avoided any transactions involving Pennsylvania lands lest "the Truth . . . be evil spoken of"; his friends in Philadelphia, however, were reported to be troubled at his negligence in allowing the money which he had in London to lie idle while his attention was absorbed in religious visits.[14]

There were Quaker traders in most of the ports with which Philadelphia had commercial relations. A number of them, like the Hills in Madeira, the Lloyds in London, the Callenders in Barbados, the Wantons in Newport, and the Franklins in New York, were related by marriage to the leading Quaker families of Philadelphia. It was wholly natural, therefore, for Quaker merchants in Philadelphia to carry on the major part of their mercantile business through correspondents of their own religious faith—Birket and Booth of Antigua, Joshua Crosby of Jamaica, John Sinclair of Charleston, William Redwood of Newport, Joseph Pike of Cork, Benjamin Coole of Bristol, and Richard Deeble of Plymouth, to mention only a few names taken from their correspondence. The merchants in London with whom the Philadelphia Friends had business dealings were almost exclu-

---

12. Henry J. Cadbury, "Intercolonial Solidarity of American Quakerism," *Pa. Mag. of Hist.*, 60 (1936), 369.
13. *Works*, 84-85.
14. John Pemberton to Israel Pemberton, 20 Nov. 1752, Pemberton Papers, VIII, 94-95; James Pemberton to John Pemberton, 18 Nov. 1752, *ibid.*, VIII, 92. Elias Bland, writing to James Pemberton, speaks of "an Interest in Trade, Established only on a Transient Religious Visit."—Letter dated 24 April 1745, *ibid.*, III, 119.

sively Quakers; they included some of the greatest traders in the metropolis—Henry Gouldney, Daniel Flexney, Sampson Lloyd, David Barclay, Andrew Pitt (immortalized in Voltaire's *Lettres philosophiques*), John Askew, Joseph Hoar, and Isaac Hunt. Of course, Philadelphia Friends also carried on a good deal of business with non-Quaker merchants such as Rip van Dam and Caleb Heathcote in New York and Andrew Faneuil in Boston.

The world of the Quaker merchants may have been largely a Quaker world, but it was far from being parochial in the geographical sense. By virtue of their commercial, religious, personal, and family contacts, the Philadelphia Quakers were in close touch with the entire north Atlantic world from Nova Scotia to Curaçao and from Hamburg to Lisbon. The intelligence which they received through their correspondents and from itinerant "public Friends" was chiefly concerned with prices current and the prosperity of Truth, but inevitably it broadened their view of the world, tending to overcome the provincialism so likely to be characteristic of a colonial people.[15]

In the organization of their business, the Quakers generally adopted, after the first few years, the same patterns which prevailed in the other colonial seaports. At the very outset, a large-scale experiment in corporate business was projected under the name of the Free Society of Traders, in which more than two hundred persons in the British Isles (including many Friends in Bristol and London) purchased stock to the amount of ten thousand pounds. The Proprietor granted it twenty thousand acres of land and certain extraordinary powers and privileges. The

---

15. This generalization needs to be qualified in one respect. There remained in the breasts of Philadelphia Friends a strong residual distrust and dislike of New Englanders; the memory of persecutions suffered by Friends at the hands of the Puritans was slow to be effaced from the Quaker memory, and Philadelphians refused to let New Englanders forget the sins of their fathers. In 1706 the Monthly Meeting sent copies of George Bishop's *New England Judged* (containing vivid accounts of the sufferings of Friends) to be distributed in Connecticut.—MS Minutes of Phila. MM, I, 255 (27 Dec. 1706). As late as 1773, Josiah Quincy found a rooted antipathy towards New England among the Quakers of Philadelphia; he was frequently and pointedly reminded, he says, of the mistreatment of their ancestors in that part of the world.—*Journal of Josiah Quincy, Jr.*, in Massachusetts Historical Society, *Proceedings*, 49 (1916), 477.

Free Society was active for a few years in stimulating immigration, and actually erected a tannery, a sawmill, a gristmill, a glassworks, and a brick kiln; it also carried on whaling operations in Delaware Bay. For various reasons, including the scarcity of money in the new colony, the inefficiency of the company's non-Quaker officers, and popular opposition to the monopolistic elements in the company's charter, the grandiose plans came to nothing. The company was obliged within a few years to discontinue its trading operations, and in 1723 the Free Society of Traders, unable even to administer its lands profitably, passed out of existence. So perished the only experiment in the corporate organization of business in early Pennsylvania.[16]

The experience of the Free Society of Traders was not calculated to give the Quakers much confidence in the joint-stock corporation as an instrument for the prosecution of trade. For the most part, they preferred to carry on their business by means of partnerships and single proprietorships. Often a family connection formed the basis of a partnership. John Reynell, for example, took his nephew Samuel Coates (1748-1830) as a partner in 1771 after carrying on his business by himself for twenty-two years. When a partner was not chosen from the merchant's own family, he was almost sure to be drawn from the membership of the Friends meeting. Partnerships were usually entered into for a specific term of years—from two to seven—at the end of which either party could withdraw. Frequently several individuals or firms, each contributing a share of the capital, jointly bought or chartered a vessel in order to send a cargo of goods to a distant market, thus reducing the risk for the individual. These "joint

---

16. Joseph S. Davis, *Essays in the Earlier History of American Corporations* (Cambridge, Mass., 1917), I, 41-45; *Pa. Mag. of Hist.*, 5 (1881), 37-50; 11 (1887), 175-80. The Philadelphia Contributionship for the Insurance of Houses from Loss by Fire, established in 1752 and incorporated in 1768 (and thus the oldest American corporation still in existence) was largely a Quaker enterprise in the beginning, its chief founder and first treasurer having been John Smith. See N.S.B. Gras, "The Oldest American Business Corporation in Existence," Business Historical Society, *Bulletin*, 10 (1936), 21-24. Interestingly enough, the oldest American business firm of any kind with a continuous history to the present day is another Philadelphia Quaker enterprise—the Francis Perot's Sons Malting Company, founded by Friend Anthony Morris in 1687. See N.S.B. Gras, "The Oldest American Business Firm," *ibid.*, 9 (1935), 97.

ventures," such as that of John Smith, Matthias Aspden, John Reynell, and Israel Pemberton, Jr., in sending the ship *Bolton* to Liverpool in 1745, were usually all-Quaker undertakings.[17]

The normal introduction to a mercantile career was an apprenticeship to an established merchant. The apprentice lived in the merchant's home, learned to keep accounts and write business letters, and performed routine tasks around the counting house, the store, or the wharf. When Elias Bland was bound apprentice to John Reynell in 1737, for example, the term of service was set at five years, and Reynell was to find the lad in meat, drink, washing, and lodging, in consideration of which the boy's father was to pay a hundred guineas and supply necessary clothing. In this instance, the apprentice was a young English Friend, sent to the colonies, as his father wrote, "to know and be known." The senior Bland wrote to Reynell by way of instructions: "I desire he may be kept fully Imployed and not have Liberty to be absent at a [*sic*] Evening or any other Time without thy Leave, in short thou art to Take as Consciencious a Care of him as if thy Own." To which Daniel Flexney, a noted London merchant and close friend of the Blands, added: "I must particularly recommend to thee not to putt him to any Business not suitable or becomming one in his Station and that thou wilt lett him in common dine at thy own Table with thyself and Family and in all things treat him as thou wouldst desire another to use a son of thy own."[18]

The next stage for the future merchant was to make a trading trip or two as supercargo, the owner consigning the goods to him and trusting him to dispose of them to the best advantage. Through this experience the youth had an opportunity to satisfy his wanderlust, to become acquainted with distant markets and merchants, to learn something of the complicated methods of making remittances, and, with the commissions which he earned, to start accumulating capital with which to set up for him-

---

17. MS Diary of John Smith, Vol. II (entry dated "Latter End of 1st mo., 1745").
18. John Bland to Reynell, 18 Aug. 1737; Flexney to Reynell, 26 Aug. 1737, Coates-Reynell Papers, 1736-37.

self. At the age of nineteen, for example, John Smith went as supercargo to Barbados on a ship belonging to his father. His motives, as he describes them, were a desire "to See the Island of Barbados, and to know the manner of living at Sea, and to survey the wonders of the Lord in the deep...."[19]

Sometimes the young trader settled down for a few months or longer in a distant port in the capacity of resident factor, as Richard Waln and Clement Biddle did in Barbados in 1759.[20] More often he opened a store in Philadelphia, where he sold goods on consignment for others until he was able to launch out on his own. Occasionally men moved over into mercantile operations from other pursuits: Samuel Powel I and Samuel Rhoads, for example, first accumulated their "stock" as carpenters and builders, and Anthony Morris I started in business as a brewer; all three later turned to foreign trade as a more lucrative and congenial occupation.

The perpetual problem facing every Philadelphia merchant was how to make remittances to England for manufactured goods. When cash or bills of exchange were not available, purchases were made on credit, and Philadelphians frequently found themselves deeply in debt to their London correspondents. There is some evidence that Quakers, mindful of the caution in the Book of Discipline against launching into business beyond one's ability to manage, made less use of credit than other merchants. Israel Pemberton I, for example, was careful never to run into debt to the English merchants; he prided himself on the fact that he never ordered any merchandise from his correspondents unless he had the money to pay for it actually in their hands or had a clear prospect of reimbursing them before the goods were shipped.[21] It is probable, in view of the constant shortage of

---

19. MS Diary, I.
20. Richard Waln to John Ladd Howell, 4 Aug. 1759, Howell Manuscripts, Friends Historical Library of Swarthmore College.
21. Israel Pemberton to John Pemberton, 30 May 1753, Pemberton Papers, IX, 9. A letter from Thomas Wharton (1730/1-1782) to Elias Bland in England suggests that not all Quaker merchants were as cautious as Israel Pemberton. "When I commenc'd Trade with thee," wrote Wharton, "[I] expected the usual terms of Credit, otherwise should not have troubled thee with my Orders

cash in the colony, that Quaker merchants, like others, were obliged to extend short-term credit to their customers in Philadelphia. Although generalization in this area would be unsafe without further evidence, one is probably justified in suggesting that in the conduct of business the Quaker merchants were extremely cautious and prudent, meticulously accurate in details, and insistent upon others being so. It is not difficult to understand how men who exhibited these traits in their commercial dealings (no matter how generous and sympathetic as individuals and as Friends) should have acquired a reputation for driving a hard bargain.

LANDS, MINES, AND MANUFACTURES

In the Quaker city, as in other colonial seaport towns, fortunes accumulated in mercantile activities soon outran the capacity of commerce to employ them. In addition to bonds and mortgages, which had the advantage of combining mobility and security, real estate, manufacturing, and mining offered the principal channels for the investment of surplus funds. Real estate produced smaller returns, but its safety and the fact that it required relatively little attention recommended it to those Quaker merchants who wished to retire and devote themselves to religious, philanthropic, and political pursuits. But for certain Quakers who had a taste for industrial pioneering, the development of mills and mines had an appeal, and in this area Friends made an important contribution to Pennsylvania's economic life.

"It is almost a proverb in this neighborhood," wrote Alexander Mackraby in 1768, "that 'Every great fortune made here within these 50 years has been by land.' "[22] In a new country, with virtually limitless space open to the westward, it was natural that land should be a favorite form of investment. With the

---

for Goods, as I am Convinc'd that as Trade is circumstanc'd at present few or none can Comply with thy Terms, which is to transmitt the Money before or as soon as [they] receive the goods."—Thomas Wharton Letter Book, 1752-59, Wharton Papers, Hist. Soc. Pa. One recalls that Elias Bland, the London Friend whose credit terms were so strict, received his business training in the counting house of John Reynell in Philadelphia.

22. Letter to Sir Philip Francis, 20 Jan. 1768, *Pa. Mag. of Hist.*, 11 (1887), 277.

great tide of immigration in the eighteenth century, the value of Pennsylvania lands appreciated rapidly. If one seeks a further motive for investment in real estate, it is not improbable that the Quaker merchants as the ruling class in the province were moved by a desire to emulate the great Whig oligarchs of contemporary England, whose wealth was largely in lands.

The greatest landholder of the first generation was undoubtedly Samuel Carpenter; he possessed much valuable real estate in Philadelphia in addition to the "Slate-Roof House" and another mansion, a bakery, two warehouses, a tavern, a coffee house, and a long wharf; a large estate in Bucks County including most of the present town of Bristol; five thousand acres on Poquessing Creek, fifteen miles north of Philadelphia; Sepviva plantation (380 acres of valuable land lying between Philadelphia and Germantown); one thousand acres in Piles Grove Township, six hundred acres on Timber Creek, and eleven hundred acres in Elsinborough, all in New Jersey; and nearly a thousand additional acres lying around "Pickering's mine." [23]

Isaac Norris I, who came to Philadelphia in 1691 with little more than one hundred pounds in his possession, was probably the most extensive landholder of the succeeding generation. In 1704, with some of the proceeds of his successful mercantile ventures, he bought part of William Penn's great manor of Williamstadt on the Schuylkill, comprising almost 7500 acres, and in 1712 he became sole owner. In the latter year he brought his holdings in the Northern Liberties of Philadelphia up to more than 850 acres, and in the following year, purchased 6000 acres of unlocated lands for £550. In addition, he owned considerable property in Philadelphia, including the "Slate-Roof House" which he had acquired from Samuel Carpenter for nine hundred pounds.[24] Inheriting all these lands from his father, Isaac Norris II went on joining house to house and laying field to field until at his death he possessed, in addition to his country estate of

23. Edward Carpenter and Louis H. Carpenter, *Samuel Carpenter and His Descendants* (Philadelphia, 1912), 17.
24. Charles P. Keith, *The Provincial Councillors of Pennsylvania* (Philadelphia, 1893), 42-43.

Fairhill, several valuable lots in Philadelphia and the plantations of Sepviva, Somerville, Springfield, Farnham, Society, Kirton, Hermitage, and Sweedland, the entire holdings being valued at forty thousand pounds.[25] Other great Quaker landholding families were the Morrises, Pembertons, Foxes, and Drinkers.[26]

In the course of their search for profitable channels of investment, the Quaker merchants presently came to be among the leading promoters of colonial manufacturing. At first their attention turned primarily to enterprises like lumbering and flour milling, which were closely associated with the export trade. As settlement extended westward, however, there began to be an emphasis (in the teeth of official British policy against colonial manufacturing) upon local self-sufficiency with a consequent diversification of industry. Friends were among those who took the lead in efforts to promote home industries during the post-war depression of the 1760's.

In the development of manufactures the most enterprising of the early merchants was Samuel Carpenter, "that honest and valuable man," Isaac Norris I called him, "whose industry and improvements has been the stock whereon much of the labours and successes of this country have been grafted." As early as 1690 Carpenter was concerned with Friend Robert Turner, William Bradford the printer, and Willem Rittinghuysen, a Mennonite papermaker, in building the first paper-mill in America on a branch of Wissahickon Creek. A decade later, he launched a project of building sawmills and gristmills on his property at Bristol in Bucks county; in good times these mills earned about four hundred pounds a year.[27] Noteworthy among

25. Besides his property in lands, Isaac Norris held notes and bonds in the amount of £5600, mortgages in the amount of £1500, and £18,000 in consolidated annuities.—"Estimate of Isaac Norris's Estate in March, 1766," manuscript in private hands.
26. Anthony Morris, dying in 1763, left lands valued at £11,157.—Inventory of Estate of Anthony Morris, Morris Papers, Coates-Reynell Collection. Israel Pemberton II left more than £25,000, much of it invested in real estate.—Pemberton Papers, VII, 139. Joseph Fox (d. 1779) owned a great deal of land in Philadelphia and held mortgages to a considerable amount in both Philadelphia and Bucks counties.—John W. Jordan, *Colonial and Revolutionary Families of Pennsylvania*, I, 320.
27. Norris to Jonathan Dickinson, 10 Aug. 1705, *Penn and Logan Correspond-*

other early Quaker manufacturers was Sybilla Masters (d. 1720), a woman Friend whose husband Thomas Masters (d. 1723) had come from Bermuda in 1687 and had bought a mill in the Northern Liberties in 1714. Sybilla had a knack for invention: she devised and patented a new process for cleaning and curing Indian corn; she contrived a method of weaving hats from palmetto leaves, chips, and straw; and she perfected a kind of hominy called "Tuscarora rice" which she offered for sale as a cure for consumption.[28] Throughout the colonial period individual Quaker merchants continued to interest themselves in industrial enterprises such as Caspar Wistar's glass works in New Jersey. Their interest increased during the decade preceding the Revolution, and many Quaker names were to be found among the subscribers to a number of ambitious but short-lived enterprises to promote colonial self-sufficiency, particularly in the manufacture of textiles.[29] Quakers thus stood in the forefront of new business enterprise in colonial Pennsylvania.

From the 1720's onward, however, the iron industry gradually came to overshadow other forms of manufacturing in Pennsylvania. The role of the Quaker merchants demands special attention, for a large share of the capital which went into the mining and manufacturing of iron had been created in Quaker mercantile enterprises, and a number of the early ironmasters came from Quaker backgrounds. It has been said of the iron industry in eighteenth-century England that the greater part of its early history could be written without passing beyond the bounds of

---

ence, II, 40; James Logan to William Penn, 3 March 1702/3, 180; Samuel Carpenter to Jonathan Dickinson, 1705, 232-35*n*; Myers, ed., *Narratives*, 305*n*.
28. Samuel H. Needles, "The Governor's Mill and the Globe Mills," *Pa. Mag. of Hist.*, 8 (1884), 285-92.
29. The following were some of the Quakers who entered into partnership with a few non-Friends in 1764 to erect and carry on a linen manufactory: Isaac Norris, Joseph Fox, Joseph Richardson, Abel James, Peter Reeve, Thomas Wharton, Samuel Rhoads, William Logan, Samuel Preston Moore, and Reuben Haines. —*Pa. Mag. of Hist.*, 18 (1894), 262-63. Six years later, the Board of Managers of a society to encourage the domestic production of silk (a favorite project of Benjamin Franklin) included the following Friends: Dr. Cadwallader Evans, Israel Pemberton, Benjamin Morgan, Moses Bartram, Samuel Rhoads, Thomas Fisher, Owen Biddle, Henry Drinker, and Edward Penington.—*Ibid.*, 16 (1892), 304-5.

the Society of Friends.[30] With an almost equal degree of truth, the same statement could be made of the Pennsylvania industry. The pioneer ironmaster in the colony was Thomas Rutter, an English Quaker who came to Pennsylvania in the early years; he became a follower of George Keith, leaving the Society of Friends in the 1690's to organize several Keithian meetings. He established Pool Forge, the first bloomery in Pennsylvania, on Manatawny Creek, about forty miles from Philadelphia. With Thomas Potts, another Friend, he was also responsible for erecting Pennsylvania's first blast furnace at nearby Colebrookdale, named for the furnace of Abraham Darby, a great English Quaker ironmaster.[31] Many of the other entrepreneurs, such as Samuel Nutt, Daniel Offley, and Stephen Paschall, were also members of Quaker families.

Quaker capital, created in commerce, early began to flow into iron. Probably the heaviest investor was Anthony Morris II. Keeping up his father's brewing and commercial interests, he helped finance several of the pioneer iron works. He was one of the founders of Durham Furnace in Bucks county, of Spring Forge in Philadelphia county, and of an iron "plantation" on the present site of Trenton, New Jersey; in addition, he owned large shares in Pool Forge and Colebrookdale.[32] James Logan was another of the founders of Durham Furnace, described by Israel Acrelius in 1758 as "the best iron works in the country"; at his death his one-fourth share passed to his son William, who operated the "plantation" under the name of William Logan and Company.[33] Quaker ships bound for England from the 1720's on frequently carried small consignments of pig and bar iron from local forges: James Logan, for example, sent three tons of pig iron to London in 1728, hoping to find a market for the

---

30. Thomas S. Ashton, *Iron and Steel in the Industrial Revolution*, 213.
31. *Forges and Furnaces in the Province of Pennsylvania*, 11-24.
32. *Ibid.*, 15, 45, 58-60; Jordan, I, 51; William Nelson, "Beginnings of the Iron Industry in Trenton, New Jersey," *Pa. Mag. of Hist.*, 35 (1911), 22ff.
33. Acrelius, *A History of New Sweden; or, The Settlements on the River Delaware*, in W. M. Reynolds, ed., Hist. Soc. Pa., *Memoirs*, 11 (1874), 165; *Logan-Story Correspondence*, 22; *Forges and Furnaces*, 57. Among other Friends concerned in the enterprise were George Fitzwater, Thomas Lindley, Griffith Owen, Samuel Powel, Lawrence Growden, and Israel Pemberton.

product of Durham Forge, but was soon lamenting that he was likely to be "intirely disappointed" in his expectations.[34] After the passage of the Iron Act in 1750, removing all duties from American pig iron, the volume in the export trade increased slightly, but throughout the colonial period, most of the product of Pennsylvania forges went into domestic manufacturing.[35] Thus by their financial support of the infant iron trade, as well as by their direct support of other manufacturing enterprises, the Philadelphia Quaker merchants gave an impetus to the industrial development of the colonies.

PAPER MONEY

Prosperity was neither uninterrupted nor universal in Pennsylvania under the benevolent rule of the Quaker oligarchy. Between 1721 and 1723, following the bursting of the South Sea Bubble, the province suffered a severe economic depression. According to Lieutenant-Governor Sir William Keith, over two hundred houses stood empty in Philadelphia, laboring people were daily forced to leave the city, shopkeepers had no money with which to replenish their stocks, and the prices of wheat, flour, bread, and other farm products fell to a point at which it was scarcely worth while for farmers to bring them to market. European goods as well as country produce, Keith maintained, were monopolized by "a Cabal of only four or five rich men, who retail'd them again on Credit at what rate they pleased . . . by which Means they soon got the whole Country into their Debt, exacting Bonds of every Body at 8 per Cent."[36]

---

34. James Logan to Nehemiah Champion, 6 Nov. 1728, Logan Letter Book, Logan Papers, 556; Logan to Story, 29 Sept. 1729, *Logan-Story Correspondence*, 22. Certain Quakers in England with whom the Philadelphia merchants were in correspondence did all they could to promote iron mining in the colony. Joshua Gee, Quaker ironmaster of Shrewsbury, appeared before the Board of Trade to ask that all duties be removed from the importation of colonial pig iron. —Arthur C. Bining, *The Pennsylvania Iron Manufacture in the Eighteenth Century*, 150.
35. Bining, 157–58. A letter of Israel Pemberton, written in 1745, makes it clear that much of the locally mined iron was used in shipbuilding.—Theodore Thayer, *Israel Pemberton*, 11.
36. *Discourse on the Medium of Commerce*, quoted in Charles P. Keith, *Chronicles of Pennsylvania*, II, 662.

Although Keith did not mention names, it is clear that he had in mind the Quaker oligarchy which was entrenched not only in financial control of the province but in political control as well, through its domination of the Council and the Assembly. There was little that could be done immediately about the economic power of the merchants or their influence in the Council, but an aroused electorate could and did turn the merchants out of the legislative house. The new Assembly wasted no time in initiating radical measures designed to ease the debt burden of the poor.

It will be instructive to examine the attitudes of the leading merchants in this critical period of economic stress and social unrest. The depression gave rise to a sharp controversy, centering around the issuance of paper money. In this controversy Quaker merchants were to be found on both sides of the question. Indeed, the relative success which attended Pennsylvania's efforts to increase the volume of currency without producing serious inflationary effects may be ascribed as much to the wise moderation of the radical Quaker wing as to the political and economic strength of the conservative Friends. The incident thus reveals in an interesting light the tension between the radical and conservative tendencies in Quaker economic thought and practice.

Most prominent among the more radical Friends who won seats in the Assembly in 1721 was Francis Rawle, a prosperous and cultivated merchant and an adherent of the popular party of David Lloyd. Rawle and his father-in-law Robert Turner, a wealthy Irish Quaker, had been followers of the schismatic George Keith in the 1690's, but Rawle had returned to the Quaker fold by 1721.[37] In this critical year he published a pamphlet entitled *Some Remedies Proposed for Restoring the Sunk Credit of the Province of Pennsylvania*. It was an attempt to provide a solution to the insistent problem of the shortage of metallic currency in the colony, occasioned by the unfavorable

---

37. Samuel Hazard, ed., *The Register of Pennsylvania*, 6 (1830), 306; T. I. Wharton, *A Memoir of William Rawle*, Hist. Soc. Pa., *Memoirs*, 4, pt. 1 (1840), 37.

balance of trade with the mother country. By virtue of its sobriety and Quaker caution, Rawle's plan stood in notable contrast to most other colonial projects for coining credit into wealth.

Rawle began by positing two essential conditions which must be met if the credit of any country was to be maintained. In the first place, its exports must be of uniformly high quality. Here he pointed out that New York flour commanded better prices in the West Indies because its weight and quality were subject to strict regulation, whereas controls had been allowed to lapse in Philadelphia.[38] In the second place, the pay of the country ought to be ready and punctual. "We find," he wrote, "it was ever the Opinion and general Custom of most Countries, where Gold and Silver was not sufficient to carry on the Domestick Trade, nothing was equal to STAMP'D PAPER, whose Value was secur'd to the Receiver by some certain Fund." The paper might be issued by a loan bank on the security of land, and the debt could be systematically retired over a period of years. With a burst of vigorous satire, he made light of the arguments of the conservatives who pointed with alarm to Boston's experience with paper currency:

Since they made *Paper Money* in *Boston* are less Fish exported? Or, fewer Vessels built? Do any refuse to receive their Bills? By what Trade can they possibly get a sufficient Stock of Silver or Gold, to supply the Country with Running Cash? And if they can no where command it, as most certainly their Trade at present cannot do it What could they do without Paper-Money? Must every Gentleman, Tradesman *&c* turn *Fish-Merchant?* What an odd Kind of Running Stock of Money must stinking Fish make? Instead of Bag or Pocket, they must hire a Cart to carry Home *Fifty Shillings;* and after all, the intrinsick Value of their Running Stock would be daily in Danger of rotting or wasting some way or other.[39]

Rawle added three important cautions, necessary in his view

---

38. It is worthy of note that the Assembly presently acted upon this recommendation and as a result Philadelphia flour soon drove the New York product out of the West Indies market.—Bridenbaugh, *Cities*, 356.

39. *Some Remedies*, 10, 12.

in order to prevent rapid depreciation: the amount of paper money should not be excessive, it must be full legal tender, and it must bear interest at a rate not less than that of gold, silver, or any other currency. Rawle served as a member of the committee which in 1722 drew up an act for issuing bills of credit, and the law as finally passed bore the unmistakable impress of his ideas. It established a public loan office administered by four commissioners who were authorized to issue fifteen thousand pounds in bills of credit secured by mortgages on land for double their value and bearing interest at 5 per cent, the bills to be legal tender for eight years during which period the loan was to be paid back in annual instalments.

There was good Quaker precedent for a scheme of this sort, for William Penn himself, twenty years before, had proposed the adoption of some form of land bank to provide paper credit.[40] Nevertheless in 1722 the mere mention of such a project was enough to send a shiver of alarm through some of the weightier Friends like Isaac Norris, James Logan, Samuel Preston, Thomas Masters, and Richard Hill, wealthy merchants who sat on the Governor's Council and represented what they conceived to be the interests of the recently deceased Founder. When the bill for paper money came before the Assembly, Norris and Logan promptly presented on behalf of a group of merchants an address criticizing the proposal and pleading for caution in the management of the currency lest creditors be ruined by depreciation. Applying Newtonian concepts to economics, these learned merchants declared that, if bills were issued on easier terms than gold or silver, they would inevitably depreciate "for credit has its own laws, as unalterable in themselves, as those of motion or gravity are, in nature."[41] The core

40. E.C.O. Beatty, *William Penn as Social Philosopher*, 204-8. Even earlier, Thomas Budd in his *Good Order Established in Pensilvania and New-Jersey* (1685) had advocated a bank of credit, evoking some enthusiasm from Penn but little from the merchants. Penn's deputy, Captain John Blackwell, another early monetary reformer, had faced a similar cool response from the Quaker merchants when he broached his scheme; of them he wrote in some vexation "Each prays for his neighbor on First Days and then preys upon him the other six."—Dorfman, *Economic Mind*, I, 95, 105.
41. The address is printed in full in Proud, *History*, II, 152-62.

of their attack lay in their objection to what appeared to be class legislation.

It was perfectly clear that the bill was inspired by the poorer farmers and debtors eager to write off a part of their indebtedness. One feels that the arguments of Norris and Logan were somewhat lacking in Quaker compassion: "If the poor only are to be the objects," they declared, "they have not security to give, or, if they had, perhaps they have as little merit as any: commonly people become wealthy by sobriety and industry, the most useful qualifications in a commonwealth, and poor by luxury, idleness and folly." This was familiar doctrine on the pages of Puritan writers like Richard Baxter, but coming from followers of George Fox and John Bellers it had an incongruous ring. The creditor status of the authors was plainly reflected in their argument that the inflation of the currency would be "the borrower's advantage; for the more easily will he pay his annuity."[42]

After the bill became law and was followed by a second act tripling the amount of paper money and another one reducing the interest rate on all debts from 8 to 6 per cent, Isaac Norris lapsed into morose silence, confiding his vexation only to his intimates.[43] Logan, on the other hand, returned to the attack in public again and again. In delivering a charge to the Grand Jury in 1723, he took occasion to offer his explanation of the poverty and want of money prevailing in the province. For the latter condition he proffered the obvious reason: the adverse balance of trade which drained the colony of metallic money. The widespread poverty he attributed to idleness, love of pleasure, and the perverse refusal of workmen to labor for

---

42. Writing to a London correspondent, Isaac Norris revealed his own financial fears: "This paper money puts me upon thinking and I must take different Measures in my Affairs. I Desire therefore thy Opinion and Judgement— What fund in England is best Safest and most Advantagious to lodge a Sum in." —Letter to John Askew, 22 May 1723, Norris Letter Book, 1716-30, 332.

43. In a letter dated 23 Sept. 1723, he wrote caustically of "This mobbish people" who were "Combining for another assembly which will Raise more paper for Unless they can Come at Something of less Vallue than they borrowed or became Indebted for their End is not answered. This is our Miserable Case —which will too probably terminate in the ruin or Great Suffering of all the frugal Industrious people who have Obtain'd any Substance." Letter to Mordecai Maddock, Norris Letter Book, 1716-30, 338.

reasonable wages. Idle men, he observed, are prone to repine and to grow envious of those whose diligence and prudence have brought them material rewards. They commence complaining about the oppression of the poor.

They grow factious and turbulent in the State; are for trying new Politics. . . . They are for Inventing new and extraordinary Measures, for their Relief and Ease: When it is certain, that nothing can prove Truly Effectual to them, but a change of their own Measures in the Exercise of those wholesome and healing Vertues. . . *Sobriety, Industry,* and *Frugality.*[44]

The fears of the conservatives were groundless. The Pennsylvania loan bank was well managed and undoubtedly helped to restore prosperity to the Philadelphia region. Indeed paper money had been current only three years in Pennsylvania before Logan found himself admitting that "to speak the Truth, it has been of great Service to the Countrey." Twenty years later, it is interesting to note, Isaac Norris II was stating his opinion that a projected issue of twenty thousand pounds in paper money was too small, and it was James Pemberton's belief in 1755 that paper money had been universally beneficial in Pennsylvania.[45]

Almost alone among colonial issues, Pennsylvania's paper money never depreciated materially, owing to the wise provisions for its redemption and to the restraint exercised in its

---

44. *The Charge Delivered from the Bench to the Grand Jury, at the Court of Quarter Sessions,* 10. Logan's objections to paper currency appear to have been less thoroughgoing than Norris's; he was chiefly concerned lest it be issued in excessive amounts "till we are in as bad Credit as they are in New England."—Letter to John Penn, 17 Nov. 1729, *Pa. Mag. of Hist.,* 34 (1910), 122. In an able discussion of the political crisis which accompanied the depression, Joseph E. Johnson plausibly argues that Logan, realizing the vanity of opposing the Assembly on the paper-money issue, decided to throw his weight behind the movement in order to insure a conservatively drawn act and perhaps forestall resort to wilder panaceas.—A Statesman of Colonial Pennsylvania, ch. 21.

45. James Logan to Joshua Gee, 14 Dec. 1726, Logan Papers, IV, 127; Norris Letter Book, 1719-59, 33-34; James Pemberton to Henton Brown, 15 Jan. 1755, Pemberton Papers, X, 57. A recent student has pointed out that the price level in Pennsylvania during the fifty-two-year period that the province was on a paper standard was more stable than the American price level has been during any succeeding fifty-year period.—Richard A. Lester, *Monetary Experiments: Early American and Recent Scandinavian,* 57.

emission. It is worth noting that those measures were integral parts of Francis Rawle's original scheme as well as being basic in the strictures of Logan and his associates. The whole incident is revealing because it reflects in a concrete instance the way in which, as material wealth came to the Quaker merchants, the two strains in their inherited economic ethic—the individualist-capitalist and the radical humanitarian—tended to diverge, each finding expression in different persons.

Rawle's contribution to the discussion of economic policy for Pennsylvania was not exhausted by his efforts on behalf of paper money. In 1725 this thoughtful merchant published a pamphlet engagingly entitled *Ways and Means for the Inhabitants of Delaware to Become Rich*. This essay deserves to be known as the first treatise on political economy produced in British America. Conceiving the entire Delaware basin as an economic unit, Rawle took what was, for its day, a statesmanlike view of its baffling problems. Paper money, he recognized, could alleviate temporary distress, but it did not constitute true wealth. "The Riches . . . of any Country," he affirmed in true mercantilist fashion, "may be said to consist in an Even Ballance to its Favour in all Trade it is engaged in with the several Countries it trades withall."[46] The Delaware region was receiving less bullion from the West Indies than it should because of the increasing consumption of Jamaica rum. If Logan could blame Philadelphia's poverty on idleness, Rawle could counter with the argument that "Riches is the Mother of Luxury and Idleness," and that "the Daughter [has] devoured the Mother." In his attitude towards luxury, based on a combination of moralistic and economic considerations, Rawle was at one with William Penn and other Quaker writers on economic subjects.[47]

The agricultural products of the Delaware watershed were,

---

46. *Ways and Means*, 12.
47. Compare *Some Fruits of Solitude*: "If all Men were so far Tenants to the Publick that the Superfluities of Gain and Expense were applied to the Exigencies thereof, it would put an End to Taxes, leave never a Beggar, and make the greatest Bank for National Trade in Europe."—*Works*, I, 854. Compare also John Woolman, "A Plea for the Poor," in *Journal and Essays*, 422.

in Rawle's mind, the "fund" from which wealth could be created. The problem was to find new markets, the old ones in the West Indies being glutted; his solution was to subsidize agricultural exports to Europe. The subsidies could be raised by taxes on rum and land; the latter would not be a burden upon the owners because the value of their lands would be enhanced by the increase in the prices of the subsidized products. Thus, more than two centuries before the United States government adopted a policy of paying agricultural subsidies, a Quaker economist was proposing that the Delaware region use this method to lift itself by the bootstraps.

There was more to Rawle's scheme, however, than this. He proposed that the governors of the Delaware colonies use their influence with the King to make a breach in the Staple Act to the extent of allowing English ships carrying wheat to Lisbon to load salt for the return voyage instead of returning in ballast. He also proposed diversifying the agriculture of the region by increasing the production of barley for brewing (thus lessening the dependence upon Jamaica rum) and raising oats, hemp, flax, and even rice; in addition, he would encourage manufacturing and the production of timber, iron, limestone, and asbestos. Finally, he suggested that the provincial government might use the interest on its loan bills to establish insurance offices.[48]

Despite its mercantilist presuppositions, or more accurately, because of the unorthodox application of them to a part of the imperial economy which was supposed to remain content with its colonial status, Rawle's proposal represented a minor assault upon the official policy of the British Empire and thus anticipated some of the economic arguments of the revolutionary generation. The essay had its weaknesses and crudities, but it revealed ingenuity, understanding of the existing economic

---

48. An answer to *Ways and Means*, entitled *A Dialogue Shewing What's Therein to Be Found*, published in 1725, has usually been ascribed to James Logan. Joseph E. Johnson, however, questions this attribution and suggests that Isaac Norris may have been the author.—A Statesman of Colonial Pennsylvania, 639-40. Rawle wrote a rejoinder called *A Just Rebuke to a Dialogue between Simon and Timothy, Shewing What's Therein to Be Found* (Philadelphia, 1726).

situation, and an open-minded willingness to experiment in the interests of all classes. Rawle may therefore stand among Quaker businessmen as a type of the pragmatic liberal, halfway between the conservatism of Norris and Logan and the Christian radicalism of Woolman and Benezet.

Chapter Six

QUAKER GRANDEES

O N the basis of fortunes accumulated in overseas trade, the Quaker merchants reared a structure of aristocratic living comparable to that of the Virginia planters, the landed gentry of the Hudson Valley, and the Puritan merchant princes of Boston. In the light of the social pronouncements of the primitive Friends, there was an element of contradiction in the very notion of a Quaker aristocracy. The contradiction was inherent, however, in the social and economic philosophy of Quakerism; and the situation in which the Friends found themselves in Pennsylvania, with great material wealth and political power in their grasp, was calculated to bring that contradiction into bold relief.

THE MUTUAL RELATIONS AMONG MEN

The primitive Friend who refused to uncover his head in the presence of magistrate or king, who said *thou* to all men irrespective of rank, and who abandoned all titles of honor, was looked upon as a dangerous radical, bent upon subverting the social order and establishing absolute equality in all social relations. William Penn, taking notice of this charge, was quick to cite Scriptural warrant for Quaker equalitarianism: "We are not to *Respect Persons*," he maintained, "And yet perhaps some will say, 'That by this we overthrow all Manner of Distinction among Men, under their several Qualities, and introduce a

Reciprocal and *Relational Respect* in the Room of it[']: But if it be so," he concluded, "I can't help it, the Apostle *James* must answer for it, who has given us this Doctrine for Christian and Apostolical."[1]

The logic of Quaker equalitarianism never issued in anything like the communism of the Hutterian Brethren; as Friends grew prosperous and achieved social respectability, the radicalism implicit in their earlier preaching was modified or sublimated into philanthropy.[2] Penn himself, in almost the same breath with his avowal of equalitarianism, made it clear that Friends did not intend to do away with social distinctions. Quakers, he submitted, were not so ill-mannered as the world believed; they had their own ways of showing respect. "But the Difference between them lies in the Nature of the Respect they perform, and the Reasons of it. The World's Respect is an empty Ceremony, no Soul or Substance in it: The Christian's is a solid Thing, whether by Obedience to Superiors, Love to Equals, or *Help* and *Countenance* to Inferiors."[3] Elsewhere Penn explicitly accepted the current social theory which assigned the several classes of men each to its proper place in the scale of being. "For tho' [God] has made of one Blood, all Nations, he has not ranged or dignified them upon the *Level*, but in a Sort of Subordination and Dependency." As the stars and planets differ in the degree of their luster, as the trees vary from the lordly cedar to the crawling bramble, as the fishes of the sea range in size from the leviathan to the sprat, so among mankind, he maintained, there is a steady progression from the scavenger at the lower end of the social scale to the king at the top.[4]

The hierarchical view of society was given classical expression for the Quakers by Robert Barclay in his great *Apology*:

I would not have any judge, that . . . we intend to destroy the *mutual* Relation, that either is betwixt *Prince* and *People*, *Master*

---

1. *No Cross No Crown*, in *Works*, I, 323-24.
2. See Eduard Bernstein, *Cromwell and Communism*, 225-52.
3. *No Cross No Crown*, in *Works*, I, 324. Note the unquestioning assumption of social superiority and inferiority.
4. *Some Fruits of Solitude*, in *Works*, I, 856.

and *Servants, Parents* and *Children;* nay, not at all: We shall evidence, that our Principle in these things hath no such tendency, and that these Natural Relations are rather better established, than any ways hurt by it. *Next,* Let not any judge, that from our opinion in these things, any necessity of *Levelling* will follow, or that all Men must have things in *Common.* Our *Principle* leaves every Man to enjoy that peaceably, which either his own Industry, or his Parents, have purchased to him; ... And further, we say not hereby that no Man may use the Creation more or less than another: For we know, that as it hath pleased God to dispense it diversly, giving to some more, and some less, so they may use it accordingly. The several Conditions, under which men are diversly stated, together with their Educations answering thereunto, do sufficiently show this: the *Servant* is not the same way Educated as the *Master;* nor the *Tenant* as the *Landlord;* nor the *Rich* as the *Poor;* nor the *Prince* as the *Peasant. ... Let the Brother of high degree rejoice in that he is abased, and such as God calls in low degree, to be content with their Condition, not envying those Brethren, who have greater abundance, knowing they have received abundance as to the inward Man;* which is chiefly to be regarded.[5]

This traditional view of social classes, arranged in their appropriate places in the chain of being, was firmly imbedded in the thinking of the Philadelphia Quakers, largely owing, no doubt, to the authority of Barclay. In 1722, when, as we have seen, a depression had brought a radical group into power in Pennsylvania politics, Philadelphia Yearly Meeting drew up a document entitled "The Antient Testimony of the People Called Quakers Reviv'd." As if wishing to disavow any imputation of radicalism attaching to the Society from its early history, the meeting, dominated by its conservative Elders, emphasized that, although the primitive Friends could not join in "the arrogant Spirit" of those who said *you* to a single person, nevertheless upon all occasions they showed "the decent Respect due to men, and maintained in the wisdom of God, the true honour and obedience due from Subjects to their Prince, inferiors to superiors, from Children to Parents, and servants to Masters, whereby the mutual

---

5. *Writings,* II, 516-17.

relations, betwixt those different Ranks and Degrees of men, have been and are asserted and endeavoured to be established after the manner that our Saviour and his Apostles were pleased to direct."[6] Nearly a half-century later, as the Revolution was approaching, and Philadelphia was beginning to witness the beginnings of a new spirit of social radicalism, John Smith, a retired Quaker merchant, quietly reiterated this traditional conservative view in the columns of a newspaper: "I am not of levelling principles," he wrote. "I think the different classes of mankind deserving of kind treatment from each other, and the higher sorts in government to be intitled to proportionable respect and rank."[7]

This hierarchical theory of society assumed that the class structure was static whereas, on the contrary, as we shall see, the society of colonial Philadelphia was highly fluid. It was not uncommon for a Quaker merchant, but one generation away from the artisan or shopkeeper, to fancy himself (and sometimes to style himself) a gentleman. Like the Virginia planters, John Smith and other Quaker merchants read such books as *The Gentleman's Calling* by the Anglican writer Richard Allestree, in which they encountered the idea that the calling of the gentleman involved clear duties towards the state and the lower classes.[8] Even this concept, however, had ample precedent in Quaker writing, for William Penn, in his widely read *No Cross No Crown*, after attacking undue pretensions based upon blood or family, had confessed that the station of a gentleman was to be preferred to "the Ranks of *Inferior People*."

The reasons Penn gave for his preference are revealing, for they correspond closely to those given by both Anglican and nonconformist divines of his day.[9] In the first place, gentlemen have more power than commoners to do good: "And if

6. MS Minutes of Phila. YM, I, 264.
7. Essay signed "Atticus," *Pennsylvania Chronicle*, 8 Feb. 1768. On John Smith and the Atticus papers, see Frederick B. Tolles, "A Literary Quaker: John Smith of Burlington and Philadelphia," *Pa. Mag. of Hist.*, 65 (1941), 300-309.
8. Compare Louis B. Wright, *The First Gentlemen of Virginia*, 133, 275, and *passim*.
9. Compare Schlatter, *Social Ideas*, 110-16.

their Hearts be equal to their Ability, they are Blessings to the People of any Country." Secondly, "the Eyes of the People are usually directed to them," and they may gain the affection of and profit from the services of the lower orders while serving as examples to them. In the third place, having more leisure, they may "polish their Passions and Tempers with Books and Conversation." Finally, they have opportunity to travel abroad, to investigate the laws and customs of other nations, and bring back for the benefit of the home government whatever is worthy of imitation. Incidentally, it is interesting to note that Penn was not oblivious of the most striking social phenomenon of his time—the rise of merchants and tradesmen (including those of his own sect) into the ranks of the gentry—although he characteristically gave it a moralistic or religious interpretation: "But because it too often happens, that Great Men do little mind to give God the Glory of their Prosperity, and to live answerable to his Mercies . . . his Hand is often seen, either in *impoverishing* or *Extinguishing* them, and raising up Men of more Virtue and Humility to their Estates and Dignity." [10] Friends had reason to believe that God had looked with special favor upon Philadelphia, for, as we shall see, He raised up many men of virtue and humility from low estates to positions of dignity and affluence.

THE RISE OF THE QUAKER ARISTOCRACY

There is good reason to believe that William Penn expected the "great Men" of his colony to be country gentlemen, living on their broad acres and visiting Philadelphia (which was itself to be a "greene Country Towne") only to transact the public business. His own preference, in spite of the months he spent at the Court of St. James, was for a rural existence, and he warned his family against being drawn into "cities and towns of concourse." "The world," he wrote, "is apt to stick close to those who have lived and got wealth there: a country life and estate I like best for my children." Like Jefferson and other agrarian philosophers of the next century, he felt that agricultural

10. *Works*, I, 333.

pursuits were "God's Trades" and were accordingly to be chosen before men's, for in the country one could study the works of God and be purified thereby, whereas urban life and the contemplation of the works of men had an inevitable corrupting tendency.[11]

On the other hand, Penn (whose ideas on landholding were a curious mixture of feudal and democratic notions) took special pains to prevent the formation of huge landed estates like the patroonships of New York by stipulating that no purchaser was to have more than a thousand acres in one place unless within three years he settled a family on each thousand acres. In the first draft of his Frame of Government, Penn again anticipated Jefferson by including a clause abolishing primogeniture; and although this clause was omitted in the final draft, measures were subsequently taken to require the equal division of property among a landholder's heirs.[12] Whether owing to these provisions or (what is more likely) to the nature of Pennsylvania's economic opportunities, the best talents and the largest amounts of capital went into business in the Delaware River port. Thus the "great Men" who dominated the social and political life of the Quaker colony were not to be landed gentry; on the contrary, almost from the beginning, they were to be men whose fortunes were made in commerce, although, to be sure, these mercantile aristocrats were soon emulating their British counterparts by purchasing lands and building country houses.

The absence, in spite of Penn's attempt to transplant feudal institutions, of most of the traditional relationships which still in large measure governed British society, together with almost unexampled opportunities for economic success, caused the society of early Philadelphia to be characterized by extreme mobility. Gabriel Thomas, the chronicler of Pennsylvania's springtime, was not always innocent of exaggeration, but, taking his words with a grain of salt, one can give some credence to his affirmation in 1698 that certain coopers "who went from Bristol

---

11. Letter to his wife and children, Aug. 1682, Janney, *Life of Penn*, 189; *Advice to His Children*, in *Works*, I, 898; *Some Fruits of Solitude*, *ibid.*, I, 830.
12. Keith, *Chronicles*, I, 149-51.

. . . that could hardly get their Livelihoods there, are now reckon'd in Pensilvania, by a modest Computation to be worth some Hundreds (if not Thousands) of Pounds."[13] There is less reason to discount the statement of Jonathan Dickinson, himself a substantial merchant, some two decades later, that "many who have come over under covenants for four years [i.e., as indentured servants] are now masters of great estates."[14] The little nucleus of merchants who had come to Philadelphia from the other British colonies in the early years[15] was constantly being augmented from the ranks of the successful artisans and shopkeepers. By the early years of the eighteenth century, Friends like George Mifflin, shopkeeper, and Samuel Powel, carpenter, had accumulated enough capital to launch mercantile ventures of their own.

The history of John Bringhurst (1691-1750) may be taken as a representative Philadelphia Quaker success story. Son of a London printer, he was apprenticed at the age of ten to a cooper in Philadelphia, whither his mother had brought him. After serving out his time and working for a few years as journeyman cooper, he concluded, in hopes of faster advancement, to go to sea. Shipping first as a cooper, he learned navigation, and made several voyages to Barbados, Curaçao, and Surinam as mate. Having accumulated about forty pounds, he decided to remain ashore and resume the cooperage business. "Under Providence," he recorded, "I got beforehand and Carried on a Trade of Merchandise with a small Stock which helped me forward into a good way of getting." Beginning to be recognized as a Friend of some weight in the affairs of the meeting, he was made an Overseer of the Poor in 1728 and two years later an Overseer of the Friends School. By 1736 he was able to purchase a one-third share in the brigantine *Joseph* which made numerous voyages to Barbados, Lisbon, and Madeira, freighted with provisions. Within a few years he was also half owner of the sloop *James*, which carried pipestaves and beeswax to the Wine Islands. Two

---

13. *Historical and Geographical Account*, in Myers, ed., *Narratives*, 327.
14. Quoted in Watson, *Annals*, II, 266.
15. See above, pp. 43-44.

years before he died, he was named an Elder of the meeting. His three sons engaged in mercantile undertakings and amassed considerable wealth; James, the second son, was to be styled "gentleman" in the city Directory.[16]

By mid-century the social complexion of Philadelphia Quakerism had altered greatly from that of the pioneer period. It will be recalled from statistics presented in an earlier chapter that of ninety men married under the care of Philadelphia Monthly Meeting during the first quarter-century, only eighteen described themselves as merchants, professional men, or gentlemen, whereas the remaining seventy-two were artisans or laborers.[17] Analysis of 189 marriages between 1743 and 1763 reveals a larger proportion of men describing themselves as merchants, besides a physician and two schoolmasters. The number of different crafts represented is actually smaller than that listed in the earlier record, although the total number of individuals involved is more than twice as great. The largest categories, the merchants apart, are the carpenters, joiners, coopers, cordwainers, and hatters, many of whom doubtless formed an aristocracy of master craftsmen. It should be recognized, too, that many who styled themselves "carpenter" like Samuel Rhoads or "joiner" like William Savery (*ca.* 1722-1787) or "silversmith" like Joseph Richardson (1711-1784) were men of substance who had large sums invested in real estate and occasionally "adventured" some of their surplus funds in trading voyages. Samuel Powel I, for example, was known as "the rich carpenter"; when he died in 1756, he owned over ninety houses in Philadelphia and a large amount of land outside the city.[18] Furthermore, it is pertinent to note that the Friends who are described in these marriage records were mostly young men, standing at the threshold of their business careers.

The testimony of contemporaries is unanimous that by mid-

---

16. Journal of John Bringhurst, Jr., in Josiah G. Leach, *History of the Bringhurst Family*, 95-105; also 24-25, 31.
17. See above, p. 41.
18. Bridenbaugh, *Rebels and Gentlemen*, 199. One recalls in this connection that Benjamin Franklin described himself in his last will and testament as "printer." —*Writings*, X, 493.

century the largest proportion of Philadelphia's wealth as well as social prestige and political power was concentrated in the hands of the Quaker merchants. Dr. Alexander Hamilton in 1744 reported that "the Quakers are the richest and the people of greatest interest in the government"; and the Reverend Robert Jenney, Rector of Christ Church, observed five years later: "the Members of our Church are not the richest in the place, the Richest generally centering in the Quakers and high Dutch, who . . . carry all before them."[19] At about the same time Professor Peter Kalm, the Swedish traveler, was writing of the Philadelphia Friends: "the majority of colonists did not look upon them as any *societas pia*, as they at first represented themselves, but as a political body. They cling together very close now, and the more well-to-do employ only Quaker artisans *if they can be found*."[20]

As these comments suggest, political hegemony went hand in hand with economic wealth. Indeed, the Quaker mercantile class possessed to a surprising degree the typical attributes of aristocracy. It was apparently part of William Penn's plan that predominant political power should rest with the Governor and his Council, the latter to be made up of men "of most note for their virtue, wisdom, and ability," the word *ability* connoting, as it often did in the seventeenth century, wealth or pecuniary power.[21] From the beginning, the Council was chiefly composed of substantial Quaker merchants friendly to the Proprietor's interests. After it was made an appointive body in 1701 (being at the same time shorn of its legislative powers), it

---

19. Bridenbaugh, *Gentleman's Progress*, 22; Robert Jenney to William Sturgeon, 26 Oct. 1749, Edgar L. Pennington, "The Work of the Bray Associates in Pennsylvania," *Pa. Mag. of Hist.*, 58 (1934), 5.

20. Adolph B. Benson, ed., *Peter Kalm's Travels in North America*, II, 652. The italics are mine; Kalm seems here to be implying that Quaker artisans were relatively few.

21. This phrase, applied to the membership of the Council, appeared in Penn's Charter of Liberties and his first Frame of Government, both produced in 1682. In the Frame of Government of 1683, it was applied to members of both Assembly and Council, and in the Charter of Privileges of 1701, when the Council had become a consultative and administrative body, it was applied only to the Assembly.—Francis N. Thorpe, ed., *The Federal and State Constitutions, Colonial Charters, and Other Organic Laws of . . . the United States of America* (Washington, 1909), V, 3048, 3050, 3055, 3064, 3066, 3078.

became even more solidly representative of the conservative Quaker merchant class; by virtue of its prerogative of tendering advice to the Governor on legislation prepared by the Assembly, it still continued by indirect means to function practically as a legislative body. The names of such wealthy Quakers as Samuel Carpenter, Samuel Richardson, John Delavall, Richard Hill, Isaac Norris, Jonathan Dickinson, James Logan, Thomas Masters and Samuel Preston appear regularly upon the membership lists of the Council; and Penn, while he was living, consciously cultivated their favor and support.[22]

Many of these Friends and their later counterparts also served as representatives of Philadelphia County in the legislative Assembly, particularly after the Founder's death, when the Quaker interest and the Proprietary interest had begun to diverge; down to 1756, as a result largely of the votes of the German sectarians in the hinterland, the Quakers dominated the lawmaking body, where they could effectively control the governor's actions. Isaac Norris II, for example, served as an Assemblyman for thirty-two years from 1734 to 1766; during the last decade and a half of his service he was, like his father before him, Speaker of the Assembly and acknowledged head of the "Quaker party." Most of the other Quaker merchants such as Israel and James Pemberton, John Smith, Anthony Morris, Francis Rawle, Edward Warner, and Joseph Fox, also served for longer or shorter periods in the Assembly.

The same Friends dominated the government of Philadelphia, which resembled the closed corporations of the English municipalities rather than the democratic town meetings of New England. In the first quarter of the eighteenth century, Philadelphia was under Quaker mayors every year except two or possibly three, and the list of mayors reads like a roll call of the great Quaker merchants of the day, for it includes Edward Shippen, Anthony Morris, Griffith Jones, Nathan Stanbury,

---

22. Penn's correspondence with his secretary and chief American representative, James Logan, is full of references to the small clique of merchants who could be counted on to uphold his interests in the Council and elsewhere. See, for example, *Penn and Logan Correspondence*, II, 80, 140, 324.

Thomas Masters, Richard Hill, Samuel Preston, Jonathan Dickinson, William Fishbourne, James Logan, Isaac Norris, and William Hudson.[23] From 1725 until the end of the colonial period, the mayor's office was occupied about half the time by Quakers, both Thomas Griffitts (d. 1746) and Benjamin Shoemaker (1704-1767) serving several terms. The mayors, like those of London, were invariably chosen from the mercantile class, and it is clear from certain practices connected with the elections that civic responsibility was consciously apportioned among the more substantial merchants and regarded as a natural concomitant of worldly wealth. The mayor was elected by the Aldermen (a self-perpetuating corporation), and any citizen who refused the honor was subject to a fine of twenty pounds. Until 1747 the office carried no salary; moreover, it was customary for the mayor, upon retiring, to provide an expensive entertainment for the gentlemen of the corporation. From 1746 on, in lieu of a banquet, the mayors usually presented a sum of money to be laid out in something permanently useful to the city. Friend William Attwood in 1747 gave sixty pounds and Benjamin Shoemaker in 1752 gave seventy-five pounds.[24] It can be seen from the size of these gifts that none but the wealthy could afford to be mayor.

The Quaker mercantile aristocrats thus exhibited a lively sense of political responsibility, and over a long period exercised political power in Pennsylvania considerably out of proportion to their numerical strength.

Intermarriage has always been a characteristic of aristocracies. In all the major colonial towns the upper class tended to consolidate its privileged position by close matrimonial alliances. This tendency was the more apparent among the Quaker grandees since the Society of Friends itself was a highly endogamous group. The Yearly Meeting in 1694 issued an unequivocal warning against unions with non-Friends: "take heed of giving your Sons and Daughters (who are Believers, and Profess, and Confess

23. A list of colonial mayors of Philadelphia is printed in John Hill Martin, *Bench and Bar of Philadelphia* (Philadelphia, 1883), 94-95.
24. Watson, *Annals*, I, 58-60, 63.

the Truth) in Marriage with Unbelievers for that was forbidden in all Ages, and was one Main Cause that brought the Wrath of God upon Old Israel."[25] The first book of discipline (1704) contained a distinct advice against marrying out of meeting, and the Yearly Meeting of 1712 cleared up any doubt that might have remained by providing that Friends who wedded "out of unity" should be admonished and advised to condemn their action in a public acknowledgment; if they remained obstinate, they were to be disowned.[26] The natural result of this testimony was to add a strong religious sanction to the practice of inter-marriage which within the circle of the merchant aristocrats also had obvious social and economic advantages to recommend it.

Thomas Lloyd, the most distinguished Friend of the first generation in Pennsylvania, was in a real sense the patriarch and progenitor of the Philadelphia Quaker aristocracy. One of the few genuine patricians to be converted to Quakerism, this descendant of an ancient Welsh family came to Penn's colony in 1683, bringing a family coat of arms with fifteen quarterings.[27] He played a prominent part in the early political life of the province, serving as President of the Council from 1684 to 1688 and as Deputy-Governor from 1691 to 1693. He was the acknowledged leader of the conservative or Proprietary party as opposed to the popular party of his distant connection David Lloyd. After his death the tradition was ably carried on by his sons-in-law Isaac Norris, Richard Hill, Samuel Preston, and John Delavall.[28] Richard Hill's second wife, Mary Stanbury, daughter of another Proprietary stalwart, later married Israel Pemberton,

---

25. MS Minutes of Phila. YM, I, 43.
26. Rayner W. Kelsey, "Early Books of Discipline of Philadelphia Yearly Meeting," Friends Hist. Assoc., *Bulletin*, 24 (1931), 19; MS Minutes of Phila. YM, I, 145-46.
27. Keith, *Provincial Councillors*, (7)-(8).
28. Always alert to promote the Proprietor's interests, James Logan frequently reminded him of the importance of cultivating the good will of this family; writing in 1708 of a vacancy among the Commissioners of Property, he observed: "Samuel Carpenter, Richard Hill, and Isaac Norris are the fittest. . . . Samuel Preston is also a very good man, and now makes a figure; and indeed Rachel [Lloyd]'s husband ought particularly to be taken notice of, for it has been too long neglected even for thy own interest."—Letter dated 17 Jan. 1708, *Penn and Logan Correspondence*, II, 308.

Jr., while a granddaughter of Thomas Lloyd married James Pemberton, thus carrying this family connection through the entire colonial period. The senior Israel Pemberton and James Logan, the two leading Philadelphia Quakers of the second quarter of the eighteenth century, married sisters; and the two daughters of James Logan became the wives of Isaac Norris II and John Smith, both of whom bore leading parts in the religious, political, and mercantile life of Philadelphia around mid-century. It would be possible to go on almost indefinitely citing examples of close marriage bonds among families in the higher social ranges of Philadelphia Quakerism.[29]

The Quaker aristocracy was not a closed circle limited to local families. Matrimonial ties were formed with wealthy Quaker families in England and in other colonies, such as the Redwoods of Newport, the Franklins of New York, and the Pleasants of Virginia. From time to time, new names and faces appeared in Philadelphia Quaker society, as Friends from other places migrated to the banks of the Delaware, launching into commerce and marrying into the older established families. Thus Richard Wells, grandson of Richard Partridge, Quaker colonial agent in London, came to Philadelphia in the middle of the eighteenth century, was apprenticed to John Smith and subsequently wedded Rachel Hill, a granddaughter of Thomas Lloyd.[30] John Reynell and Joshua Crosby, merchants of Jamaica, who removed to Philadelphia a little earlier, were likewise soon accepted and assimilated.

Quaker physicians moved freely in the circles of the mercantile aristocracy. Medical men were held in high repute by the Quakers because of the humanitarian nature of their calling; indeed *Doctor* was the only honorific title in general use among Friends. Dr. Thomas Wynne (d. 1691) and Dr. Griffith Owen (d. 1717), two prominent physicians among the early Welsh

---

29. It may be noted in passing that similar intermarriage was equally characteristic of the wealthy Quaker families of England; the Darbys, Lloyds, Pembertons, Barclays, and Gees, families prominent in the iron industry, for example, were all interrelated.—Ashton, *Iron and Steel*, 214-17, 231-32.

30. John Jay Smith, ed., *Letters of Doctor Richard Hill and His Children*, vi, xviii.

immigrants, figured importantly in the religious and political life of early Philadelphia; Dr. Wynne was Speaker of the first provincial Assembly and Dr. Owen, in addition to carrying on an extensive practice, was recorded as a ministering Friend, and sat for many years on the Governor's Council.[31] Among the most distinguished Quaker practitioners in the middle of the eighteenth century were Dr. Samuel Preston Moore, Dr. Charles Moore (1724-1801) and Dr. Lloyd Zachary (1701-1756); all grandsons of Thomas Lloyd, they lived on the same scale as the merchant princes, owning country houses and participating actively in civic and humanitarian affairs.

For nearly a half century, lawyers figured hardly at all in Philadelphia society. Friends still regarded the bar in much the same light that George Fox had when he spoke of seeing "the lawyers black, their black robe as a puddle, and like a black pit, almost covered over with blackness."[32] There was little need for lawyers so long as disputes continued to be settled under the aegis of the meeting. Until 1722 it was actually illegal to practice law for money in Pennsylvania.[33] As time passed, however, and a more complex economic life begain to require legal services, the prejudice abated, and a few members of weighty Quaker families commenced to enter the law. Francis Rawle was admitted to practice late in life, and John Kinsey, who studied law in Burlington, moving to Philadelphia in 1730, was so highly regarded by his co-religionists that he served them for many years in the dual role of Clerk of Philadelphia Yearly Meeting and Speaker of the Provincial Assembly.[34] Nicholas Waln, later a well-known minister and Clerk of the Yearly Meeting, studied at the Inns of Court and had a lucrative practice in Philadelphia until he gave it up in 1772, along with his fashionable dress and

---

31. Myers, ed., *Narratives*, 228n; Proud, *History*, II, 99n.
32. *The Law of God* (London, 1658).
33. Keith, *Provincial Councillors*, 126.
34. Jordan, *Colonial Families*, I, 149; Sharpless, *Political Leaders*, 156-80. David Lloyd, perhaps the most learned lawyer in the province during the first half century, had studied under Chief Justice Jeffries in England before being "convinced" as a Quaker.—Burton A. Konkle, David Lloyd and the First Half Century of Pennsylvania (MS at Friends Historical Library of Swarthmore College), 11.

mundane interests, to turn his attention wholly to religious concerns.[35] By that time, however, the great period of the Quaker aristocracy in Philadelphia was over; indeed Nicholas Waln's dramatic renunciation of worldly pride and riches was symbolic of the end of an era in the history of the Philadelphia Quaker aristocracy.

"OF THE BEST SORT BUT PLAIN"

Along with the increase of material wealth and the habituation to political power, there was a sort of social osmosis, a subtle but constantly growing tendency, more noticeable among some Friends than others, towards conformity to the world against which the primitive Friends had so vigorously and persistently protested. As worldliness grew, as departures from "the simplicity of Truth" became more apparent, at least so the plainer Friends maintained, spiritual power and sensitiveness to the promptings of the Inner Word declined. In 1764 John Smith, an aged minister from Marlborough in Chester County, stood up in the Yearly Meeting of Ministers and Elders in Philadelphia and "appearing to be under a great exercise of Spirit," summarized the history of Philadelphia Quakerism since the beginning of the century. He well remembered, he declared, that in the early years

Friends were a plain lowly minded people and that there was much tenderness and Contrition in their meetings and That at the end of twenty years from that time the society increasing in wealth and in some degree conforming to the fashions of the World, true Humility decreased and their meetings in general were not so lively and Edifying That at the end of Forty years many of the Society were grown rich, that wearing of fine costly Garments and with fashionable furniture, silver watches became customary with many and with their sons and daughters. And as these things prevailed in the Society and appeared in our Meetings of Ministers and Elders; so the powerful overshadowings of the Holy Spirit were less manifested amongst us that there had been an increase of outward greatness till now, and that

---

35. Bowden, *History of the Society of Friends in America*, II, 404-5; E. Alfred Jones, *American Members of the Inns of Court* (London, 1924), 212-13.

the weakness amongst us in not living up to our principles and supporting the Testimony of Truth in Faithfulness was matter of much Sorrow.[36]

Philadelphia Friends were not wholly unaware of the mundane spirit creeping in amongst them: indeed some were ready to defend the thesis that, as wealth and prestige grew, material comforts and luxuries might justifiably increase in proportion, and that one's scale of living should reflect the amount of one's worldly goods. A frank avowal of this theory was offered by Isaac Norris I as early as 1707/8 in a letter to Joseph Pike, a weighty Friend of Cork Meeting in Ireland. Irish Friends were notable for strict discipline, and it is probable that Norris's correspondent had taken him and his family to task for indulging, while on a visit to the British Isles, in a degree of ostentation and luxury inconsistent with Truth. Norris was willing to acknowledge some departure from plainness: "It is not improbable but upon this occasion of our furnishing ourselves and family from England, something of what thou fears may have happened; but if it be, it will wear off; and yet I hope it is so little as hardly to be noticed."[37] Continuing in more philosophic vein, Norris set forth his views on the proper scale of living (or "use of the creation" in Barclay's phrase) in relation to one's social and economic status:

I confess my own thoughts are too general, but universal, in these cases, to be very narrow in that way; yet I believe consideration is safest to that side where it gives most self-denial; and example, as thou hints, goes a great way to draw on others, whose abilities are not the same; yet I cannot see it reasonable that Joseph Pike and Samuel Combe should wear the same and live at the same rate within-doors. Thus, then, every man ought soberly and discreetly to set bounds to himself, and avoid extremes, still bearing due regard to the society he is of.[38]

---

36. *Journal and Essays of John Woolman*, 267.
37. Deborah Norris Logan, who transcribed this letter in the *Penn and Logan Correspondence*, reads *punishing; furnishing*, however, seems a more likely reading.
38. Samuel Combe was a cooper who had removed from Bristol to Cork and thence, recently, to Philadelphia. His certificate from Cork Monthly Meeting explained that "although he was observed to be a Laborious painfull man, the

Pursuing his argument (or self-justification) one step further, he adumbrated the philosophy which was becoming dominant among Philadelphia Friends, a philosophy which diverged sharply from the strict disciplinary views characteristic of Irish and of rural Pennsylvania Quakerism:

And since I am thus led into these considerations, give me leave, dear Joseph, to give thee one thought more, which I often have, which is, that if we will be instrumental to the more general spreading of our noble principles, the light and manifestation of our blessed Lord . . . we must not appear too narrow in other things to be particular. In what I mean by too narrow, might require more room than I shall take here; but that far I would venture to say, that, although in conversation among Friends it may be very well to be very particular in such thoughts, yet for standing and public orders, and rules from churches and meetings, there should be a great care, and an eye always to the universal good and unity of the same believers in divers nations.[39]

Whether as a result of conscious policy, as Isaac Norris suggested, or of emulation of "the world's people" with whom they were in constant association, or as a natural consequence of the possession of wealth, the Philadelphia Quakers early departed from primitive plainness and accommodated their manner of living by degrees to that of "the world."

The process of assimilation was soon apparent to the eye in the external appearance of the merchants and their families. By clear implication in the Yearly Meeting's testimony of 1695 one can find a description of the fashionable apparel which some Friends were even then beginning to adopt. With revealing specificity it was urged:

that all that profess the Truth, and their Children, whether Young or Grown up, keep to Plainness in Apparell As becomes the Truth and that none Wear long lapp'd Sleeves or Coates gathered at the Sides, or Superfluous Buttons, Or Broad Ribbons about their Hatts, or long curled Perriwiggs and that no Women,

world favoured him not with Success."—Myers, *Quaker Arrivals*, 43. For Barclay's view see above, pp. 110-11.
39. *Penn and Logan Correspondence*, II, 259. On Joseph Pike and the strict discipline of Irish Quakerism, see Braithwaite, *Second Period*, 501-10; and Isabel Grubb, *Quakers in Ireland, 1654-1900* (London, 1927), 81-98.

their Children, or Servants, Dress their Heads Immodestly, or Wear their Garments undecently As it is too Common, nor Wear long Scarves, and that all be Careful about Makeing, Buying, or Wearing (as much as they can) Striped or Flower'd Stuffs, or other useless and Superfluous Things....[40]

"Plainness" at this period in Philadelphia Quakerism did not connote the uniform drab-colored "plain dress" later characteristic of Friends; it implied simply the ordinary garb of the day stripped of superfluous ornaments and useless fripperies like lace and ribbons.[41] Margaret Fox, wife of the founder of Quakerism, had spoken her mind concerning the legalistic spirit creeping into the discipline of the Society of Friends in Ireland and other quarters, which insisted, as she put it, that "we must not look at no colours, nor make any thing that is changeable colours, as the hills are, nor sell them, nor wear them. But we must be all in one dress and one colour."[42] Women Friends in Philadelphia tended to agree with her that this was "a silly poor gospel." They regularly wore aprons of green and blue, and their gowns were not infrequently of brilliant colors. Portraits of three generations of women in the Norris family may be cited in evidence. Mary Norris, daughter of Thomas Lloyd and wife of Isaac Norris I was painted in a blue gown relieved with crimson. Sarah, daughter of James Logan and wife of Isaac Norris II, appears in a portrait attired in deep blue. And Mary Norris, who became the wife of John Dickinson, was dressed for her portrait in a gown of dark crimson.[43] Most women Friends, however, did eschew the more gaudy and obvious adornments affected by their more worldly contemporaries.

Wives and daughters of the Quaker grandees compensated for their self-denial in the matter of ornaments by having their garments made only of the finest and most expensive stuffs.

---

40. MS Minutes of Phila. YM, I, 54.
41. See Amelia Mott Gummere, *The Quaker: A Study in Costume*, 10-24, and *passim.*
42. Braithwaite, 518.
43. Agnes Repplier, *Philadelphia: The Place and the People*, 132. Miss Repplier points out that it is not until we reach Maria Dickinson Logan, born in the year the Revolution ended, that we encounter the dove-colored "plain dress" usually associated with Friends.

Christopher Sower, the Dunker printer, observed in 1724 that plainness was still noticeable in Quaker garb "except that the material is very costly, or is even velvet."[44] And Peter Kalm, attending a Quaker meeting a quarter-century later, offered similar testimony:

the women have no clothing that differs from that of the other English [ladies], except that I do not remember having seen them wear cuffs, and although they censure all adornments I have seen them wear just as gaudy shoes as other Englishwomen. . . . Although they pretend not to have their clothes made after the latest fashion, or to wear cuffs and be dressed as gaily as others, they strangely enough have their garments made of the finest and costliest materials that can be procured.[45]

In domestic architecture the same tendencies were apparent. The brick town houses of the Quakers, built, except for a few early examples, in the simple classicism of the rebuilt London or the quiet elegance of early Georgian, were as large and as comfortable as those of the most fashionable Anglicans.[46] The only distinctive characteristic of the Quaker dwellings was a certain austerity and economy in detail, and even this quality was not invariably present. Doorways were often high and narrow, lacking the sidelights typical of New England Georgian houses, and usually surmounted, as at James Logan's Stenton, by a plain flat arch of brick or, more often, by a simple unsupported door hood. Windows likewise tended to be simply framed, without elaborate pediments, and there was relatively little use of Palladian arches, rusticated quoins, and other purely decorative members.[47]

---

44. Rayner Kelsey, ed., "An Early Description of Pennsylvania," *Pa. Mag. of Hist.*, 45 (1921), 252-53.
45. *Travels*, II. 651.
46. See, for example, the description of the town house of Charles Norris (1712-1766) in Scharf and Westcott, *History of Philadelphia*, II, 870. The conclusion of two architectural historians is that basically "little difference is distinguishable between the houses of Quakers and 'World's People' and that the distinctive characteristics of the colonial architecture of Philadelphia are more or less common to all buildings of the period."—Frank Cousins and Phil M. Riley, *The Colonial Architecture of Philadelphia*, 14.
47. An interesting comparison can be made between Stenton and William Byrd's Westover in Virginia. The two houses, both superb examples of early Georgian, were built within a year or two of each other, *ca.* 1725. Their general external appearance is remarkably similar. The most striking difference lies in

Beyond these subtle distinctions, however, there was little observable difference in grandeur and elegance between the homes of Quaker merchants and those of wealthy families of other denominations. There was equally little difference in the interior furnishings. The tendency towards conspicuous consumption in this respect did not go unobserved by the Elders and Overseers of the Meeting. The Yearly Meeting of Women Friends in 1698 uttered a warning "that no superfluous furniture be in your houses, as great fringes about your valances, and double valances, and double curtains, and many such like needless things; which the Truth maketh manifest to the humble minded."[48] Here, as in the matter of clothing, it was easy to obey the letter of the discipline without curtailing extravagant impulses. John Reynell in 1738 wrote to Daniel Flexney in London for "A Handsome plain Looking Glass for my Self, Cost about £4 and 2 raised Japan'd Black Corner Cubbards, with 2 Doors to each, no Red in 'em, *of the best Sort, but Plain.*"[49]

Inventories of estates provide interesting evidence concerning the manner in which the Quaker grandees furnished their homes. Among the pieces in Jonathan Dickinson's best parlor in 1722 (when exotic woods were not common in the colonies) was a "Mohogany Chest of Drawers and Table." In the front parlor stood a "5 foot Mohogany Table," a clock and case valued at £22/10, and a "Mohogany Cloathes Press." Dickinson's household goods as a whole were valued at £1017/15/10. No doubt many of the elegant mahogany highboys and chairs fashioned by William Savery and now so greatly prized by collectors were originally made on the orders of Savery's wealthy fellow Quakers. Charles Norris's house boasted Turkey carpets, and the walls of John Smith's parlor were adorned with "a painted cloth. . .11 feet by 9, painted on one side with black and marbled Chequers and on the other brown."[50]

---

the doorways: the entrance to Westover is capped by a fan light and a rather elaborate scroll pediment, whereas Stenton's is unadorned.

48. Epistle dated 21 Sept., copy in Quaker Collection, Haverford College Library.

49. Letter dated 25 Nov. 1738, Reynell Letter Book, 1738-41 (italics mine).

50. Inventory of the Goods and Chattles of Jonathan Dickinson . . . taken this

Silversmiths like Francis Richardson (1681-1729) and his son Joseph (1711-1787) did a thriving business turning out silver tankards, braziers, porringers, salvers, candlesticks, teapots, and similar articles for Quaker patrons. It was customary for merchants to conserve part of their extra money in the form of plate, for when, as with Jonathan Dickinson's plate (worth more than two hundred pounds), it bore the family arms, it was easily identifiable if stolen. Designs executed for Quakers like Samuel Powel, Thomas Griffitts, William Logan, Samuel Emlen, Isaac Norris, John Smith, and Anthony Morris, were usually simple: the tankards, for example, lacked the ornamental finials characteristic of New England silver.[51] In the eyes of a consistent Friend like John Woolman, however, it was impossible to achieve true simplicity while making any use of silver and gold. "The Customary use of Silver Vessels about houses," he stated in 1770, "hath deeply affected my mind of late years, and under a living Concern I have frequently laboured in Families, and Sometimes more publickly to disswade from the Use of these things, in which there is a manifest conformity to Outward shew and greatness."[52]

Although the fine arts were officially proscribed by Quaker discipline, the esthetic impulse (or the desire to have one's features recorded for posterity) could not be so easily rooted out. Isaac Norris I gave the following interesting instructions to his son as he left on a voyage to England in 1722:

If thou Should meet with—by any Accident Cheap a Good Landscape or Two—the prospect Geometrically Extended—

---

twentieth day of fifth Month Anno Domini 1722, Hist. Soc. Pa.; Scharf and Westcott, II, 870; John Smith to Elias Bland, 31 Jan. 1750, Smith MSS, Library Company of Philadelphia.

51. See Clara L. Avery, *Early American Silver*, 188. The names of the Quaker merchants listed in the text all appear in the day books of Joseph Richardson, Hist. Soc. Pa.

52. MS dated 20 Nov. 1770, Friends Historical Library of Swarthmore College. So far did Woolman carry his aversion to silver utensils that on one occasion, being at the home of a wealthy Friend (conjectured by Amelia M. Gummere to have been John Smith), when "drink was brought in Silver Vessels and not in any other," he found himself unable to touch it, although he was thirsty: "I . . . told him my case with weeping," he writes, "and he ordered some drink for me in another vessel."—*Journal*, 310.

Well and beautifully Shaded—and good painting in which thou may take Judgment of Somebody of Skill—I did not Care If thou bought them—for my Garden Closett—but as thou Remembers my begun designs on the Chimney piece there—think of Such as may be Coppy'd for my finishing and well Shading the figures rivers hills fields &c.[53]

A quarter of a century later, two young Quakers, John Smith and William Logan, are found "viewing" the pictures which Robert Feke was then exhibiting in Philadelphia, and still later, young Friends like Elizabeth Sandwith and Hannah Callender were frequent visitors at Bush Hill where they admired James Hamilton's fine collection of paintings.[54]

Benjamin Franklin once confided to Lord Kames that he knew of some eminent Quakers who "have had their pictures privately drawn and deposited with trusty friends. . . ."[55] It is doubtful whether the Norris family was so secretive; at any rate, several members of the family had their portraits painted by fashionable artists while in England. Although the stricter Friends tended to frown upon oil paintings, they had not the same objection to silhouettes, since the cutting of profiles entailed little expense and the elimination of color tended towards simplicity; consequently the features of many of the eighteenth-century Friends have come down to us only in this form.[56]

Like the ownership of a yacht or a private airplane today, possession of an elaborate equipage was a sign of having "arrived" in colonial society. An old Philadelphian, whose memory reached back to the third decade of the eighteenth century, told John Fanning Watson, the annalist, that in his childhood the only four-wheeled carriages in the colony were those of Governor Gordon, Andrew Hamilton, Council President Anthony Palmer (three non-Friends), Jonathan Dickinson, Isaac Norris, James Logan, David Lloyd, and Lawrence Growden (all Friends).[57]

53. Letter to Isaac Norris II, 10 April 1722, Norris Letter Book, 1716-30, 303.
54. MS Diary of John Smith, Vol. X (entry for 7 June 1750); Bridenbaugh, *Rebels and Gentlemen*, 214.
55. Letter dated 3 Jan. 1760, *Writings*, IV, 6.
56. Anna Brinton, "Quaker Profiles," Friends Hist. Assoc., *Bulletin*, 29 (1940), 10.
57. *Annals*, I, 208.

Isaac Norris in 1713 ordered a coach from England "like Jonathan Dickinson's," emblazoned with his coat of arms; a few weeks later, however, he reconsidered this latter bit of ostentation, saying that on second thought, he "would have only I N in Cypher the rest all plaine." Before long we find Norris writing again to England: "I am not for a Livery, but my wife has a mind that the Servants who drive and go with the Coach Should be distinguisht from the Others"; he therefore ordered liveries "Strong and Cheap, Either of a Dark Gray or Sad Coullour ... or any Grave Coullour thou likes."[58] Around the middle of the century, a provincial poetess, with a touch of snobbery, wrote the following halting verses:

> Judge Allen drove a coach and four
>   Of handsome dappled grays,
> Shippens, Penns, Pembertons, and Morrises,
> Powels, Cadwaladers, and Norrises
>   Drove only pairs of blacks and bays.[59]

The last five names were those of Quaker families. By 1772, with the widespread growth in prosperity, there were no less than eighty-four private equipages in Philadelphia. Looking at the list of carriage-owners carefully compiled by Pierre Eugène du Simitière, one discovers that thirty-three were Friends.[60] If the

---

58. Letters to John Askew, 30 May, 26 June 1713, Norris Letter Book, 1709-16, pp. 389, 393; 6 May 1720, Norris Letter Book, 1716-30, 224.
59. Dixon Wecter, *The Saga of American Society*, 65.
60. The list is printed in Scharf and Westcott, II, 880-81n. The names of the Quakers come at the end, indicating that du Simitière thought of them as a separate element in Philadelphia "society." Since this forms as good a basis as any for a sort of Social Register of Philadelphia Quakerism just before the Revolution, the list of Friends may be given in full:

William Logan	Reese Meredith	Richard Wistar
James Logan, Jr.	Abel James	Samuel Emlen, Jr.
Israel Pemberton	Henry Drinker	George Emlen, Jr.
James Pemberton	Thomas Clifford	James Bringhurst
John Pemberton	John Reynell	Samuel Noble
Samuel Preston Moore	Samuel Pleasants	John Mifflin
Henry Hill	Joseph Wharton	Anthony Morris
Joseph Fox	Thomas Wharton	Joshua Fisher
Hugh Roberts	Joseph Wharton, Jr.	Elizabeth Norris
Samuel Shoemaker	Jacob Lewis	Widow Greenleaf
Joshua Howell	Christian Samuel Morris	Samuel Smith

ownership of a coach may be taken as a sort of *cachet* of nobility, or at least as a rough index of social standing, the obvious conclusion is that the Quaker grandees differed little from their aristocratic Anglican or Presbyterian neighbors in the outward trappings of wealth, and that the actual number of Quakers in the higher social ranges increased considerably during the eighteenth century, although the Friends formed a progressively smaller proportion of the total aristocratic class as they did of the population at large.

COUNTRY LIFE

Every Quaker merchant, as soon as he was able to afford it, built a country house outside the city, where he and his family could escape the heat of the Philadelphia summer. In so doing he was but following the example of many *parvenus* in the mother country who, having prospered in trade, sought to ape the customs and manners of the gentry. As non-Friends joined in the trend to the country, the environs of the Quaker City came to exhibit by mid-century the "most nearly perfect replica of English country life that it was possible for the New World to produce."[61] Most of the "plantation" houses were small, having few or no bedrooms, and were located within easy driving distance of Philadelphia since they were designed only for a day's, or at most a weekend's outing. A few of the wealthier merchants like James Logan and Isaac Norris built large mansions in the country to which they retired upon their withdrawal, at an early age, from active business.

The custom of maintaining "plantations" arose early in Philadelphia, stimulated perhaps by the example of William Penn's splendid country estate at Pennsbury, about twenty-four miles up the Delaware. Samuel Carpenter, for example, retired from his multifarious business activities in 1704, and settled down on his "plantation" in Bucks County.[62] Some of the merchants made a practice of accumulating country estates. Israel Pember-

---

61. Bridenbaugh, *Rebels and Gentlemen*, 191.
62. Letter of Isaac Norris I to Jonathan Dickinson (?), 28 July 1704, Norris Family Letters, II, 10.

ton I, who inherited Bolton Farm in Bucks County from his father, also owned a town house on Water Street, and a "plantation" on the south side of Philadelphia. His son Israel II moved to a larger dwelling—Clarke Hall—on Chestnut Street, where his family lived during most of the year; the summer months were usually spent at Bolton, but for the sake of an occasional day in the country, he also maintained a "plantation" in Germantown.[63]

Isaac Norris's mansion at Fairhill on the road to Germantown (built ca. 1716) was a two-story house with a cupola surmounted by an imported weathercock; there were several outbuildings, including one which housed his library, and an extensive garden, formally laid out with gravel walks and parterres. The window sashes (unusual in that day of casements) were imported from England, as were the marble hearths and a clock with a walnut case. According to Deborah Norris Logan, Fairhill was built on the plan of Dolobran in Wales, the ancestral seat of Thomas Lloyd, whose daughter the first Isaac Norris had married.[64] Here at Fairhill "instead of the beautifull prospects of Enclosures and gay Improvements," wrote Norris to a friend in England, "we are surrounded with Woods and all nature in its rough dress." A quarter of a century later, Isaac Norris II, having inherited the estate, withdrew from trade and retired to Fairhill where he lived "downright in the Country way." There in the summertime he occupied himself with his gardens, his fishponds, and his meadows, after the manner of the English rural gentry. For the rest, he observed, not without an appropriate Virgilian quotation, "*Rura Gelu cum claudit Hyems* I keep my Self as warm as I can in the Green house Chimney Corner [,] poor amusement to the Splendor of Courts but such as I believe will now be my Station while I live." He went seldom to town, except for his legislative duties; he had not retired from politics,

---

63. "Last Will and Testament of Israel Pemberton," Pemberton Papers, VII, 138; Thayer, *Israel Pemberton*, 3, 195.
64. Fairhill was burned during the Revolution. A description of it by Deborah Norris Logan may conveniently be consulted in Charles J. Stillé, *The Life and Times of John Dickinson* (Philadelphia, 1891), 311-12.

he explained, because of his sense of duty to the people.[65]

More typical were the unpretentious villas of the less opulent merchants—Callenders, Whartons, Mifflins, Richardsons, Walns, and others—which lay within a ten-mile radius of Philadelphia and can easily be located on the Scull and Heap map of 1750. "Plantation" on the east bank of the Schuylkill, the country house successively of John Kinsey, Quaker Speaker of the Assembly, and of James Pemberton, younger brother of Israel II, may be considered as representative of these smaller villas. Standing in the midst of natural surroundings modified only by the presence of a few shrubs and a kitchen garden, it was a substantial two-story brick building, its sloping roof pierced by dormer windows and crowned by a balustrade and two chimneys. There were four rooms on each floor, divided by a wide hall; the kitchen was in the basement. Except for its squat balusters and rather heavy lintels over the windows, it was bare of ornament, giving an impression of solidity rather than of grace.

For a description of the surroundings of a typical Quaker "plantation" we may turn to Hannah Callender's account of Richmond Seat, her father's country estate, situated on the Delaware at Point-no-Point, north of Philadelphia, near the estates of John Smith, Edward Warner, and Joseph Fox. The property comprised sixty acres, half upland and half meadow. The little house was on the upland, set in the midst of a small garden interspersed with fruit trees. The larger garden, lying alongside the meadow, was described by the young Quakeress in these terms:

By three descents of grass steps, you are led to the bottom in a walk lengthways of the garden. On one side a fine cut hedge encloses from the meadow, the other a high green bank shaded with spruce, the meadows and river lying open to the eye, looking to the house covered with trees: honeysuckle on the fences, low hedges to part the flower and kitchen gardens, and a fine barn just at the side of the wood. A small space of woods around

65. Isaac Norris I to Benjamin Coole, 11 March 1716/7, Norris Letter Book, 1716-30, 60; Isaac Norris II to Robert Charles (?), 22 June 1743, Norris Letter Book, 1719-56, 14.

it is cleared from brush underneath. The whole a little romantic rural scene.[66]

"INNOCENT DIVERTISEMENTS"

The chief diversions of the Quaker merchants and their families were gardening and the pleasures of the table, and Quaker gardens were as famous for their beauty as Quaker dinners for their abundance. "To follow after gardening" was mentioned by Robert Barclay as one of the few "innocent Divertisements" permitted to Friends, and Philadelphians proceeded to make the most of it.[67] As early as 1698, there were reported to be "very fine and delightful Gardens and Orchards" in the neighborhood of Philadelphia. Edward Shippen's estate on Second Street, with its broad lawn descending to Dock Creek and its herd of grazing deer, was a veritable *rus in urbe;* its garden was singled out for especial notice for its abundance of "Tulips, Pinks, Carnations, Roses (of several sorts), Lilies, not to mention those that grow wild in the Fields." Israel Pemberton's garden was a show place of the Quaker City; Alexander Graydon later described it as being "laid out in the old fashioned style of uniformity, with walks and allies nodding to their brothers, and decorated with a number of evergreens, carefully clipped into pyramidal and conical forms."[68] Most of the descriptions indicate that the vogue for formal Italianate gardens persisted among Philadelphia Quakers throughout the colonial period, although on some of the country estates a taste for romantic or naturalistic effects was beginning to prevail.[69]

Professor Peter Kalm, who visited the Quaker City in 1749, found that Friends were regarded by their fellow Philadelphians

---

66. George Vaux, ed., "Extracts from the Diary of Hannah Callender," *Pa. Mag. of Hist.,* 12 (1888), 448.

67. *Apology,* Prop. XV, sec. ix, *Writings,* II, 540-41.

68. Gabriel Thomas, *Historical and Geographical Account,* in Myers, ed., *Narratives,* 332; Watson, *Annals,* I, 39; Graydon, *Memoirs of a Life Chiefly Passed in Pennsylvania* (Harrisburg, 1811), 34-35.

69. John Smith's garden at Point-no-Point, although carefully terraced and bordered with "privy Hedges," was planted with watermelons, strawberries, and gooseberries as well as tulips, pinks, and Sweet Williams; it also contained a pond fed by a ditch from a nearby creek. —MS Diary, II, *passim* (especially entries for 10 and 12 May 1746).

as gourmets or "semi-Epicureans." "No other people," he reported, "want such choice and well-prepared food as the Quakers."[70] Marriages were occasions for great feasts, not only on the
day of the wedding, but also on the two days, a month apart,
when the couple "passed meeting." Again and again the Elders
were forced to issue admonitions against making "extraordinary
provisions" at such times.[71] Every other autumn, when Yearly
Meeting was held in Philadelphia (it convened in Burlington
across the river in the intervening years), the town was filled
with country Friends who took this opportunity to bring their
farm produce to market; they were entertained with great hospitality in the spacious homes of the city merchants, who endeavored to outdo each other in the liberality of their dinners.[72]

Weighty and wealthy Friends like the Pembertons made a
special point of entertaining traveling ministers from distant
places; this was one of the virtues which led Daniel Stanton to
refer to the first Israel Pemberton with approbation as "a bright
pattern and elder in the church of Christ, given to hospitality and
good works."[73] The great banquets were not only for Friends,
however; John Adams, though a New England Congregation-
alist, was regaled with many a "sinful feast" in the homes of plain
Friends in 1774, while attending the Continental Congress. Miers
Fisher (1748-1819), a young Quaker lawyer, provided a repast
which included so many dishes that Adams wearied of itemizing
them all in his diary: "ducks, hams, chickens, beef, pig, tarts,

---

70. *Travels*, II, 651. Although total abstinence from alcoholic liquors had not
yet become a recognized Quaker testimony, Kalm observed that Friends practiced restraint in drinking. —*Ibid.*, 652.

71. Watson, *Annals*, I, 178; MS Minutes of Phila. YM, I, 176 (1716). In 1705
it was the advice of the Monthly Meeting that at the "passing" of each marriage
two Friends be appointed "to see that all things be carried on soberly and that
nothing of Rudeness or Extravagancy, or the world's vain Customs be made
use of."—MS Minutes of Phila. MM, I, 202. The widely prevalent custom of
presenting gloves at burials and weddings was discouraged by the Monthly
Meeting in 1737. —*Ibid.*, II, 281-82.

72. Myers, *Immigration of the Irish Quakers*, 221. Elizabeth Wilkinson, an English "public Friend," felt obliged in 1763 to caution Anthony Morris and his
family against trying to surpass their neighbors "in the Grandeur of their
Houses, Tables, Entertainment, &ca." —Friends Hist. Assoc., *Bulletin*, 18
(1929), 90.

73. *A Journal of the Life, Travels, and Gospel Labours of a Faithful Minister
of Jesus Christ, Daniel Stanton* (Philadelphia, 1772), 64.

creams, custards, jellies, fools, trifles, floating islands, beer, porter, punch, wine, and a long &c." [74] If this is a sample menu, it would appear that at dinnertime Friends made an exception to their general rule of "using the creation with moderation"!

In their avoidance of most forms of diversion, Friends stood apart from the majority of "the world's people" in Philadelphia. The Discipline took a stern view of any pastime which had no practical use or entailed a waste of precious time. The Overseers were directed to deal with "such as run Races, either on Horse back or on Foot; lay Wagers, or use any Gaming, or needless and vain Sports and pastimes; for our time Swiftly passeth away, and our pleasure and delight ought to be in the Law of the Lord." The meeting took vigorous action to stamp out such temptations to frivolity as dancing schools and theaters. [75] When Isaac Norris I ordered some battledores and shuttlecocks ("to Exercise my Children in the hall in Cold Weather and keep 'em out of the dirt"), he revealed by the very deviousness with which he broached the subject his anticipation of the frowns of stricter Friends: "If I could tell thee without seeing it wrote," he told John Askew in London, "I would wisper to send a pair of battle doors and some Shuttle Cocks of the best make. . . ." [76]

It should not be supposed, however, that Quaker youths had no means of enjoying themselves: on the contrary, the diaries of young Friends like John Smith and Elizabeth Sandwith are full of tea-parties, skating parties, sleighing parties, and similar innocent amusements. Most of the scions of the weightier merchant families, nevertheless, looked askance at the horse-racing, fox-hunting set to which Jacob Hiltzheimer and several backsliding young Friends belonged. [77] To be sure, Isaac Norris, his brother Charles, Griffith Owen II, Thomas Masters, and Lloyd Zachary were among the ten young men who were concerned in

---

74. Charles Francis Adams, ed., *The Works of John Adams*, II, 369 (entry for 7 Sept. 1774).

75. MS Book of Discipline, 22-23; MS Minutes of Phila. MM, I, 216 (26 April 1706); Ezra K. Maxfield, "Friendly Testimony Regarding Stage Plays," Friends Hist. Assoc., *Bulletin*, 14 (1925), 18-19.

76. Letter dated 2 Mar. 1716/17, Norris Letter Book, 1716-30, 55.

77. See Jacob Cox Parsons, ed., *Extracts from the Diary of Jacob Hiltzheimer, passim*.

building the famous Bachelors' Hall, a square one-room club-house located in Kensington, just outside the town limits. The meeting, apprehensive lest this "house of Recreation or diversion . . . prove of Pernicious Consequence" to its youth, appointed a committee to dissuade the young Friends from proceeding further with it. The young men politely informed the committee that the project was too far advanced for them to withdraw, but that they would surely abandon it if they found its influence corrupting.[78] It may be doubted, however, whether the group ever indulged in much unQuakerly revelry. George Webb, who celebrated this "proud Dome on Delaware's stream" in stumbling verse, foresaw that perhaps on occasion

> . . . the all-inspiring bowl
> To laughter shall provoke and cheer the soul;
> The jocund tale to humor shall invite,
> And dedicate to wit a jovial night.

Nevertheless he took pains to make it clear that

> 'Tis not a revel or lascivious night,
> That to this hall the Batchelors invite.

Far otherwise: the real purpose of the club was "to mend the heart and cultivate the mind." Philosophy and natural science were to be the topics of discussion and a botanical garden was to be maintained for the cultivation of medicinal plants, "whose virtues none, or none but Indians know."[79]

No doubt John Smith spoke for most other young Quakers when he made the following comment in his diary after a social occasion on which he and his friends had been "very merry together":

I Cannot think the Reflection on spending our time in Mirth Occasioned by trifling talk &Ca Can afterwards yield any Satisfaction—for my part tho' I love a free sociable Conversation as

78. MS Minutes of Phila. MM, II, 191 (31 July 1731); Isaac Norris to William (?), 1730, Norris Letter Book, 1730-33, 5; Charles Norris to Isaac Norris, 5 Apr. 1734, Norris Family Letters, I, 25.
79. "Batchelors' Hall" (1731), in Evert A. and George L. Duyckinck, eds., *The Cyclopaedia of American Literature* (Philadelphia, 1875), I, 111-12.

well as anybody, Yet I would have it turn upon such subjects as are Improving at the same time they Entertain. . . .[80]

There is no doubt that the sobriety of the Friends, supplemented after 1740 by the latter-day Puritanism of the Great Awakening, made Philadelphia down to the Revolutionary War the most sedate and decorous of colonial towns. Dr. Alexander Hamilton, at least, found it so in 1744: never, this urbane traveler declared, had he been in a place "where the *gout* for publick gay diversions prevailed so little."[81]

"WET QUAKERS"

For all their aloofness from the worldlier aspects of eighteenth-century civilization, the Quaker aristocrats were far from provincial. We have already seen how their far-flung commercial and religious interests kept them in touch with the rest of the Atlantic world. Feeling that the education of even a Quaker aristocrat was not complete without the crowning experience of the Grand Tour, several of the merchants sent their sons off to Europe for a year or two of travel before the counting house finally claimed them. Francis Rawle, a grandson of the advocate of paper money, has been credited with initiating the custom in Philadelphia in 1748, and he was followed, a number of years later, by George and Thomas Mifflin.[82] Long before this, Quaker merchants had been in the habit of sending their sons to England to make the acquaintance of weighty figures in the parent Yearly Meeting, many of them traders with whom presently they would be carrying on business correspondence. Thus Israel Pemberton II was sent to Great Britain on business in 1735 at the age of twenty. His overzealous buying in London caused his cautious father considerable embarrassment before all the bills were paid; and this experience may have led the elder Pemberton to acquiesce in his second son James' resolution of "avoiding to engage in much business" when he went abroad at the age of twenty-five. John Pemberton, youngest of the three sons, first

---

80. Entry dated 27 Mar. 1746.
81. Bridenbaugh, *Gentleman's Progress*, 22.
82. Bridenbaugh, *Rebels and Gentlemen*, 194; Keith, *Provincial Councillors*, 363.

went abroad at the age of twenty-two, primarily for the sake of his health. Paying little heed to business, he spent his time visiting Quaker meetings in company with John Churchman of Nottingham, Pennsylvania, a "public Friend" traveling "in the service of Truth." In the course of his journeyings Pemberton made his own first hesitant "appearance in the ministry" at Penzance in Cornwall.[83]

Parents often expressed concern lest their sons, by associating with foreigners and foreign ways, might lose their Quaker plainness. Isaac Norris I, no doubt remembering the satisfaction of Philadelphia Friends at seeing "the same Isaac Norris to return" from his own trip to England in 1707, gave his twenty-one-year-old son explicit cautions as he set sail for the mother country in 1722:

In thy Clothing be plain, and frugal, Careing only to be Decent and Cleanly,—and on thy Return avoid the fluttering Gaudy Coullours or Shew which the Empty and Weak heads appear in —which turns them to Ridicule with people of Sence and judgment—Thy own hair with the Care the London Barbers may take of it, will be an observable Ornament to thee. I will not name them [;] thou may Collect what Vallue or Reputation Some Young fellows have obtain'd with their Light Wiggs, and Gay Dress on their return from England.[84]

For some Quaker youths the richness of European life and society overcame the inherited concern for plainness, and they returned from their travels glittering young dandies laden with spoils picked up from Florentine art dealers, London haberdashers, and Parisian perfumers and jewelers. This was the experience of Samuel Powel, grandson of the "rich carpenter," who spent the years from 1760 to 1767 in Europe in quest of culture and enjoyment. In London he had an audience with George II and in Rome with Pope Clement XIII. With the avidity of a man

---

83. Thayer, 5-7; John Pemberton to James Pemberton, 31 Dec. 1748, Pemberton Papers, V, 14; W[illiam] H[odgson], Jr., ed., *The Life and Travels of John Pemberton*, 2-6.
84. Isaac Norris I to Joseph Pike, 25 Feb. 1717/18, *Penn and Logan Correspondence*, II, 259; Isaac Norris I to Isaac Norris II, 10 Apr. 1722, Norris Letter Book, 1716-30, 300.

starved for sensuous beauty, he drank in the glories of Italian sculpture, architecture, and painting, and, falling in with the *cognoscenti* in Rome, became a member of the "Arcadian Society of Belles Lettres." This young aristocrat, like his companion, Dr. John Morgan, shed his Quakerism in the course of acquiring a cosmopolitan polish; returning to his native city in 1767, he was baptized by the Reverend Richard Peters and became a communicant of fashionable St. Peter's Church.[85]

On a less dramatic scale, this was the story of many a scion of Philadelphia Quaker families. It was a shrewd observation of Ralph Waldo Emerson that "no dissenter rides in his coach for three generations; he infallibly falls into the Establishment."[86] Throughout the colonial period one finds Friends in their new-found prosperity revolting against the rigorous discipline of the meeting with its tiresome iteration of the ideal of plainness, and drifting over to the Church of England where they found a ritual satisfying to their senses and a type of preaching which did not dwell overmuch on the vanity of worldly possessions and show. A number of prosperous Quakers such as Robert Turner and Charles Read followed George Keith in his "separation" from the Friends in the 1690's and later went with him into the Anglican Church.[87] In 1716 the Reverend George Ross observed that "though we and the Quakers do differ widely, yet 'tis observable that when any of them do leave their own way and become Christians, they generally make their application" to the Anglican minister instead of going to any of the dissenting pastors "who, though ten to one of us, do not count one Quaker to ten that come over to the Church."[88] Many of the leading citizens of Philadelphia who petitioned the Proprietors in 1754 for land on

85. Bridenbaugh, *Rebels and Gentlemen*, 207-12.
86. Edward Waldo Forbes and Waldo Emerson Forbes, eds., *The Journals of Ralph Waldo Emerson* (New York, 1909-14), VII, 359.
87. Keith, *Chronicles*, 210-42; Ethyn W. Kirby, *George Keith*, 93. When the Reverend Thomas Clayton arrived in Philadelphia at the end of the decade, there were only 50 Anglicans in the town, but within two years the number had increased to 700, largely as a result of the accession of the Keithians. See Ernest Hawkins, *Historical Notices of the Missions of the Church of England in the North American Colonies* (London, 1845), 16.
88. Quoted by Sharpless, *Quaker Experiment*, 91n.

which to build the new Anglican church of St. Peter's were wealthy merchants who had once been Quakers; among them were William Plumsted, Phineas and Thomas Bond, Amos Strettell, and Joseph Redman.[89]

Even among those who remained within the fold, there grew up a distinction between the more "consistent" or strict Friends and those who tended to give way to mundane fashions and customs. The latter, who came to be known as "wet Quakers," were, according to a French visitor, allowed to attend meeting for worship, but not Monthly or Quarterly Meetings for discipline.[90] These Friends no doubt represented the "younger and politer" circles in which Silas Deane was to move just before the Revolution, when he observed that they were "not distinguishable, but in a very few particulars from other people."[91] The division apparent within Philadelphia Quaker society was even more marked as between the wealthy merchants of the city and the plainer, more traditional Friends from the rural areas, where life was simple and contacts with the "world" were fewer. Country Friends on their regular pilgrimages to the metropolis for Yearly Meeting were deeply conscious of the social gulf beginning to open up between themselves and their worldlier co-religionists.[92] This was not a phenomenon peculiar to Philadelphia; it could also be observed in the British Isles, where Friends from

---

89. *Pa. Mag. of Hist.*, 47 (1923), 343-44.

90. Brissot de Warville, *Nouveau Voyage*, II, 173. The term "wet Quaker" appears to have been in use in England as well as in America. An English actress of a Quaker family speaks *ca.* 1750 of dressing without "the studied formality of a rigid Quaker," but only so plainly and neatly as to entitle her to the appellation of a "*wet* Quaker, a distinction that arises chiefly from the latter's wearing ribbons, gauzes, and laces." —*An Apology for the Life of George Anne Bellamy* (London, 1785), quoted in Friends Hist. Soc., *Journal*, 17 (1920), 47. Barbé-Marbois, who visited Philadelphia in 1779, uses the expression "white Quakers" with the same general meaning. —Eugene P. Chase, *Our Revolutionary Forefathers*, 139. Is it possible that the word *wet* sounded like *white* to French ears?

91. Letter to Elizabeth Deane, 23 Sept. 1774, *Deane Papers*, New York Historical Society, *Collections*, 19 (1886), 30.

92. See John Woolman, "Conversations on the True Harmony of Mankind," *Journal and Essays*, 460-66, for a reflection of this social differentiation. The divergence was to continue, becoming ultimately one of the grounds of the "separation" of 1827. —See Elbert Russell, *The History of Quakerism*, 285-87.

the country districts and from Ireland were noticeably stricter and more exclusive than those of London and Bristol.

Refusing to cut themselves off in monastic or Anabaptist fashion from the "world," remaining indeed resolutely in the midst of the world, but holding always before themselves an ethic of perfection, the Quakers subjected themselves to mental and moral tensions which sometimes became intolerable. Some, as we have seen, chose to give up the struggle, and capitulated to the "world," entering the Anglican communion, or at least, as "wet Quakers," joining wholeheartedly in the gaiety and extravagance which characterized Philadelphia society during and after the Revolutionary period. Others like Nicholas Waln chose to abandon the "world" completely, and, becoming plain Friends in dress and address, confined themselves to religious and humanitarian concerns. The rest, living just within that margin of tolerance between the letter of the discipline and its actual enforcement, gradually curtailed the outward splendor of their manner of living in the years preceding the war and devoted more and more of their wealth and energy to philanthropic activity. By the end of the American Revolution, the great days of the Quaker grandees were over, and a new atmosphere of sober piety, earnest private philanthropy, and concern for doctrinal orthodoxy settled over Philadelphia Quakerism.

ATTITUDES TOWARDS READING

HAVE but few Books, but let them be well chosen and well read, whether of Religious or Civil Subjects . . . reading many Books is but a taking off the Mind too much from Meditation. Reading your selves and Nature, in the Dealings and Conduct of Men, is the truest human wisdom. The Spirit of a Man knows the Things of Man, and more true Knowledge comes by Meditation and just Reflection than by Reading; for much Reading is an Oppression of the Mind, and extinguishes the natural Candle; which is the Reason of so many senseless Scholars in the World.[1]

Such was William Penn's advice to his children in the matter of reading, but like many another moralist, he failed to follow his own advice. Although primarily a man of action, he spent many hours in the realm of books; indeed some of his writings cause one to wonder whether he did not sometimes allow booklearning to extinguish the candle of his own natural reason. The second half of *No Cross No Crown*, for example, is little more than a *catena* of passages culled from an extraordinary range of authors, classical, patristic, and modern, including Demosthenes, Aristotle, Epictetus, Seneca, St. Augustine, St. Chrysostom, Machiavelli, Montaigne, Raleigh, Grotius, and Abraham Cowley.[2] In somewhat more temperate vein, he once listed for a

---

1. *The Advice of William Penn to His Children*, in *Works*, I, 898-99.
2. [Henry Portsmouth], *An Index to William Penn's Works* (n.p., n.d.), which

young English Quaker the books which he considered "most valuable for a modest library." The list included, in addition to the Bible and "Friends' Books," titles like Augustine's *City of God*, *The Imitation of Christ*, Jeremy Taylor's *Liberty of Prophesying*, Raleigh's *History of the World*, Plutarch's *Lives*, the histories of Thucydides, More's *Utopia*, Coke's *Institutes*, Robert Boyle's scientific works, and Leybourn on mathematics— a list which would have constituted a library worthy of any cultivated English gentleman.[3]

No complete catalogue exists of William Penn's own library, but there is evidence that it was both large and well selected. Just before leaving England on his second voyage to Pennsylvania in 1699, he placed an order with his bookseller for sixty-eight titles including all the major writings of his friend John Locke, the *Discourses Concerning Government* of another friend, Algernon Sidney, Sir William Temple's *Observations upon the United Provinces of the Netherlands*, the works of Milton and Machiavelli, the *Sermons* of the Cambridge Platonist Benjamin Whichcote, the voyages of William Dampier and Louis Hennepin, *Don Quixote*, Livy, Suetonius, and Diodorus Siculus.[4] A collection of books bearing Penn's bookplate with the date 1703 was sold at auction in 1872. It was an equally varied assortment, ranging from religious books such as Chillingworth's *Religion of Protestants a Safe Way to Salvation* (a work of Anglican divinity), the *De religione gentilium* of Lord Herbert of Cherbury, precursor of the Deists, and the *Works* of Isaac Penington, Penn's relative by marriage, to practical manuals like *The Country-Man's Recreation; or, The Art of Planting, Graffing, and Gardening* and Dr. John Schroeder's *Chymical Dis-*

---

lists most of the authors quoted by Penn, gives some indication of the range of his erudition.

3. Penn to Sir John Rodes, Oct. 1693, Mrs. Godfrey Locker-Lampson, ed., *A Quaker Post-Bag* (London, 1910), 4-6.

4. Invoice dated Feb. 1699, Taylor Papers, 3309, Hist. Soc. Pa. I am indebted for this reference to Professor Henry J. Cadbury of Harvard University. The fact that Penn purchased several copies of many of these titles (for example, six of Locke's *Essay Concerning Human Understanding* and four of *The Reasonableness of Christianity*) suggests that he may have been buying books for his friends in Pennsylvania.

pensatory, Treating of All Sorts of Metals, Precious Stones, Minerals, Vegetables, Animals, etc., Very Proper for All Merchants, Druggists, etc.[5] We know that part of his library at least was in America, for there is a letter extant from his secretary James Logan, telling of the theft of Raleigh's *History of the World*, *Purchas His Pilgrims*, and Richard Brathwait's *English Gentleman* from the manor at Pennsbury.[6] In spite of his feeling that "much reading is an Oppression of the Mind" and that it should give way to meditation, it is clear that William Penn was a highly literate, not to say erudite, person, whose reading tastes were those which one would expect in a wealthy gentleman and former student at Oxford, Saumur, and Lincoln's Inn.

The attitude of the Philadelphia Quakers, particularly during the first half century, towards the reading of books was similarly ambivalent: on the one hand they were convinced that it was profitless for salvation and, except for devotional or practical manuals, a waste of precious time; on the other hand, as they achieved leisure, they began to accumulate libraries remarkable for their catholicity and to spend a considerable portion of their time in reading. Thomas Chalkley gave expression to the former of these views in 1727 in writing to his son-in-law: "I perceive thou art inclined to read pretty much: I pray thee, that thy chief Study in Books may be the holy Scriptures. Let all other Books (tho' of Use, and good in their Places) be subservient to them."[7]

It seems somewhat incongruous in the light of attitudes like these that one of the three largest and best libraries in the American colonies, rivaling those of the Puritan Cotton Mather and the Virginia gentleman William Byrd, should have been collected and owned by a Quaker. One can only explain it by suggesting that James Logan, who came to Philadelphia as William Penn's secretary, followed his master's example rather than his advice. "It may seem strange," wrote Logan to a correspondent in Ham-

---

5. *Catalogue of Books, Manuscripts, Maps, Charts, and Engravings, from the Libraries of William Penn, Founder of Pennsylvania and His Descendants. To be sold by Messrs Puttick and Simpson, London* (London, 1872), *passim*.
6. Letter dated 22 Nov. 1704, *Penn and Logan Correspondence*, I, 347.
7. *Journal*, in *Works*, 210.

burg from whom he hoped to obtain some Greek and Latin books, ". . . to find an American Bearskin Merchant troubling himself with such books, but they have been my delight and . . . will I believe continue my best entertainment in my advancing years." A few years later, as he prepared to retire to a leisurely scholar's life in his newly-built mansion at Stenton, he acknowl-edged that the collecting and reading of books was his "Disease": "they are soon to be my only amusement," he forecast, and then, as if feeling under the necessity of an apology to his Quaker cor-respondent, added, "they are better however than either Tavern Expenses abroad or Merid. Clubs &c." And nearly twenty years after this, when he was over seventy, he wrote to his friend Ben-jamin Franklin that, old as he was, "and much fail'd in all re-spects," he yet wished to lay out about two hundred pounds in books.[8] He lamented his sons' apparent lack of interest in the magnificent library he had collected, but Thomas Story (1662-1742), "public Friend" and son-in-law of the great Quaker mer-chant Edward Shippen, seeking to comfort him, pointed out, in the spirit of the earlier Friends, that books and learning are "gen-erally speculative and so barren (as to us), that they cannot af-ford us one morsell, for support of a short, uncertain life in this teezing World." Nevertheless, he went on, he would not have Logan think him an enemy to learning; he conceded that "that field [affords] great variety for contemplation, and much de-light to the mind therein."[9]

By the end of the colonial period the merchants had pretty well settled the matter with their Quaker consciences, and no longer regarded the reading of non-Quaker and secular books (so long as it was indulged in with suitable moderation) as a danger-ous snare or a failing which required apology. "To read for de-light and profit," wrote one of the most literate of the Quaker merchants, "is a most rational way of employing a part of our

8. Letter to Frederick Schomaker, 14 Nov. 1721, Logan Letter Book, 1717-31, 215; letter to James Steel, 3 Dec. 1729, Logan Papers, I, 93; letter to Benjamin Franklin, 13 July 1747, Sparks MSS, XIX, opp. p. 31, Harvard University Li-brary.
9. Story to Logan, 21 Jan. 1734, *Logan-Story Correspondence,* 50.

time, and is what in this happy age and country, people of all classes, that can read at all, may do, in greater or less variety." This Friend's views on the selection of books were notably catholic: "there ought to be in every family," he averred, "some good books to be always at hand, not merely systematic treatises, to support the particular tenets of any sect or party . . . but such as are designed to enlarge the understanding and mend the heart. . . ."[10]

Towards the end of the colonial period, a sophisticated Anglican clergyman wrote of the Quaker town: "You would be surprised . . . at the general taste for books which prevails among all orders and ranks of people in this city."[11] Philadelphia's rapid growth into one of the chief cultural centers in the colonies, and its eventual maturing into the intellectual capital of the American republic, was a result in no small part of the presence there of a group of highly literate Quaker merchants with a catholic taste in reading and the leisure to indulge it.[12]

EDUCATIONAL THEORY AND PRACTICE

It is not necessary to devote many words to disproving the hoary legend that Quakerism was uncompromisingly hostile to education and learning. The testimony of Thomas Ellwood, John Milton's Quaker amanuensis, should put an end to all question on this subject: ". . . when I was a boy I had made some good progress in learning, and lost it all again before I came to be a man; nor was I rightly sensible of my loss therein untill I came amongst the Quakers. But then I both saw my loss and lamented

---

10. [John Smith], letter signed "Atticus," *Pennsylvania Chronicle,* 24 Oct. 1768.
11. [Jacob Duché], *Caspipina's Letters,* I, 13.
12. T. J. Wertenbaker's statement in *The Founding of American Civilization: The Middle Colonies,* 209, that Philadelphia's development as a cultural center was chiefly owing to the efforts of non-Quaker groups—the Anglicans, Presbyterians, and Lutherans—thus needs some qualification; likewise his opinion, expressed in *The Golden Age of Colonial Culture,* 83, that the Quakers contributed only a tolerant atmosphere in which others could develop a cultural life seems too negative. Bridenbaugh appears closer to the mark when, speaking of colonial intellectual life, he observes that, even in its first decade, "Philadelphia gave ample indication of a promising future, and nothing is further from the truth than the charge that Quaker domination . . . proved a stultifying influence in the early years." —*Cities,* 134.

it; and applied myself with utmost diligence, at all leisure times, to recover it: so false I found that charge to be which in those times was cast as a reproach upon the Quakers, that they despised and decried all human learning, because they denied it to be essentially necessary to a gospel ministry, which was one of the controversies of those times."[13] Although George Fox, in common with other sectarian preachers of the Commonwealth period, had fulminated against the universities, and although William Penn had attacked them as "Signal Places for Idleness, Looseness, Prophaneness, Prodigality, and gross Ignorance," the town of Philadelphia in its infancy was not without its university-trained leaders. Penn and Thomas Lloyd were Oxford men, George Keith a Master of Arts from Marischall College, Aberdeen, and Francis Daniel Pastorius had been educated at the universities of Altdorf, Strasburg, Basel, and Jena. It is true that Friends, having no specially trained clergy, saw no need for a college and established none in colonial Pennsylvania; it is also true, however, that they insisted upon an ideal of universal elementary education for their children and maintained a system of public schools said to have been superior to those of Bristol and Norwich in England.[14] The Quaker philosophy of education, although subject to the limitations implicit in the phrase "a religiously guarded education," was far from illiberal or narrowly sectarian. As Ellis Hookes and Christopher Taylor, the latter one of the earliest Philadelphia schoolmasters, put it, "We deny nothing for children's learning that may be honest and useful for them to know, whether relating to divine principles or that may be outwardly serviceable for them to learn in regard to the outward creation."[15]

The first impetus to education in Pennsylvania came from Governor Penn and the Provincial Council who in 1683 authorized one Enoch Flower to open a school for the teaching of reading and writing and casting accounts. The Council's interest

---

13. C. G. Crump, ed., *The History of the Life of Thomas Ellwood* (London, 1900), 87.
14. Bridenbaugh, *Cities*, 289.
15. Elbert Russell, *Early Friends and Education* (Philadelphia, 1925), 10.

in promoting education soon lapsed, but the concern passed to the Monthly Meeting, and in 1689 a secondary school was established, which soon developed into an educational *system* culminating in a Latin School.[16] From the beginning there was a strong practical and realistic emphasis in the curriculum of the Quaker institutions; this emphasis reigned particularly in the "English School" where Anthony Benezet was a teacher. Literary and linguistic attainments were not neglected, however; Latin was taught as early as 1698, and by the 1740's the Latin School had emerged as a distinctly classical institution, calculated to equip the children of the wealthier merchants with the graces of a literary education. The Reverend Jacob Duché observed in 1774 that the Quaker merchants "now think it no more a crime to send their children to school to learn Greek and Latin, Mathematicks and Natural Philosophy, than to put them to Merchants or Mechanicks to be instructed in the several arts and mysteries."[17]

So far had the tendency towards an aristocratic ideal of education progressed in the Friends educational system by 1769 that one of the tutors, John Wilson, felt obliged to resign from the Latin School in protest against teaching the "uncouth terms and intricate distinctions of dead Languages" and other "learned Trifles" to boys intended by their parents for "Mercantile or Mechanick Employments." Wilson's attack on what he conceived to be, in the circumstances, a useless and pernicious type of education was made in the name of the older realistic and pietistic theory of Quaker education: "instead of dissipating your

16. James Mulhern, *A History of Secondary Education in Pennsylvania*, 30-37.
17. *Caspipina's Letters*, I, 64. James Logan sent his son William to the Friends school in Bristol, England (where he and his father had been teachers) to be instructed in Latin by Alexander Arscott, an Oxford graduate and a Quaker. Writing to Arscott in 1731, he expressed the hope that the boys were required to speak only Latin in school, giving as his reason that "to a man of business, Speaking of Latin with ease and freedom . . . may be of more Service than to be able to compose one of Tully's Orations in the Closet and out of it to Stammer in bringing out 2 Sentences by which many learned Englishmen abroad have rendered themselves ridiculous." —Letter dated 9 Oct. 1731, Logan Letter Book, 1731-32, 15. Several letters written in Latin by Isaac Norris to correspondents in Europe are extant. See Norris Letter Book, 1734-53, pp. 14, 19.

Revenues," he conjured the Overseers of the school, "in humouring the Pride of rich men and debauching their offspring with the rubbish of Paganism let it be your study as it will be your happiness to promote the increase of Christian knowledge."[18] This tirade reflected a reaction from excessive accommodation to "the world," a reaction which was quite general in Quaker circles by the end of the 1760's and which was bound to be felt in the school system.

Two Friends—James Logan and Dr. Lloyd Zachary—were among the original Trustees of the Academy which later became the College of Philadelphia. Upon Logan's death, his son-in-law Isaac Norris was elected to fill his place. Their participation appears to have been purely nominal, however, for neither Logan nor Norris attended more than one meeting apiece. Dr. Zachary, on the other hand, was fairly constant in attendance. Although some Quaker merchants, including James Pemberton and Abel James, contributed financially to the Academy, attracted, no doubt, by the practical and non-sectarian emphasis in Franklin's *Proposals Relating to the Education of Youth in Pennsylvania*, their interest seems to have cooled when the inauguration ceremonies were accompanied by a formal Anglican service and a set sermon by the Reverend Richard Peters. When the Academy developed into a college in 1755, Quaker interest turned into hostility. Not only did Friends recognize no necessity for higher education, but they began to see in the movement which led to the College a threat to their own political hegemony.[19] Another full century was to pass before Philadelphia Quakers were to feel the need for an institution of higher learning.

Knowledge of French was regarded as a desirable acquirement for the children of Quaker aristocrats, more particularly for the girls. Isaac Norris II began studying French in his late teens; his father lent him encouragement by pointing out that

---

18. Mulhern, 42-44, 122, 129.
19. Thomas H. Montgomery, *A History of the University of Pennsylvania from Its Foundation to A. D. 1770* (Philadelphia, 1900), 43-45, 118; Samuel X. Radbill, "Dr. Lloyd Zachary, 1701-1756," *Annals of Medical History*, 3d ser., 1 (1939), 515; Bridenbaugh, *Rebels and Gentlemen*, 42-43.

whatever he acquired beyond a superficial acquaintance with languages would be both "advantage and Ornament" to him.[20] He added many French books to those which his father had collected at Fairhill and he occasionally penned a letter in French to his correspondent Andrew Faneuil in Boston.[21] His wife, the daughter of James Logan, had been introduced to the French language along with needlework at the age of nine, and her learned father even insisted upon giving her a smattering of Hebrew.[22] Polly Norris, later the wife of John Dickinson, commenced the study of French before she was ten years old, and lived for a period in a French-speaking family in Philadelphia to acquire facility in speaking the language.[23] Anthony Benezet was employed in 1742 to teach French in the English School under the care of the Monthly Meeting; undoubtedly he also included this subject in the curriculum of the Girls' School where he taught after 1754.[24] Thus in most respects the education of Quaker aristocrats was not essentially different from that of the sons and daughters of Virginia planters or Boston Brahmins.

THE AVAILABILITY OF BOOKS

For men and women educated in this manner books were a necessity. Starting with the small personal libraries (consisting usually of a Bible and a few "Friends' books") brought over in the baggage of the first immigrants, the Philadelphia Quakers

---

20. Isaac Norris I to William Keen, 9 Apr. 1722, Norris Letter Book, 1716-30, 289; Isaac Norris I to Isaac Norris II, 10 April 1722, *ibid.*, 300.
21. See, for example, Norris Letter Book, 1730-33, 69.
22. Logan to Story, 25 Oct. 1724, *Logan-Story Correspondence*, 20. Logan himself had learned Greek, along with Latin and Hebrew, before he was thirteen years old. As he grew older, he improved himself in Greek and added French, Italian, and Spanish to his linguistic accomplishments.—Autobiography in Myers, *Immigration*, 238-39. His library at Stenton contained lexicons and grammars of Anglo-Saxon, Portuguese, Dutch, Polish, Magyar, German, Arabic, Turkish, Syriac, Samaritan, Ethiopian, and Persian.
23. Isaac Norris II to Susanna Wright, 14 Sept. 1746, Norris Family Letters, II, 45; to Dr. William Logan, 17 Nov. 1748, Norris Letter Book, 1735-55, 53; to Charles Norris, 7 Aug. 1749, *ibid.*, 58.
24. Mulhern, 44; Brookes, *Benezet*, 40. Elizabeth Sandwith Drinker's diary supplies ample evidence that French remained a major element in the education of Quaker girls in Philadelphia throughout the remainder of the colonial period. See Henry D. Biddle, ed., *Extracts from the Journal of Elizabeth Drinker*, 14, 16, and *passim*.

were supplied with an increasing flow of reading matter from the mother country and presently from colonial presses.

Since the Society of Friends has always been concerned to "publish the Truth" through the printed as well as the spoken word, it was natural that Philadelphia Monthly Meeting should have taken steps very early to provide for the printing and distribution of Quaker literature. By 1686 William Bradford was installed as official printer for the Yearly Meeting. In 1690 an arrangement was made whereby the Yearly Meeting agreed to take from him two hundred copies of all books published by its advice and with its approval, and all Monthly Meetings were instructed to contribute towards the support of his press. Under such successors as Reinier Jansen, Jacob Taylor, and Andrew Bradford, the Yearly Meeting's press regularly turned out epistles, journals of "public Friends," and works of Quaker devotion, doctrine, discipline, and history.[25] In addition to supporting its own press, the Yearly Meeting in 1690 agreed to take six copies of each book published under the care of the parent Yearly Meeting in England. In 1723, four prominent merchants in Philadelphia Monthly Meeting, Richard Hill, Isaac Norris, James Logan, and William Hudson, were appointed to make arrangements for printing Willem Sewel's *History of the Rise, Increase, and Progress of the Christian People Called Quakers* and to take subscriptions for it; five years later, this folio volume finally came off the press of the struggling Samuel Keimer, who had been obliged to turn the printing of the last quarter of the book over to an ambitious young man named Benjamin Franklin.[26]

The Monthly Meeting also provided its members a lending library: one finds a minute as early as 1705 to the effect that "George Fox's Journal is lent to Richard Armitt for one month."

---

25. "The first ninety years of printing activity in Philadelphia," says the leading authority on this subject, "[was] devoted to the service of the Society of Friends." —Douglas C. McMurtrie, *A History of Printing in the United States,* II, 24.

26. MS Minutes of Phila. YM, I, 23; MS Minutes of Phila. MM, II, 98 (26 July 1723); Franklin, *Autobiography,* in *Writings,* I, 300-301; Charles R. Hildeburn, *The Issues of the Pennsylvania Press, 1685-1784,* I, 92-93.

In 1742 the little meeting library received a notable accession when it fell heir to Thomas Chalkley's collection of 111 volumes. The books were kept in the home first of Robert Jordan, a ministering Friend, and later of Anthony Benezet.[27] When a new building was erected for the Latin School in 1744, the library was housed in a special room designed for that purpose. A remarkable addition to the collection was a gift from Peter Collinson, F.R.S., the famous Quaker merchant-botanist of London. The gift consisted of more than two hundred titles, including Foxe's *Book of Martyrs*, Bishop Latimer's sermons, Burton's *Anatomy of Melancholy*, Bunyan's *Life and Death of Mr. Badman*, George Wither's *Abuses Stript and Whipt*, Prynne's *Histriomastix*, and editions of Virgil and Marcus Aurelius, as well as Quaker books by George Fox, Robert Barclay, William Penn, and Thomas Lawson.[28] As a result of these vigorous efforts by the meeting and by individuals, there was hardly a Quaker home without an adequate supply of suitable literature. We have the testimony of a hard-pressed missionary of the Society for the Propagation of the Gospel *ca.* 1710 that "there were Variety of Books sent and placed in almost every *Quaker* Family, especially *Barclay's* Apology, to fortify the People in their Errors, and furnish them with Arguments against the Faith; whereas in the Houses of the Church People, few or no Books were to be seen."[29]

Besides the Monthly Meeting library, the Latin School had its own collection of books which included in 1752 such works of secular history as Sir Paul Rycaut's *History of the Turks*, Pufendorf's *Introduction to the History of the Principal Kingdoms and States of Europe*, and memoirs of the Duke of Marl-

---

27. MS Minutes of Phila. MM, I, 210 (30 Nov. 1705); II, 339 (30 April 1742), 340 (28 May 1742), 365 (24 Feb. 1743).
28. Norman G. Brett-James, *The Life of Peter Collinson*, 169. Other contributions came to the Monthly Meeting library from Dr. John Fothergill and David Barclay of London, and it is possible that Anthony Benezet gave some of his own books to the library while it was under his care.—George Vaux, "Friends Library, Philadelphia, Pennsylvania," Friends. Hist. Soc., *Jour.*, I (1904), 124-27; Henry J. Cadbury, "The Passing of Friends' Library," *The Friend*, 103 (1930), 459-61.
29. Quoted in David Humphreys, *An Historical Account of the Incorporated Society for the Propagation of the Gospel in Foreign Parts* (London, 1730), 153.

borough, as well as Humphrey Prideaux's *Life of Mahomet*, William Law's *Serious Call to a Devout and Holy Life*, and Cave's *Primitive Christianity*.[30]

Individual Friends were active in the formation and support of library companies, of which Philadelphia could boast four, founded in the quarter-century between 1732 and 1757. Several of the first Directors of Franklin's original Library Company were Quakers; this fact was clearly reflected in the early minutes in an objection on the part of "those who had accustomed themselves to what is called the 'plain language'" to the style of an address designed to solicit the Proprietor's support.[31] Established by a group of young tradesmen and mechanics for their own self-improvement, the Library Company soon attracted men of means, anxious to keep themselves *au courant* with the latest books; in fact, the time soon came when it attracted only the wealthier class, since the cost of a share increased by ten shillings each year.[32] Analysis of the list of shareholders during the first thirty years discloses that well-nigh half were Quakers. Virtually all the prominent names in Philadelphia's Quaker aristocracy appear on the list, such names, for example, as Joseph Wharton, Francis Richardson, William Rawle, George Emlen, Isaac Norris, Charles Norris, Samuel Coates, Israel Pemberton, Jr., Samuel Rhoads, William Callender, John Smith, John Reynell, Abel James, and William Logan.[33]

---

30. "List of Books delivered to Robert Willan for the use of the Latin School, 8th 11 mo, 1752," Mulhern, 54-55.
31. MS Minutes, quoted in George M. Abbott, *A Short History of the Library Company of Philadelphia*, 7. Thomas Cadwalader, John Jones, Jr., William Coleman, and Joseph Breintnall were the Directors who can be identified as having Quaker backgrounds. It might be pointed out as indicative of further Quaker influence in the early history of this enterprise that the first books were chosen with the advice of James Logan, the most learned man in the province, and that Israel Pemberton acted as agent in purchasing books for the Library Company on his trip to England in 1733. —Abbott, 5; Thayer, *Israel Pemberton*, 6.
32. E. V. Lamberton, "Colonial Libraries of Pennsylvania," *Pa. Mag. of Hist.*, 42 (1918), 194.
33. A Chronological Register of the Names of the Members of the Library Company of Philadelphia, MS at the Library Company of Philadelphia. Of the 191 individuals who had purchased shares up to the end of 1763, 79 can be identified as Friends in good standing, and 12 more were non-members who were children of Quaker parents or who had been disowned by the meeting.

When the price of shares in the Library Company had risen from the original forty shillings to nine pounds in 1746, a group of prosperous young shopkeepers and artisans, mostly Quakers, formed the Union Library Company, offering shares at three pounds.[34] Ten years later another group of successful tradesmen and craftsmen, again chiefly Quakers, excluded from the other library companies by the rising cost of shares, subscribed twenty shillings each to found the Association Library.[35] By 1769 the three younger libraries were merged in the original Library Company. The previous year had seen the Loganian Library, bequeathed to the city by its Quaker owner, James Logan, opened to the public. Philadelphia could now boast of the finest public and semi-public library facilities in the colonies. Although the original impulse had come from Boston-born Benjamin Franklin, he had been ably abetted and his example had been enthusiastically followed by the Quakers of his adopted city, who, although a minority in the population, seem to have expressed a livelier interest than other groups in this means of promoting the intellectual life.

The wealthier merchants were able, of course, to purchase books and build up private collections of their own. There was a bookshop in Philadelphia as early as 1714; by 1724 there were five, and by the end of the colonial period there were more than thirty.[36] Quaker merchants regularly patronized the well-stocked shops of James Chattin, David Hall, James Rivington, Robert Bell, and others; nevertheless, we find Isaac Norris II in 1738

---

34. MS Records of the Union Library Company, Library Company of Philadelphia. Of the 26 members who signed the Articles of Agreement in 1747, 20 appear to have been Quakers. At least 22 of the additional 34 charter members were Friends. Most of them signed as "shopkeeper," "brass founder," "biscuit baker," etc., but some of the signers, such as Thomas Clifford and Reuben Haines, were men who were soon to become importing merchants.

35. The list of subscribers is printed in Lamberton, "Colonial Libraries," 201-2. At least 68 Friends, including members of the Wharton, Mifflin, Wistar, Drinker, Dillwyn, and Biddle families, were among the 107 subscribers. The fourth Philadelphia library company, the Amicable, was organized in 1758; since it was, as the Bridenbaughs have pointed out, "more nearly a workingmen's library," it probably contained fewer Quaker members than the other groups.—*Rebels and Gentlemen*, 88.

36. Carl Bridenbaugh, "The Press and the Book in Eighteenth-Century Philadelphia," *Pa. Mag. of Hist.*, 65 (1941), 13.

envying the London merchants who live "so near the fountain" where they may get books every day, and complaining that Philadelphians "may want, but Cant purchase books here at any price unless by accident."[37]

For books not available in the local bookshops, one relied upon his London correspondents. Many a business letter devoted mainly to detailed instructions about cargoes of oznabrigs, calicoes, hats, and cutlery contained an additional note requesting the purchase of a recent book or magazine. When James Pemberton was in London in 1749, he received this suggestion from his brother Israel: "if thou hast leisure time on thy hands, [I] wish thou would Spend two or three afternoons in Moorfield's[,] Little Brittain or some others of the Places noted for Second hand books, and if thou could lay out 10 or 15 £ in good Books for me I should be pleas'd therewith."[38] James Logan, an omnivorous and erudite reader, ranged far and wide in his search for books. He corresponded directly with Bateman, Osborne, Innys, and other London booksellers and made use of the services of the learned William Reading, librarian of Sion College, London, as an agent in buying books in the English market. On the Continent, Theodorus Hodson in Amsterdam and Frederick Schomaker in Hamburg kept him supplied with the best scholarly editions of the classics.[39]

THE BOOKS OF THE FIRST SETTLERS

The great Quaker libraries at Stenton, Fairhill, and elsewhere were collected over a long period of years and reached

---

37. Letter to Charles Norris, 29 March 1738, Norris Letter Book, 1734-39.
38. Letter dated 29 April 1749, Pemberton Papers, V, 77.
39. See Logan Letter Books, especially 1717-1723 and 1721-1733, *passim*. The purchase of books abroad was beset with the same difficulties and hazards that affected other transatlantic dealings. One shipment of books which Logan ordered from England was lost in Delaware Bay in the winter of 1728. The ship, of which Logan was half owner, was plundered after being wrecked. Logan concluded that the trunk containing his books had been destroyed "for a minister of those parts Saw a leaf of Pool [no doubt Matthew Poole's *Synopsis*, a compendium of Biblical commentaries] that was pick'd up on the Shoar from whence I judge that the Robbers upon opening the Trunk finding those useless Latin books in it which might only help to discover them threw them into the Sea. . . ."—James Logan to J. Reading, 12 May 1729, Logan Letter Books, III, 233.

impressive proportions only towards the middle of the eighteenth century. The earliest immigrants brought relatively few books with them; indeed in the midst of making new homes they had little time for collecting and reading books. Study of the inventories of estates left by the first generation of Quaker settlers shows that the average immigrant possessed a Bible, the works of two or three of the first Quaker "Publishers of Truth," and a few other books, mostly of a practical sort. Philip Richards, for example, dying in 1698, left nine books, John Whitpain left eleven in 1696, and Elizabeth Fox, a widow, left twelve in 1702. John Hunt, a ship captain, had a somewhat larger collection amounting to twenty-five volumes, and the library of John Jones, merchant, consisted of fifteen titles in addition to "Sundry Smal bound and Stitcht books." Edward Shippen, affluent merchant from Boston, had thirty-four books at his death in 1714; Christopher Taylor, the schoolmaster, who died in 1686, had more than forty, not including duplicate Testaments and primers intended for the use of his pupils; and George Emlen's library in 1711 contained upwards of fifty volumes. One of the largest collections of the early years was that of Jonathan Dickinson, which was not itemized but which was valued at £25/8/6.[40]

Robert Barclay's *Apology for the True Christian Divinity* ("the glory and Alcoran of Friends," as one Anglican missionary termed it) was found in many an early Philadelphia home, being regarded by Quakers as virtually indispensable.[41] Equally ubiquitous was George Fox's *Journal*, the personal record of the founder of Quakerism. The collected works of Isaac Penington,

---

40. Philadelphia Wills and Inventories, 1682-1719, photostats, Genealogical Society of Pennsylvania (originals at Philadelphia Registry of Wills). The library of Francis Daniel Pastorius, the German Friend of Germantown, comprising over 250 volumes, was undoubtedly the largest in the colony in the first half-century. A list of his books appears in Marion D. Learned, *The Life of Francis Daniel Pastorius*, 274-84.

41. Barclay's works proved unexpectedly useful to Jonathan Dickinson and his companions, shipwrecked on the coast of Florida in 1696 and beset by man-eating savages. After stripping the luckless Quakers of their clothes, Dickinson relates, the Indians spied a Bible and "a large book of Robert Barclay's"; tearing out the pages, they gave each of the shivering Friends a leaf to cover his nakedness.—Evangeline W. Andrews and Charles M. Andrews, eds., *Jonathan Dickinson's Journal; or, God's Protecting Providence.* (New Haven, 1945), 44.

Edward Burrough, George Fox the Younger, William Bayley, Samuel Fisher, Francis Howgill, and William Smith, all published between 1662 and 1681, were present in one or another of the early libraries.[42] Foxe's *Book of Martyrs*, Bunyan's *Pilgrim's Progress*, and Richard Baxter's *Saints' Everlasting Rest* were among the non-Quaker religious books listed in one or more libraries.[43] The utilitarian manuals, of which almost every library had one or two, included Michael Dalton's *Countrey Justice, The Surveyor, in Foure Bookes* by Aaron Rathborne, the "Rational Physicians Library," "Mercator's atlas," and Richard Blome's *Gentleman's Recreation* (an "encyclopedy of the arts and sciences" with special sections on horsemanship, hunting, fishing, and agriculture).[44] Among the other titles of special interest listed in these early inventories were Father Paul Sarpi's *History of the Council of Trent* in the small library of the first Anthony Morris; Josephus' *History of the Jews* belonging to Thomas Wharton, founder of another notable Quaker family; Camden's *Britannia*, Selden's *Mare Clausum*, and a history of Edward III in the library of Captain John Hunt; and "a book of dreams and visions" in the possession of John Whitpain.

The largest libraries in the early years were no doubt found in the homes of the circle of wealthy merchants who came to Philadelphia from other colonies.[45] Unfortunately, no complete itemized lists of any of these libraries have survived. A partial inventory of Edward Shippen's library, however, reveals reading interests of fairly wide scope. In addition to Fox's *Journal* and *The Standard of the Quakers Examined*, an anti-Quaker tract by the apostate George Keith, this former New Englander owned the Latin works of John Milton, *Poems on Affairs of State from*

---

42. Inventories of John Day (1696), John Whitpain (1696), Robert Ewer (1697), Philip Richards (1698/9), Elizabeth Fox (1702), John Jones (1708), Susanna Worrall (1710), George Emlen (1711).

43. Inventories of Robert Wade (1698), John Whitpain (1696), John Jones (1708), John Hunt (1708), Samuel Carpenter (1714). John Day's inventory (1696) lists works of John Everard and William Dell, two non-Quaker writers in great favor among Friends.

44. Inventories of Samuel Spencer (1705), Jane Peart (1706), John Whitpain (1696), Philip Richards (1698/9), Christopher Taylor (1696).

45. See above, pp. 43-44.

the Time of Oliver Cromwell to the Year 1707 (a volume of political satires), five volumes of the popular *Letters of a Turkish Spy*, Sir Matthew Hale's *Primitive Origination of Mankind Considered and Examined According to the Light of Reason*, the Jansenist *Essays* of the Messieurs du Port Royal, a history of Florence (Machiavelli's?), a volume of "Voyages to America," "Parks Defensive War by sea" (strange title for a Quaker library!), and twenty-four more books not itemized. Jonathan Dickinson's tastes (insofar as we can reconstruct them from his correspondence) ran chiefly to law and history. In 1715 he requested his London correspondent to purchase for him Clarendon's *History of the Rebellion*, the *Annals of Queen Anne*, and the *Votes of Parliament*, in addition to *The Practical Physician* by the great Dr. Thomas Sydenham, John Mortimer's *Whole Art of Husbandry*, and complete files of the *Tatler* and *Spectator*.[46]

From this imperfect evidence it is clear that Quaker Philadelphia, even in its earliest days, when the building of houses and the establishment of means of livelihood were the first order of business, was not devoid of books or of a disposition to read them.

---

46. For his expression of his personal tastes see letter to Clement Plumsted, 11 Oct. 1715, Dickinson Letter Book, 1715-21, 50, Library Company of Philadelphia. Also Memorandum to John Askew, 1715, *ibid.*, 40. For his familiarity with recent Quaker literature, see letter to C.D., 14 May 1698, Dickinson Letter Book, 1698-1701, Hist. Soc. Pa.

Chapter Eight

READING FOR DELIGHT
AND PROFIT

IT is time now to turn our attention to the collections of books built up by three generations of Quaker merchants whose lives fell principally in the first six decades of the eighteenth century. The evidence upon which any reconstruction of their libraries can be based is scattered and fragmentary, but it will suffice to establish the main outlines of the reading interests of the Quaker grandees.

There is little reliable evidence regarding the size of these private libraries. James Logan's collection, when it was turned over to the city of Philadelphia after his death, is said to have numbered upwards of two thousand volumes. This did not represent Logan's entire collection, however, for some of his books were apparently bequeathed to his son who later gave them, together with others collected by himself or acquired from an uncle in Bristol, England, to the Loganian Library.[1] Isaac Norris II had a special building of several rooms in his garden at Fairhill to house his collection of books. John Adams, visiting Fairhill in 1774, after Norris's death, pronounced the library "very grand."[2] After the Revolution, when John Dickinson, who had married Norris's daughter, wanted to make a suitable gift to the college

---

1. *Catalogue of the Books belonging to the Loganian Library* (Philadelphia, 1837), v; Carl L. Cannon, *American Book Collectors and Collecting* (New York, 1941), 36. Friend Richard Hockley estimated the value of Logan's library in 1743 as at least £1000.—Keith, *Provincial Councillors*, 13.
2. *Diary*, in *Works*, II, 379 (entry for 12 Sept. 1774).

which had just been named for him, he chose from his father-in-law's library, according to a contemporary account, "about 1500 volumes upon the most important subjects."[3] It is certain, however, that this donation represented only a part of the Norris library. No complete catalogue of John Smith's books is extant, but it is possible to list nearly 250 which he almost certainly read. Dr. Lloyd Zachary's library consisted of 197 items, more than half being medical books. A number of other eighteenth-century Quaker libraries are now known to us only through a family tradition or a descriptive phrase, as, for example, Francis Rawle's, which is said to have been "extensive, especially in classical literature," Robert Strettell's, which included "Greek, Latin, and French authors," and Miers Fisher's, which a visiting Bostonian deigned to call "clever."[4]

For purposes of analysis the available data on the books read by the Philadelphia Quaker merchants have been divided into six categories: Religion; Philosophy and Conduct; Politics and Law; Science, Medicine, and Practical Arts; History, Biography, and Travel; and Belles-Lettres. These categories, though admittedly arbitrary, will serve as convenient guideposts. The fact that a merchant ordered or owned a given volume does not, I am aware, mean necessarily that he read it; at the very least, however, it does reflect the direction in which his interests lay. Moreover, the expense and difficulty involved in importing books from England and the official attitude of Friends towards possessions acquired merely for display were such that one can assume that books were normally purchased to be used rather than for ornament or ostentation.[5] With these prefatory observations, we may

---

3. *Pennsylvania Gazette*, 27 Oct. 1784.
4. Harold D. Eberlein and Cortlandt Hubbard, *Portrait of a Colonial City: Philadelphia 1670-1838*, 293; *Pa. Mag. of Hist.*, 1 (1877), 241n.; John Adams, *Diary*, in *Works*, II, 369.
5. Partial exception should perhaps be made for the two greatest book collectors among the eighteenth-century Friends—James Logan and Isaac Norris. Logan confessed in 1732, after acquiring a large number of volumes at auction in New York, that he had bought several of them "rather thro' my Love to books and a good Edition than to any Want of them."—Letter to James Alexander, 8 June 1732, Logan Letter Book, 1731-32, p. 69. Isaac Norris II was something of a connoisseur of fine printing; he possessed several volumes printed in Paris by Simon de Collines and by members of the Estienne family, the great-

turn to an analysis of the reading interests of the Quaker merchants.

RELIGION

Most of the Quaker merchants faithfully followed William Penn's advice, building their libraries around a nucleus of the Bible and "Friends' Books." The King James Version was found in virtually every library, although by the end of the colonial period Friends were able to obtain the translation made by the Quaker Anthony Purver.[6] Friends had access to the Scriptures in foreign languages too. John Pemberton in 1748 requested his brother James in London to procure for him "a french Testament and Bible separate."[7] Dr. Lloyd Zachary's estate included the New Testament in both Greek and Latin. Isaac Norris II began learning Hebrew after his retirement to Fairhill in order to be able to read the Old Testament in the original tongue; he owned a number of Bibles in foreign languages, including the so-called London polyglot of 1657 in eight folio volumes with Edmund Castell's great lexicon of Hebrew, Chaldaic, Syriac, Samaritan, Ethiopic, Arabic, and Persian.[8] By far the most impressive collection of Bibles in Philadelphia and perhaps in the American colonies was that of the erudite James Logan, in whose library at Stenton were more than thirty versions of the entire Bible, or parts of it, in Latin, Greek, Hebrew, Arabic, Chaldaic, Syriac, German, Bohemian, Italian, French, Spanish, Polish, Danish, and "the Virginian Language" (John Eliot's Algonkian translation of 1663). In addition, Logan owned such curiosities as a work containing "the Lord's Prayer in above a hundred Languages, Versions and Characters, by Benjamin Mott," and the Psalms and other books of the Bible done into Latin, Greek, and Italian verse.

---

est typographers of the seventeenth century; his bibliophilic interests are further evidenced by notations inside the covers on the lives and achievements of the printers.

6. Israel Pemberton's estate, for example, contained a copy of Purver's translation.—Pemberton Papers, XXXIII, 97.

7. Letter dated 2 Feb. 1748, *ibid.*, V, 21.

8. Letter to Robert Charles, 5 March 1744/5, Norris Letter Book, 1719-56, 17.

The charge was often brought against Friends by other Protestants that they slighted the Scriptures. If the presence of the Bible in virtually every Quaker library were not sufficient proof to the contrary, perhaps such proof could be found in the notable frequency with which the titles of commentaries, concordances, and other tools of Biblical study appear in the inventories, catalogues, and letters of the Quaker merchants of Philadelphia. William Rawle, for example, bought a concordance at a vendue in 1736, and William Fishbourne's effects included four Bibles (one in Latin), a concordance, and Daniel Tossanus' commentary on the Evangelists. John Smith possessed Thomas Wilson's *Christian Directory*, an early concordance; Daniel Whitby's *Paraphrase and Commentary on the New Testament*, and Richard Blome's *History of the Old and New Testaments*. The *Sacred History* of Thomas Ellwood, a compendium of Biblical chronology, was also a popular book among Philadelphia Friends.[9] James Logan possessed numerous commentaries, mostly written in Latin by European scholars such as his friend Johann Albertus Fabricius of Hamburg and Hugo Grotius, the great Dutch jurist, theologian, and exegete. Both Isaac Norris II and his father-in-law Logan had copies of the *De legibus Hebraeorum ritualibus et earum rationibus* of Dr. John Spencer, Master of Corpus Christi College, and Norris had a copy of the same author's *Dissertatio de Urim et Thummim*. Logan's library at Stenton also contained works of Biblical scholarship by two learned Puritan divines—the *Synopsis criticorum* of Matthew Poole and John Downame's *Concordance*.

Quaker controversialists and devotional writers were naturally well represented in Philadelphia private libraries. The works of Richard Claridge, who had been successively an Anglican priest, a Baptist preacher, and a Quaker minister, were quite popular; perhaps his learning and literary skill caused his writings to appeal to urbane tastes more than the cruder and less

---

9. Isaac Norris I gave a copy of it to Samuel Preston in 1707.—Letter dated 26 March 1707, Norris Letter Book, 1706-09, 48. John Smith also owned a copy.

polished works of the primitive Friends.[10] Nevertheless, the writings of Edward Burrough ("son of thunder and consolation," as the title page of his *Works* proclaimed him), John Burnyeat, John Crooks, Steven Crisp, Richard Hubberthorne, Isaac Penington, William Penn, and other early Friends were staple items in most Quaker libraries. Barclay's *Apology* was never missing: Israel Pemberton, Jr., had two copies of the Baskerville edition of 1765, James Logan had a Spanish translation, and Caspar Wistar had "a Dutch Barclay" bound by Benjamin Franklin in 1734.[11] Devotional works of a Quietist tinge like Hugh Turford's *Grounds of a Holy Life* and Alexander Arscott's Quaker attack on the Deists, *Some Considerations Relating to the Present State of the Christian Religion,* were widely read in Philadelphia Quaker circles.

From the time when the first "general meeting" held in England in 1656 had ordered that records of the sufferings of Friends under persecution be set down and collected, Quakers have been diligent recorders and readers of their own history. When the *History of the Rise, Increase, and Progress of the Christian People Called Quakers* by the Dutch Friend Willem Sewel was published in England in 1722, most of the wealthy Quaker merchants, as well as many of the "middle sort" of Friends, subscribed with Andrew Bradford for copies, Richard Hill taking five, and William Hudson, James Logan, Isaac Norris, and William Fishbourne two apiece.[12] Similarly, when Dr. John Rutty's *History of the Rise and Progress of the People Called Quakers in Ireland* was issued in 1751, most of the more substantial Friends again ordered copies: William Logan wrote to John Pemberton that he thought the book well compiled and service-

---

10. John Pemberton to James Pemberton, 2 Feb. 1748, Pemberton Papers, V, 21.

11. Pemberton Papers, XXXIII, 97; George S. Eddy, ed., *Account Books Kept by Benjamin Franklin: Ledger, 1728-1739; Journal, 1730-1737* (New York, 1928), 41.

12. Subscription list in Logan Papers, VIII, 125. In the next year, as we have seen (above, p. 153), Philadelphia Monthly Meeting took measures to have Sewel's work reprinted for local distribution.

able, especially for young Friends, whose eyes might be opened and their hearts "tendered" by the recollection of the trials and afflictions which their forefathers had suffered "for the propagation of the Truth."[13] Joseph Besse's *Collection of the Sufferings of the People Called Quakers*, designed for precisely this purpose and published in the very year in which Logan was writing, became a standard item in most Quaker libraries.

Another source of historical information and edification lay in the journals kept by "public Friends" and published after their death as patterns to posterity and means of furthering the progress of the Truth. John Smith, for example, read a good many of these spiritual autobiographies. The dramatic *Journal* of George Fox was of course on his shelves. By way of contrast to Fox's enthusiasm he could read the pedestrian *Journal* of the respectable George Whitehead, leader of the Society of Friends after the founder's death. He also read, among others, the journals of William Edmundson, the apostle of Irish Quakerism; Richard Davies, the Welsh hatter; John Burnyeat, early preacher of the gospel of the Inner Light to an unfriendly New England; John Fothergill, father of the famous physician; Thomas Story, who had lived for sixteen years in Pennsylvania as member of the Council, Keeper of the Great Seal, and Master of the Rolls; and Thomas Chalkley, the seafaring Friend whose salty *Journal* Smith himself saw through the press of Franklin and Hall in 1749. Smith's reading in this area was fairly typical of that of the average Quaker merchants of his day.

It should not be assumed, however, that the merchants restricted their religious reading to the Scriptures and the writings of Friends; on the contrary, they displayed a remarkable catholicity and range of acquaintance with the literature of religion. Editions of all the major Church Fathers were to be found in the library at Stenton, and an interchange of letters between Logan and the learned English Quaker Josiah Martin regarding the translation of a passage in Clement of Alexandria proves that Logan

---

13. Letter dated 10 May 1753, Pemberton Papers, VIII, 157.

was actually familiar with the contents of the patristic writings.[14] He possessed two complete texts of St. Augustine, the Paris edition of 1571 in eight volumes and the Leyden edition of 1693 in seventeen volumes. The works of the Pseudo-Dionysius and of the other early mystics in the Neo-Platonic tradition—Iamblichus, Proclus, Porphyry, and Hermes Trismegistus—were also in Logan's library in the edition of the great Humanist, Marsilio Ficino. Isaac Norris's array of patristic writings was not so extensive as his father-in-law's, but it boasted editions of Tertullian, Athanasius, Lactantius, Theodoret, and Gregory of Nyssa.

Quaker views on Roman Catholicism tended to coincide in large measure with those of their fellow Protestants, being represented (and to some extent formed) by such books as George Fox's *Arraignment of Popery*.[15] Nevertheless, whether they read to learn or to refute, the more scholarly Friends occasionally perused works of Catholic theology. The *Summa theologiae* of Thomas Aquinas (in the Douai edition of 1614) was to be found in Logan's library, as were the works of Bernard of Clairvaux, Thomas à Kempis, Pico della Mirandola, and Cardinal Bellarmine, the great Jesuit controversialist. Isaac Norris had a genuine curiosity about the history and dogma of Catholicism as shown by his possession of books like the *Histoire du droit canonique* by J. Doujat, professor of canon law and royal historiographer in France; Lorenzo Valla's exposé of the Donation of Constan-

---

14. Logan Letter Book, 1731-32, 48a.
15. William Rawle purchased a copy of this book in 1736. Dr. Lloyd Zachary's library contained two anti-Catholic polemics—Bishop Usher's *Answer to a Challenge Made by a Jesuit* and Daniel Whitby's *Protestant Reconciler*. Logan possessed a copy of the *Treatise of the Corruption of Scripture, Counsels, and Fathers by the Church of Rome*, by Thomas James, first librarian of the Bodleian. Isaac Norris II in 1745 ordered Sir Richard Steele's *Account of the State of the Roman Catholic Religion throughout the World* and Conyers Middleton's *Letter from Rome Shewing the Exact Conformity between Popery and Paganism.*—Letter to William Griffitts, 18 May 1745, Norris Letter Book, 1735-55, 41; letter to Robert Charles, 5 March 1744/5, Norris Letter Book, 1719-56, 17. Thomas Chalkley's library contained a copy of *Arrowes against Babylon; or, Certain Quaeries Serving to a Cleere Discovery of the Mystery of Iniquitie*, a blast against the churches of Rome and England, by John Pendarves, a Puritan controversialist. Although Catholics were tolerated in Pennsylvania, the presence of these and other anti-Catholic books in the libraries of Friends would seem to indicate that prejudice against the Catholic religion was not absent from their outlook.

tine; and (most surprising for a Quaker) the *Calendarium perpetuum ad divinum officium quotidie recitandum* of M. Antonius Olivanus, published at Cahors in 1626. Fénélon, the most popular French writer in eighteenth-century Philadelphia, was a special favorite among Friends, because his mysticism was consonant with the growing Quietism in the Society.[16] John Smith's library, for instance, contained *The Characters and Properties of True Charity Display'd;* the *Dissertation on Pure Love,* translated by the Quaker Josiah Martin; the ubiquitous *Télémaque;* and a volume of "Cambrays Letters."

Reformation theologians were represented in Logan's library by Calvin's *Institutes* and Luther's *Catechism* (in Swedish and an American Indian dialect). Of a rather special interest are the works of three other Reformed theologians which found a place on Logan's shelves: William Ames's *Medulla theologiae,* Wollebius' *Compendium theologiae Christianae,* and Zacharias Ursinus' *Corpus doctrinae Christianae ecclesiae reformatae.* These works, representing that modification of Calvinism known as the "federal" theology, were regularly found in the libraries of New England Puritan ministers; their presence in the library of a Quaker merchant-politician is evidence of genuine breadth of intellectual interests. Both Logan and Norris appear to have been interested in the literature of the Socinian controversy, for both owned copies of the *Traité de la divinité de nôtre seigneur Jésus Christ* by Jacques Abbadie, a Swiss Protestant divine; Norris had, in addition, at least six anti-Socinian works in Latin, mostly by Roman Catholic theologians. The writings of nonconformist clergymen found some favor among Friends: for example, Isaac Watts's poems (which John Smith owned) and Philip Dodd-

---

16. Howard M. Jones finds, on the basis of booksellers' advertisements, that Fénélon led all other French authors of the sixteenth and seventeenth centuries in popularity in Philadelphia between 1750 and 1800.—"The Importation of French Books in Philadelphia, 1750-1800," *Modern Philology,* 32 (1934), 160. Quaker interest in Fénélon dated back to his own lifetime: Bishop Bossuet exclaimed in 1698, when Fénélon's *Maxims of the Saints* was just off the press: "The Quakers are ordering M. de Cambray's book so fast that it has been necessary to stop the circulation."—Dorothy L. Gilbert and Russell Pope, "Quakerism and French Quietism," Friends Hist. Assoc., *Bull.,* 29 (1940), 95.

ridge's sermons (which James Pemberton requested in 1761 from a friend in Reading).[17]

The writings of Anglican divines seem, rather oddly, to have attracted many Quaker readers; perhaps this was owing to the fact that the Society of Friends, as Douglas V. Steere has pointed out, shared with the Church of England a fondness for devotional reading, while other Protestant groups condemned it as smacking dangerously of "works" and Popery.[18] Logan's collection contained works by Bishop Latimer, Gilbert Burnet, Edward Stillingfleet, Richard Hooker, Jeremy Taylor, Ralph Cudworth, and the learned Isaac Barrow.[19] Isaac Norris I, writing in 1704 to a young woman brought up in the Church of England, was able to recommend Taylor's *Holy Living and Holy Dying*, *The Whole Duty of Man*, *The Lady's Calling*, and "any of Dr. Tillotsons Sermons."[20] John Smith knew the works of a number of High-Church divines, including Bishop Atterbury, William Sherlock, and Robert South. Conning the sermons of South, he was at first "well pleased with them", but as he got deeper into them, he noted in his diary: "The more I read him The less I like him"; finally he put them down in evident disgust, with the revealing explanation: "find he was a Rigid Tory."[21] On the whole Friends appear to have perferred the more liberal Anglicans like Archbishop Tillotson, whom Smith endeavored at the age of eighteen to vindicate against Jonathan Edwards' charge that he denied the eternity of Hell torments. After searching

---

17. Letter to James Read, 16 June 1761, Pemberton Papers, XIV, 152.
18. George F. Thomas, ed., *The Vitality of the Christian Tradition* (New York, 1944), 202-3.
19. Logan indicated in a letter written in 1732 that Taylor's *Holy Living and Holy Dying* was for his daughter's edification.—Letter to Lawrence Williams, 6 May 1732, Logan Letter Book, 1731-32, 55. Dr. Zachary also owned copies of these twin works of the English Chrysostom, and John Smith records in his diary that he read "Dr. Jer. Taylors imitation of Christ" (probably *The Great Exemplar*).
20. Letter to Prudence Weamouth, 28 Sept. 1704, Copies of letters, Norris Papers, I, 110-11. A good Quaker, overlooking no chance to propagate the Truth, Norris added: "if thou would look into any of our Friends Books, I recommend William Penn's No Cross No Crown, Robert Barclays Apology and W[illiam] P[enn]'s Key [Opening the Way to Every Common Understanding]."
21. MS Diary, II (entries for Feb. 1745/6).

Tillotson's works "to See whether Dr. Edwards Charges against him were true or not," he concluded with all the ponderousness that could be mustered by a provincial Quaker youth setting himself up as an arbitrator between the Archbishop of Canterbury and the most profound Calvinist theologian of the day: "Although I think there are Several Errors and Imperfections In Tillotson's Works Yet I Think Edwards has not done him Justice. . . ."[22]

There were certain non-Quaker theologians and divines whom the eighteenth-century Friends read with special pleasure because they spoke a cognate language of the spirit. Such was William Dell, a seventeenth-century forerunner of Quakerism, whom Thomas Chalkley called "a wise and learned Man, and one who had a large Sense of the Power of God."[23] Dell had emphasized in his writings what was to be the characteristic Quaker conception of "the living and Eternal Word . . . in our hearts" as against the outward Word of the Scriptures. Recognizing the unison between this spirit and their own, the Friends adopted him as one of themselves; thus we find Chalkley recommending his *Doctrine of Baptism* and Israel Pemberton possessing a copy of his *Several Sermons*.[24] Dr. John Everard, another seventeenth-century Anglican mystic who had written in Quaker-like language, "if ye once know the truth experimentally after the Spirit ye will no longer make such a stir about Forms, Disciplines and Externals," proved to be another favorite of Philadelphia Friends. His volume entitled *Some Gospel Treasures Opened*, republished in 1757 by Christopher Sower and described by Anthony Benezet as "a Book in the reading of which of Light and, I think I may say some degree of Life has been communicated," was in John Smith's library and undoubtedly in many others.[25]

---

22. Letter to E[lias] B[land], 15 May 1740, *ibid.*
23. *Journal*, in *Works*, 125.
24. Pemberton's copy bearing his signature is in the Friends Historical Library of Swarthmore College.
25. Anthony Benezet to Samuel Fothergill, 17 Oct. 1756, Brookes, 223. Here it may be noted that the little collection of books assembled in Mount Holly by the saintly John Woolman contained Sower's edition of Everard along with *The Imitation of Christ*, the Spanish mystical dialogue *Desiderius* (which John Smith also read), one or two volumes by William Law, and the works of the

The Puritan mystic Francis Rous was still another earlier writer of whom the Quakers approved. His *Academia Coelestis: The Heavenly University*, published by Tacy Sowle, the London Quaker printer, was among Thomas Chalkley's books; it was appropriate that this volume should have been housed after Chalkley's death in the Friends School, for Rous, although Provost of Eton, had insisted in common with Friends that the really important education is gained only in "the heavenly Academy—the High School of [religious] Experience." The mystical writings of William Law were widely read among Friends. One of Anthony Benezet's projects was the reprinting and circulating of extracts from Law's *Spirit of Prayer*, along with several treatises of Dell, and Thomas Hartley's *Discourse on Mistakes Concerning Religion, Enthusiasm, Experiences, &c.*, the work of an Anglican rector whose religious sympathies had passed from evangelicalism to mysticism.[26]

In the light of the frequent charge that Quakerism, in its simplification of theology and its hostility to the clergy was tantamount to Deism, it is interesting to notice the attitude of certain Philadelphia Quakers towards the Deists and writers on natural religion who were so numerous in the early eighteenth century.[27] In 1707 Isaac Norris I, on a visit to England, came upon *The Rights of the Christian Church Asserted*, an early work of Matthew Tindal, calculated, in its author's words, to "make the clergy mad." Norris reported that "the High Fliers and *Jure Divino* men" were mightily alarmed by Tindal's argument that the Church of England was a mere creature of the civil power. The book dealt, said Norris in obvious approval, with "the original natural rights of Government upon Sidney's and Locke's

---

occult German mystic Jakob Boehme. Comparison of Woolman's library of religious and utilitarian manuals with the much larger and more varied collections of the Philadelphia merchants reveals a significant divergence of temperament and interests.—See Frederick B. Tolles, "John Woolman's List of 'Books Lent,'" Friends Hist. Assoc., *Bull.*, 31 (1942), 72-81.

26. Benezet to John Smith, 8 Feb. 1760, Brookes, 236-37.

27. For charges of Deism, see, for example, George Keith, *The Deism of William Penn and His Brethren Destructive to the Christian Religion* (London, 1699). Some rough notes for a reply to this book are found in Logan Papers, II, 113.

principles" and revealed "such strength of reasoning, depth of learning and adventurous boldness, that the like is scarce to be met with." The Quaker's final comment hinted at a readiness to take advantage of the arguments of a Deist when they happened to support Quaker traditions: "To read some parts gives me to admire the Providence that has cast our Friends into such a discipline by unlearned instruments, as can be learnedly vindicated and fairly proved to be according to primitive institution."[28]

James Logan followed the controversy over Deism with great interest from the vantage point of his library at Stenton. In 1718 he ordered from England copies of the *Letter to Mr. Dodwell* and the *Scripture Doctrine of the Trinity* by the Reverend Samuel Clarke, the liberal Anglican divine, who was accused by his contemporaries of crypto-Deism and Arianism.[29] A few years later he was reading the recently published *Religion of Nature Delineated*, a mild Deist work by William Wollaston. Logan could not conceal his approval of the book: it was, he said, "a piece for which one may justly . . . congratulate the age."[30] Logan's fullest and most revealing account of his attitude towards Deism was occasioned by the publication of Matthew Tindal's *Christianity as Old as the Creation*, the book which marked, as Leslie Stephen has observed, "the culminating point of the whole deist controversy."[31] Logan referred to it in the year of its publication as a "wicked Book," but suggested that by discrediting the Established Church, it might well play into the hands of the Quakers: "for as Man has naturally a Propensity to Religion . . . they will find none other left for them than the Spiritual," or in other words, the religion of Friends.[32] Among the thirty-odd re-

28. Letter to Joseph Pike, 24 April 1707, *Penn and Logan Correspondence*, II, 210-11. The printed version reads "natural *lights* of government."
29. Logan to Josiah Martin, 26 Oct. 1718, Logan Letter Book, 1717-31, 40.
30. Letter to William Burnet, 7 Nov. 1726, Logan Letter Book, 1721-1723, 59-60. The library at Stenton contained not only the English edition but also a French translation of Wollaston's work. Incidentally, Logan got from this book the germ of the idea which led to his major contribution in the field of natural science: see below, pp. 215-17.
31. *History of English Thought in the Eighteenth Century* (London, 1881), I, 134.
32. Letter to Thomas Story, 22 Dec. 1730, *Logan-Story Correspondence*, 34.

plies which Tindal's book evoked was one by Alexander Arscott, a Quaker of Bristol, in whose hands Logan had placed the education of his son William. Logan and Israel Pemberton read Arscott's rejoinder, *Some Considerations Relating to the Present State of the Christian Religion*, and were instrumental in having it reprinted in Philadelphia. Logan felt that both Tindal's and Arscott's books would further the progress of Truth, Tindal's "as a purgative to carry off the peccant humours" and Arscott's "as a Restorative or at least what may help to the only true and solid Nutrition." Tindal's book, in Logan's opinion, would "throw more work on [the] Clergy's hands than they will ever be able to dispatch otherwise than by the mere dint of Power or by coming truly to own and teach and practice the only great fundamental Truth in Religion which their trade is to oppose."[33] In the course of his argument Tindal had dealt rather irreverently with the Inner Light of the Quakers, calling it a "senseless notion" and "one of their ugliest Brats." Arscott had taken umbrage at this latter phrase, but Logan tried to mollify him:

I was pleas'd ... with that part ... with which thou art offended, where he so scurvily treats our friends, for I should not have wish'd, that in a piece design'd to batter all Reveal'd Religion and particularly the Xian, we should have found any better Quarter, for had he mention'd the Profession with respect, it would appear as a Confirmation of the Charge that Quakers are no Christians.[34]

The keen interest of the Philadelphia Friends in the Deist controversy as it unfolded is further reflected by the presence in their libraries of many other books on both sides of the question. John Locke's *Reasonableness of Christianity*, a work by which the great philosopher had unwittingly become the "progenitor of

---

33. Letter to Alexander Arscott, 14 Dec. 1730, Logan Letter Books, IV, 203-4. In a letter of 9 Oct. 1731, Logan expresses disappointment that the philosophical portions of Arscott's second volume are "too drily managed," adding that "Tyndal . . . should either have been otherwise handled or let alone."
34. Letter to Alexander Arscott, 14 Feb. 1731/2, Logan Letter Book, 1731-32, 40. Logan added a bit of gossip to the effect that Tindal's use of the offensive expression had been dictated by his pique at Friends' not having "come into the Subscription"; Tindal was alleged to have requested financial aid for his projected book from a number of Friends, and to have been turnd down.

the whole generation of eighteenth-century iconoclasts,"[35] was on Logan's shelves, and his son William added a copy of Henry Dodwell's *Christianity not Founded on Argument*, an essentially skeptical work, written at the end of the Deist controversy, which undermined the Lockean effort to prove the rationality of the Christian religion and ostensibly asserted a Quaker-like doctrine of an inward and divine light as the source of religious authority. Whether Friends accepted Dodwell's argument at face value or perceived his subtle and destructive irony does not appear. One of the few known titles in the library of Charles Norris, brother of Isaac II, was Conyers Middleton's *Free Inquiry into the Miraculous Powers Which Are Supposed to Have Existed in the Christian Church through Several Successive Ages*, an attack upon the argument from miracles, one of the key positions in the orthodox Christian apologetic.[36] James Logan, Dr. Lloyd Zachary, and Isaac Norris II all possessed copies of William Derham's *Physico-Theology* and John Ray's *Wisdom of God Manifested in the Works of the Creation*, two books which anticipated Paley's classic exercises in demonstrating the existence of God from the presence of design in the Creation.

This interest in Deist writers is related, no doubt, to the rationalist strain which existed in unresolved tension with the dominant mystical tendency of Quaker thought.[37] Logan resembled his patron William Penn in the free play which upon occasion he allowed to this side of his mind, but the fact that he also owned and presumably read several orthodox replies to Tindal and Toland suggests that even a Friend who sat so loose to his inherited faith as did James Logan never confused the basic postulates of Quakerism with those of the Deists. The presence of all these discussions of Deism on Quaker bookshelves argues a lively interest in the vital theological issues of the day and effectually demonstrates the falsity of the notion that Friends read only religious works designed to bolster their own faith.[38]

---

35. Stephen, I, 94.
36. Charles Norris to James Wright, 19 April 1759, Norris of Fairhill MSS, Miscellaneous, 24.
37. See below, pp. 210-12.
38. It may be added that Logan also read widely in the literature of non-

PHILOSOPHY AND CONDUCT

Of all the Quaker merchants James Logan was most given to philosophical speculation; it was therefore natural that his library should contain the largest array of philosophical books. No less than four complete editions of Aristotle in both Greek and Latin stood upon his shelves, together with separate editions of the *Nicomachean Ethics*, the *Politics*, and the *History of Animals;* alongside them were three editions of Plato, including a recension of Ficino's text, published at Basel in 1539. The writings of the Stoic philosophers Seneca and Marcus Aurelius, Plutarch's *Morals*, and the *De consolatione philosophiae* of Boethius were also in the library at Stenton. Of the major modern thinkers Logan had the works of Descartes and of the anti-Cartesian Gassendi, the *Recherche de la vérité* of Malebranche, Spinoza's *Tractatus theologico-politicus*, and Locke's *Essay Concerning Human Understanding*.

Logan's familiarity with contemporary philosophy is clearly evidenced by his own unpublished treatise on "The Duties of Man Deduced from Nature," of which his *Charge Delivered from the Bench to the Grand Inquest*, published by Franklin in 1736, was a sort of synopsis. As he completed successive chapters of this lengthy treatise, he sent them for criticism to his scientific and philosophical friends in England—Peter Collinson, the Quaker botanist, William Jones, the eminent mathematician, Dr. Richard Mead, one of the most learned physicians of the day, and Sir Hans Sloane, president of the Royal Society; he also submitted them to Benjamin Franklin for comment.[39] The Quaker

---

Christian religions, having in his library two copies of the Koran, the works of Confucius, the *Porta Mosis* of Moses Maimonides, the great Talmudist, and numerous works on the history of Oriental religions. His conclusions from his studies in this field seem to have been akin to those of the exponents of "natural religion," except that he conceived the supposed common substratum of all religions to be mystical rather than rational: "I shall die," he wrote, "in the faith that in the main . . . [the religion of the Inner Light] will one day be the only Religion of the World. Nay it already is so amongst all the judicious of every Profession, as well amongst the Mahometans and such as own or know not the Christian Name as those who are best acquainted with it."—Letter to John Hoop, 15 May 1729, Logan Letter Books, III, 235.

39. Logan to William Jones, 25 July 1737, Stephen J. Rigaud, ed., *Correspondence of Scientific Men in the Seventeenth Century*, I, 317-18; Franklin to

thinker took issue with Hobbes's position that the state of nature was a state of war, and showed his thorough acquaintance with current speculation on the ethical role of reason and the "moral sense" in his discussion of Shaftesbury, Clarke, Wollaston, and Hutcheson.[40] Although recognizing that "every man conceives the best opinion of his own notions," Logan was rash enough to assert that he had "seen somewhat farther into this affair, tho' of very unequal abilities, than any or all of them."

His main thesis was that the "affections" (which he regarded as remains of the divine image not wholly vitiated by the Fall of Man) are the springs of conduct, and that reason is merely a regulator or monitor, standing guard over the affections of the heart, as a chemist stands guard over his fires, stills, and bottles. This relationship of head and heart, he concluded, was the basis of morality; "and when there is joyned to this a true Sense of our dependance on the Supreme and Divine Author of all things, a constant contemplation of his Wisdom and Goodness, and a Sincere Love springing from thence . . . this is true Religion and Holiness." Logan denied his friend Story's contention (grounded, no doubt, upon Barclay's treatment of reason and conscience in the *Apology*) that reason and the affections were unsafe guides in moral and religious matters except when enlightened by the divine Light. He was enough of a Quaker, however, to believe that "something divine attends Mankind," operating upon the natural conscience (which Logan, departing from most contemporary moralists, ranged among the affections), and that "when ardent desires are roused in the heart to know the Will of God, to be enabled to perform it, and to have some communion with him, it purifies, animates, and strengthens." Logan's quarrel was only with those Quietist Friends who insisted that "all the thoughts,

---

Logan, n.d., Sparks MSS, Harvard University Library. Drafts of various parts of the treatise exist in the Logan Papers.

40. See the significant letter to Samuel Blunston, 11 Jan. 1735/6, Friends Historical Library of Swarthmore College. In this letter he also mentions "Dean Berkeley's Notion of all being Spirit," and quotes some lines from Sophocles' *Ajax* (apparently translated by himself) to convey his unsympathetic view of Berkeleyan idealism.

suggested (as in preaching) from a sense of that Love are the dictates of the Spirit."[41]

Although Logan was the only Philadelphia Quaker who ventured to take up his pen as a technical philosopher, his fellow merchants showed considerable interest in both ancient and contemporary thought. Isaac Norris I, for example, quoted Socrates, "the Sententious Seneca," and the Cynic philosopher Stilpo in his letters. On the shelves of his library at Fairhill were Locke's famous *Essay Concerning Human Understanding* and Shaftesbury's *Characteristics*.[42] John Smith knew Plato's dialogues (in an English translation of André Dacier's French version) and the Stoic moralists, Seneca and Epictetus. Francis Hutcheson's *Inquiry into the Original of Our Ideas of Beauty and Virtue* was popular philosophical fare, perhaps because its theory of the "moral sense" leading to a life of disinterested benevolence seemed to harmonize with Quaker philanthropic impulses.[43] The inventory of Dr. Lloyd Zachary's books shows that he possessed *The Fable of the Bees* by Bernard Mandeville, whose cynical view of human nature contrasted sharply with that held by Shaftesbury and Hutcheson.

Most Quaker libraries, like those of the gentlemen of Virginia, contained one or more practical guides to conduct.[44] John Smith's collection may be taken as typical. Early in his career as a merchant, he read a little book called *A Present for an Apprentice*, the subtitle of which was *A Sure Guide to Gain Both Esteem and Estate*. This curious medley of Christianity and commerce, published in 1740, was written by Sir John Barnard, Lord

---

41. Letter to Thomas Story, 15 Nov. 1737, *Logan-Story Correspondence*, 61-62, 65. Compare Rufus M. Jones, *The Later Periods of Quakerism*, I, 92-100 for a discussion of the Quietist theory against which Logan argued. In a subsequent letter Logan attempts to allay any lingering fears Story might have about his essential Quakerism by stating his belief that the Inward Light is "the ONLY source of true happiness attainable in this life."—Letter dated 19 Nov. 1738, *Logan-Story Correspondence*, 69.
42. Norris Papers, I, 36; Norris Letter Book, 1716-30, 147, 357, 387.
43. Logan, Smith, and William Rawle all had copies of this work of Hutcheson; Logan also had Hutcheson's *Essay on the Nature and Conduct of the Passions and Affections*.
44. Compare Wright, *First Gentlemen*, index under "Conduct Books."

Mayor of London; John Smith described it as "A piece wrote with so much Judgment and persuasion to Industry and Virtue that 'tis a Pity but they were more Common."[45] Two popular collections of Polonian precepts, Dr. Thomas Fuller's *Introductio ad prudentiam* and *Introductio ad sapientiam*, Smith read as a young man just embarking upon a business career. We do not know at what period of his life he first read *The Gentleman's Calling*, which was listed among his books, but it may well have been after his retirement to Franklin Park, his country estate in Burlington where, in the midst of his spacious park with its herd of a hundred deer, he did his best to emulate the life of an English country gentleman.

POLITICS AND LAW

Being actively engaged in the governing of men, most of the Quaker merchants naturally interested themselves in both the theoretical and practical aspects of politics. There is hardly a major classic of political theory which was not to be found in the private collection of one or another of the Philadelphia Quakers. The catalogues of Logan's library at Stenton yield *inter alia* the following titles: Plato's *Republic,* the *Politics* of Aristotle, the *De republica* of Jean Bodin, the works of Machiavelli (including *Il principe* in Italian), the *Politica methodice digesta* of Althusius, the political writings of James I, Harrington's *Commonwealth of Oceana*, Hobbes's *Leviathan,* and John Locke's *Two Treatises of Government.* Isaac Norris II owned, in addition to many of the foregoing titles, a copy of the *Vindiciae contra tyrannos,* the classic Calvinist statement of the right of resistance to unjust rulers.

The sympathies of the Quaker merchants in relation to current British politics can perhaps be judged by their persistent fondness for Trenchard and Gordon's *Independent Whig* and *Cato's Letters,* two series of Whig apologetics whose influence in popularizing the ideas of liberty and representative government in the American colonies was incalculable. The elder Isaac

45. MS Diary, II (entry for 12 Feb. 1745/6).

Norris asked to have copies of *The Independent Whig* sent to him from London as they appeared in 1721. William Fishbourne had a set of these same partisan political papers, and John Smith's library contained both series in bound volumes. We have only hints of Smith's own political leanings, but they lead us to surmise that, like John Dickinson, whose "Farmer's Letters" ran concurrently in the *Pennsylvania Chronicle* with his non-political "Atticus Papers," he was Whiggish in sympathies but inclined to draw back as the application of Whig ideas seemed about to issue in violence.[46]

Dr. Lloyd Zachary owned a treatise on government by Sir Robert Filmer (perhaps the *Patriarcha*, the work which evoked Locke's *Two Treatises*) and Locke's *Letter upon Toleration*. That politically conscious Quakers shared their century's interest in the law of nature and of nations is shown by the popularity of works like Montesquieu's *Spirit of Laws*, Pufendorf's *De jure naturae et gentium*, and Burlamaqui's *Principles of Politic Law*.[47] Samuel Morris in 1763 read an unnamed work of Jean Jacques Rousseau, and commented to his nephew Samuel Powel: "he's a fine writer, I wish he was as much a Christian."[48]

As lawgivers and magistrates the merchants needed a working knowledge of legislative and judicial practice and precedent. The *Votes of the Pennsylvania Assembly* and the laws of the neighboring colonies were usually on their shelves for ready reference. British legal reports were also useful to those who were called upon to serve as Justices of the Peace; and books such as the *Lex mercatoria rediviva* of Windham Beawes (ordered from England by John Reynell in 1762) were essential to the merchant in the conduct of his business.[49] Chief Justice James Logan's law library, like his collections in the other fields of his

46. Letter to John Askew, 9 July 1721, Norris Letter Book, 1716-30, 274; Inventory of William Fishbourne's estate, 1742, Philadelphia Registry of Wills. For an oblique indication of Smith's attitude, see the letter of "Atticus" in the *Pennsylvania Chronicle*, 27 Feb. 1769, quoted in Tolles, "Literary Quaker," 309.
47. Montesquieu was certainly read by John Smith and Dr. Richard Hill.— See Smith, ed., *Letters of Dr. Richard Hill*, 147. Pufendorf was read by Zachary, Isaac Norris II, and James Logan, and Burlamaqui by John Smith.
48. Letter dated 4 July 1763, *Pa. Mag. of Hist.*, 15 (1891), 379.
49. Letter to Mildred and Roberts, 15 Nov. 1762, Reynell Letter Book, 1762-67.

wide-ranging scholarly interests, was extensive, embracing the *Institutes* of Justinian, the *De jure belli et pacis* of Grotius, Sir John Fortescue's *Learned Commendation of the Politic Lawes of England*, and the ever-present Coke upon Littleton. Isaac Norris II inherited from his father a large number of lawbooks, valued at £56, to which he made many additions. In 1752 he placed an order with Thomas Osborne in London for fifty titles chosen from the catalogues of the great Harleian library, then being dispersed and sold; these included, in addition to a number of law books a great many treatises on the rights and powers of the British Parliament.[50] Whatever may have been the case earlier, it behooved the eighteenth-century Quaker, deeply involved as he was in worldly affairs, to be learned in the law and the prerogatives of legislative bodies.

A few treatises upon political economy were to be found in Quaker libraries. Logan, for example, had Charles Davenant's *Essay upon the Probable Means of Making People Gainers in the Ballance of Trade*, a work which, accepting most of the basic premises of mercantilism, nevertheless argued for relative freedom of trade, and John Locke's *Papers Relating to Money, Interest and Trade*, in which the philosopher criticized proposals for the depreciation of the currency.[51] Logan also read at least one of the treatises of John Bellers, the English Quaker economist and social reformer.[52] In 1755, when the first part of John Huske's *Present State of North America* appeared in England, Friend Thomas Wharton ordered it, with a view, no doubt, to countering its provocative arguments against the French.[53] The very

50. Will of Isaac Norris I, Logan Papers, VII, 119; Isaac Norris II to Thomas Osborne, 16 March 1752, Norris Letter Book, 1735-55, 70. This letter was kindly brought to my attention by Mr. James W. Phillips of the Dickinson College Library.

51. W. R. Shepherd suggests that Logan and Norris may have got their anti-paper-money ideas from Sir Henry Pollexfen's *Discourse of Trade, Coyn, and Paper Credit*, a copy of which was in Logan's library.—*History of Proprietary Government in Pennsylvania* (New York, 1896), 406n.

52. See Logan to John Bellers, 29 July 1726, Logan Letter Book, 1717-31, 143, in which Logan acknowledges receipt of a book of Bellers and expresses his pleasure in reading it.

53. Letter to Thomas Crowley, 4 Oct. 1755, Thomas Wharton Letter Book, 1752-59.

titles of these books in the field of politics, economics, and public law are sufficient in themselves to suggest the degree to which the Quaker merchants were immersed in the mundane world of human government and jurisprudence.

SCIENCE, MEDICINE, AND PRACTICAL ARTS

The activities of the Quakers in promoting scientific enterprises in colonial Philadelphia are discussed in the next chapter, where an effort is made to explain their concern with these phases of knowledge. Here it is proposed merely to show the extent of their interest in science, medicine, and practical arts as reflected in the books on their shelves.

In the transfer of the European Enlightenment to America, a process to which Philadelphia made a greater contribution than any other town, the scientific books at Stenton played no inconsiderable part.[54] The first copy of Isaac Newton's *Principia mathematica* to arrive in the colonies appears to have been that which Logan acquired in 1708.[55] The pains which Logan took to build up a mathematical collection second to none in the colonies are reflected in his will, an extract from which was published after his death in the *Gentleman's Magazine*:

In my library [he wrote] ... [are] All the old Greek Mathematicians, viz, *Archimedes, Euclid, Ptolemy*, both his Geography and Almagest, which I had in *Greek* (with *Theon's* Commentary in folio, above 700 pages) from my learned friend *Fabricius*, who published 14 volumes of his Greek *Bibliotheque* in quarto, in which, after he had finished his account of *Ptolemy*, on my enquiring of him at *Hamburgh* in 1722 how I should find it, having long sought for it in vain in *England;* he sent it to me out of his own library, telling me it was so scarce, that neither prayers or

---

54. On Philadelphia's scientific primacy and her role in mediating the Enlightenment to America, see Bridenbaugh, *Rebels and Gentlemen*, 27-28, 304-58.
55. Frederick E. Brasch, "James Logan, a Colonial Mathematical Scholar, and the First Copy of Newton's *Principia* to Arrive in the Colonies," American Philosophical Society, *Proceedings*, 86 (1943), 3-12. Logan's tribute to Newton, incorporated in a letter to William Jones, F.R.S., Sir Isaac's friend and editor is worth quoting: "the world, as long as there remains in it any regard for science and sound knowledge must ever revere that wonderful man's memory, and acknowledge him the greatest genius in that way that has ever been known to this day."—Letter dated 25 July 1737, Rigaud, ed., *Correspondence*, I, 316.

price could purchase it; Besides, there are many of the most valuable *Latin awthors*, and a great number of modern mathematicians, with all three editions of *Newton*, Dr. *Wallis, Halley*, &c.[56]

In addition to the works of Ptolemy, Logan had a copy of the *De revolutionibus orbium coelestium*, in which Copernicus had upset the Ptolemaic conception of the universe. Alongside Copernicus were ranged the foundation works of modern astronomy—the treatises of Tycho Brahe, Galileo, and Kepler, as well as of the English astronomer John Flamsteed, to whom Logan referred as "my good friend (while living)."[57] To list the other scientific writers whose works crowded Logan's shelves would be simply to call the roll of most of the great names in the history of science and many of the lesser ones. Let it suffice to note the major works of Roger Bacon and Francis Bacon; of William Gilbert, pioneer investigator of magnetism; of Marcello Malpighi, William Harvey, and Nehemiah Grew, founders of the sciences of plant and animal physiology; of Robert Hooke and Robert Boyle, early workers in the fields of physics and chemistry. Where else in the American colonies, where, indeed, in the English-speaking world of the early eighteenth century, outside of the libraries of a few universities and learned societies, could such a collection of scientific classics have been found?

The library at Fairhill almost matched the collection at Stenton in this field, for it boasted more than 175 scientific titles. Galileo's *Siderius nuncius*, in which the Italian astronomer had reported his first discoveries with the newly invented telescope, was there; and in his copy of the *Systema cosmicum* Norris neatly inscribed some notes on Galileo's life and his experiences with the Inquisition. The *Dioptrice* of Kepler had its place on Norris's shelves alongside later works such as Pascal's *Traitez de l'équilibre des liqueurs et de la pesanteur de la masse de l'air;* Robert Boyle's account of his experiments on the "spring and weight" of air; Edmé Marriotte's *Premier essay de la végétation des*

---

56. *Gentleman's Magazine*, 36 (1766), 529.
57. Letter to James Steel, 3 Dec. 1729, Logan Papers, I, 93.

182

plantes, a pioneer work in plant physiology; Gassendi's *Institutio astronomica;* and William Whiston's *Praelectiones physico-mathematicae.* A letter from Isaac Norris I to James Logan in 1723 is extant, requesting the purchase of "Sir Isaac Newtons treatise of Light and Collours"; this could have been any one of Newton's important treatises on optics. Norris was one of three Philadelphia Quakers (the others being Logan and Griffith Owen) who ordered a copy of Henry Pemberton's *View of Sir Isaac Newton's Philosophy* before publication.[58]

Dr. Lloyd Zachary had, in addition to his extensive medical library, a number of general scientific works, including a treatise by the Dutch geographer and cartographer Hermann Moll, and the *Historia plantarum* of John Ray, who first introduced a precise definition of species into botanical science. Charles Pemberton, youngest of the four sons of Israel Pemberton, Senior, appears to have had scientific leanings, for after his early death at the age of nineteen, we find James Logan requesting from among his effects a copy of *La figure de la terre* by Maupertuis and other French savants who, on an expedition to northern Sweden, had established the fact that the form of the earth was that of an oblate spheroid.[59] John Smith's small library of scientific books included Sir Hans Sloane's *Voyage to the Islands of Madera, Barbados, Nieves, St. Christophers, and Jamaica, with the Natural History . . . of the Last of Those Islands;* a four-volume work of pre-Linnaean natural history called *Le spectacle de la nature; or, Nature Display'd;* and Andrew Baxter's *Matho; or Cosmotheoria puerilis,* a simple exposition of astronomy. Probably there was no private Quaker library of any size in Philadelphia which did not include some scientific books.

It is hardly surprising to find excellent medical libraries in the possession of Quaker physicians. Dr. Lloyd Zachary left, at his death in 1756, 103 medical works, collected during his student days abroad; nearly half of them went to the Pennsylvania Hos-

---

58. Norris to Logan, 16 Dec. 1723, Norris Letter Book, 1716-30, 367; Logan to Sylvanus Bevan, 7 Feb. 1726/7, Logan Letter Book, 1721-33, 65.
59. Logan to John Pemberton, 29 Aug. 1749, Pemberton Papers, V, 155.

pital in 1767 to form the nucleus of its library. In the same year the Hospital received the gift of fifty-five volumes acquired by Dr. Benjamin Morris during his period of study at the University of Leyden.[60] Nor is it surprising, in spite of the fact that Philadelphia was better supplied with trained physicians than most colonial towns, to find that virtually every Quaker merchant possessed a few general handbooks as a basis for self-treatment. Dr. George Cheyne's works were especially popular: his *Essay of Health and Long Life*, which preached the virtues of temperance, exercise, and vegetarianism, and his *English Malady*, a treatise on nervous diseases, were in several libraries. Isaac Norris I also read Cheyne's *Observations Concerning the Nature and Due Methods of Treating the Gout* and faithfully followed its prescription of brimstone "to dilute the blood." Norris's motive in spending what he confessed to be a great deal of time and money upon medical books appears to have been partly hypochondria and partly intellectual curiosity. After a severe attack of gout, he recorded, he formed a resolution to do everything in his power as a reasonable creature towards making his life more easy:

I thought one proper Step was to Enquire as far as I had Opportunity or power into the frame of our bodys, and by looking into Some of the best treatises I could in this country come at on that head—have found Even by the little Glimerings I have been able to obtain, not only a Satisfaction but real pleasure in Seeing in part the Wonderful contrivance of our Bodies and the providentiall Care over us and for us, in all our Wants and Necessities.[61]

Only a consuming intellectual curiosity (or a really serious case of hypochondria) can account for the extraordinary inter-

60. Thomas G. Morton, *The History of the Pennsylvania Hospital*, 347.
61. Letter to Joseph Pike, 28 Nov. 1724, Norris Letter Book, 1716-30, 405. See also Isaac Norris I to James Logan, 16 Dec. 1723, *ibid*, 379, where, after ordering Cheyne on the gout, he gives further evidence of hypochrondria by asking Logan to procure for him a copy of Dr. Richard Mead's iatrochemical treatise *De imperio solis ac lunae in corpora humana et morbis inde oriundis*, in which the popular London physician tried to show on Newton's principles how the heavenly bodies affect the human body even as they affect one another. Norris's revealing comment was: "I've a mind to See what he Says for I'm Sure I feel their Effects at full and Change."

est in technical phases of medicine reflected in the library at Fairhill. It was no ordinary collection of popular manuals, but consisted of nearly 150 specialized treatises (insofar as medicine can
be said to have been specialized in the eighteenth century),
chiefly in Latin, the international language of science, or in
French.[62] A random sampling discloses such titles as the *Schedula
monitoria de novae febris ingressu* of the great clinician Thomas
Sydenham; an important treatise on infantile diseases by Sydenham's disciple Walter Harris; the Dutch physician Regner de
Graaf's pioneer study of the male genitalia; several works by
Martin Lister on medicinal waters; Thomas Willis's *Pharmaceu-
tica rationalis,* an epitome of the seventeenth-century *materia
medica;* a work on the anatomy of the brain by Niels Stensen, a
Danish physician-priest; the Delphic aphorisms of the great Hermann Boerhaave; and William Harvey's epochal work on the
circulation of the blood. There can be no doubt that these books
were read with care, for many of them contain notations in Latin
and French in the younger Norris's hand. It is unlikely that many
practicing physicians in the colonies had absorbed so much medical lore as this merchant and politician in his ivy-covered study
at Fairhill.

The libraries of even the most learned or pious Quakers were
not without a number of purely utilitarian manuals. Alongside
the Greek and Latin classics and abstruse scientific tomes at
Stenton were such books as *The Compleat Shipwright;* John
Collins' *Navigation by the Mariner's Plain Scale, New Plained;*
a French treatise on beekeeping; another French book entitled
La mécanique du feu, dealing with a new type of chimney; and
Richard Bradley's *New Improvements of Planting and Gardening, Both Philosophical and Practical.*[63] Logan's copy of the *De re*

---

62. It is probably impossible now to distinguish between the books acquired
by the father and the son. Evidence of the elder Norris's preoccupation with
medicine has already been given. The best proof of the son's similar interest
lies in the fact that, after Dr. Zachary's death, Isaac Norris II asked the executors of the estate for the opportunity to purchase some thirty volumes on
medical subjects.—See Isaac Norris II to Hugh Roberts and Samuel Neave, 1
Jan. 1757, Logan Papers, XXII, 22.
63. Some rather surprising titles to find in a Quaker's library are Thomas
Salmon's *Essay to the Advancement of Musick,* de Piles' *Art of Painting and*

metallica of Agricola was acquired partly for practical reasons and partly to satisfy his itch for learning. "I wanted that author," he wrote to a correspondent in Amsterdam who had procured the book for him, "because I am somewhat concerned in mines, but more particularly in Iron works, yet there is something more in it for I confess a Book has from my Infancy been my Diversion."[64]

Garden books, particularly those of Bradley and Miller, were in demand especially by those merchants who maintained "plantations" in the country. John Smith, for example, borrowed from his brother-in-law William Logan a copy of Bradley's *New Improvements*, a treatise based on the proposition that gardening was an enterprise for "expert philosophers and reasonable men"; others, like Isaac Norris II and Thomas Wharton preferred Philip Miller's less technical but more expensive *Gardener's Dictionary*.[65] Although Thomas Chalkley's reading was largely in religious tracts, he found a use for T. Langford's *Plain and Full Instructions to Raise All Sorts of Fruit Trees*.[66] Some of the smaller libraries may have been composed principally of just such utilitarian works. Although no inventory of John Reynell's books has survived, most of the references in his correspondence are to such works as *The Gentleman and Builder's Repository*, *The Hertfordshire Husbandman*, Bailey's *Dictionary*, a cook book for his wife, and Daniel Defoe's *Compleat English Tradesman* ("a Book well worth thy Reading," he observed to his former apprentice, "when thou has Leisure").[67]

Most private Quaker libraries included at least one all-em-

the *Lives of the Painters*, Vegetius' *De re militari*, and Sir Jonas Moore's *Modern Fortification*. In explanation of the presence of the last two titles it may be pointed out that Logan, unlike most of his fellow Quakers, believed in defensive war.

64. Letter to Theodorus Hodson, 12 Jan. 1725/6, Logan Letter Book, 1717-31, 410.

65. Isaac Norris to Robert Charles, 8 Nov. 1753, Norris Letter Book, 1719-59, 43; Thomas Wharton to Thomas Crowley, 28 April 1756, Wharton Letter Book.

66. His copy is now in the Haverford College Library.

67. John Reynell to Daniel Flexney, 5 April 1739, Reynell Letter Book, 1738-41; to Elias Bland, 4 Dec. 1743, Reynell Letter Book, 1741-44; to Daniel Flexney, 29 May 1744, *ibid.*; Elias Bland to John Reynell, 17 Sept. 1743, Reynell Papers, 1742-43.

bracing compendium of useful information such as John Harris's *Lexicon Technicum* or Ephraim Chambers' giant *Cyclopedia*. Both James Pemberton and John Smith were familiar with Chambers; indeed, Smith actually spent a good part of his spare time in the month of January, 1746/7, reading consecutively its thousands of alphabetical entries on every conceivable subject from commerce to metaphysics and from meteorology to painting.[68] Intellectual curiosity could hardly go further!

HISTORY, BIOGRAPHY, AND TRAVEL

One of the "innocent Divertisements" which Robert Barclay recommended in his *Apology* as suitable "for Relaxation of the Mind" was "to hear or read History; to speak soberly of the present or past Transactions."[69] With this warrant Friends felt easy in devoting time to history and (by a slight extension of Barclay's meaning) the allied fields of biography and travel. No doubt such books supplied some of the qualities of drama and color and excitement lacking in the quiet life of Quaker Philadelphia.

The collections at Stenton and Fairhill, the two largest Quaker libraries, were well stocked with historical works. Most of the Greek and Roman historians, including many relatively minor ones such as Arrian, Dionysius of Halicarnassus, and Velleius Paterculus, were on Logan's shelves along with medieval writers like Procopius, the Venerable Bede, William of Malmesbury, Geoffrey of Monmouth, Saxo Grammaticus, and Froissart. There was a profusion of works on modern history, of which the following list is representative:

Francisco Guicciardini, *Historia d'Italia*
Juan de Mariana, *General History of Spain*
François Hotman, *Franco-Gallia*
J. Henley, *History of Sweden*
Sir William Temple, *Observations upon the United Provinces of the Netherlands*

---

68. Elias Bland to James Pemberton, 23 Nov. 1743, Pemberton Papers, III, 99; MS Diary of John Smith, III, *passim*.
69. Prop. XV, sec. ix, *Writings*, II, 540-41.

Geoffrey Keating, *General History of Ireland*
William Camden, *Britannia*
John Smith, *The Generall Historie of Virginia, New England and the Summer Isles*
Rapin de Thoyras, *The History of England*
Gilbert Burnet, *History of My Own Time*
Edward Hyde, Earl of Clarendon, *History of the Rebellion*
John Oldmixon, *The British Empire in America*[70]

In addition to these secular histories Logan possessed well over fifty titles in church history, ranging from the *Historia ecclesiastica* of Eusebius to John Spottiswoode's *History of the Church of Scotland*.

Isaac Norris's history collection was only slightly less imposing than Logan's, and contained many of the same works. A few additional titles may be mentioned, however, for their special interest. Norris's copies of Machiavelli's *History of Florence*, Father Paul Sarpi's *History of the Council of Trent*, and the *Histoire du Wiclifianisme* by Varillas are still in existence. In 1764 Norris ordered from London Frederick the Great's "Memoires of the House of Brandenburg And his (or Voltairs) Anti-Machiavel The best French Edition." He looked at Pierre Bayle's iconoclastic *Historical and Critical Dictionary* (which his more patient brother-in-law John Smith read in its entirety), but found it "tiresome"; nevertheless, he used it as a principal source of the biographical data about authors which he copied into many of his books. Interest in the great French colony to the northward, stimulated no doubt by his participation in the great conferences with the Iroquois, is reflected in his possession of the *History of New France* by the Jesuit Charlevoix. Writing to Thomas Hutchinson, the historian of Massachusetts Bay Colony in 1747, he discussed the curiously persistent legend of the "Welsh Indians," a mythical race of bearded white savages supposed to have mi-

---

70. After reading Oldmixon's book, a year after its publication, Logan commented to William Penn that with respect to Pennsylvania he was "very much misinformed."—Letter dated 14 June 1709, *Penn and Logan Correspondence*, II, 353. Similar dissatisfaction with Oldmixon's inaccuracies had led another scholarly colonist, Robert Beverley, to write his *History and Present State of Virginia*.

grated from Wales in the twelfth century; as pertinent sources he mentioned the following works: Peter Heylin's *Cosmographia*, James Howell's *Epistolae Ho-Elianae*, Captain John Smith's *Generall Historie of Virginia*, and David Powell's *History of Wales*. This display of antiquarian knowledge, while it may not indicate profundity, still suggests something more than a mere dilettante's interest in history.[71]

John Smith's acquaintance with history was less extensive than that of Norris or Logan, and was therefore, no doubt, more representative of normal Quaker reading habits. He possessed Tacitus in the standard eighteenth-century version of Thomas Gordon, under whose hands the Roman historian virtually became an apologist for English Whiggery. Bossuet's *Universal History*, and Pufendorf's *Introduction to the History of the Principal Kingdoms and States of Europe*, afforded a smattering of world history. His special interests seem to have centered in English history, for his diary shows him reading Camden's *Britannia*, Rapin's multivolumed *History of England* (borrowed from his business partner John Reynell), and Burnet's *History of My Own Time*. An interest in the American West would seem to be indicated by his reading the *History of Louisiana* by Le Page du Pratz.

A few scraps of information about the historical reading of other Quaker merchants can be added. Francis Rawle in his *Ways and Means* quoted from a "Hist. of Russia, by G. Fl" (no doubt the book of that title by Giles Fletcher, British ambassador to Russia).[72] Thomas Griffitts, whose thirst for learning seems to have exceeded his literary acquirements, had a copy of the compendious *History of All Religions in the World from the Creation Down to This Present Time* by William Turner, in which he inscribed this jingle:

> Thomas Griffiths his Book,
> God give him Grace theirin to loock,

---

71. Isaac Norris to C. and O. Hanbury, 2 April 1764, Norris Letter Book, 1756-66, 142; to Susanna Wright, 14 Sept. 1746, Norris Family Letters, II, 45; to Thomas Hutchinson, 24 March 1746/7, Norris Letter Book, 1734-53, 7.
72. *Ways and Means*, 34.

Not only loock but understand,
Larning is bater than Hous and land,
When Hous and land is gon and spent,
Larning is most excelent.[73]

Dr. Zachary's library included only two history books: Pufendorf's *Introduction* and Meredith Hanmer's *Auncient Ecclesiasticall Histories*, a translation of Eusebius, Socrates, and Evagrius.

Biographies of Pope Alexander VI and his son Cesare Borgia, of the Prince of Savoy and the Duke of Marlborough, of Richelieu and of Fénélon, of Tycho Brahe and Copernicus, of Henry VIII and William III, stood on James Logan's shelves along with Diogenes Laertius' *Lives of the Philosophers* and Anthony à Wood's *Athenae Oxonienses*, the latter a biographical dictionary of Oxford writers and bishops. Isaac Norris's curiosity about the Roman Catholic Church was reflected in his possession of a eulogy of St. Francis of Sales and a collection of "Lives of the Popes"; he also had a life of the Reformer Melancthon by Joachim Camerarius and Peter Barwick's Latin biography of his older brother John Barwick, Royalist Dean of St. Paul's.

Among the few books of William Rawle whose titles have survived was *The Lives of All the Lords Chancellors, Lords Keepers, and Lords Commissioners, of the Great Seal of England ... but More Especially of Those Two Great Opposites, Edward Earl of Clarendon and Bulstrode Lord Whitlock* written "by an impartial hand"; Rawle probably noted with special interest the comments on Bulstrode Whitelock, who had been an intimate of William Penn and a useful friend at court for the early Quakers. Some rather unusual biographies figured in John Smith's reading. In 1745 he perused Samuel Mather's life of his father Cotton Mather, who had never shown much sympathy for the Quakers; he commented drily in his diary that sons who write lives of their fathers usually present "the best part of them" and therefore can "scarcely be Impartial Historians." In 1763 a Quaker correspondent in London sent him Oliver Goldsmith's recently published life of Beau Nash, thinking that this "person

---

73. *Pa. Mag. of Hist.*, 24 (1900), 119.

so eminent among the Great Vulgar, and trifling part of Mankind may at least excite thy Curiosity." Smith did not record his thoughts upon this book, but his reaction to the biography of another worldling—the notorious courtesan Constantia Phillips—was quick and characteristic: "having upon an Extraordinary Character given of the Apology for Con. Phillips's Life sent for a sett of them, I having read them and Concluded the general tendency of them to Encourage and Apologize for Vice, I this Evening burnt them."[74]

The rich literature of travel was popular among all English readers in the eighteenth century and the Philadelphia Quakers proved no exception. It may not be too far-fetched to suggest that the appeal of English travel books to Friends arose from their way (to quote the words of an appreciative modern writer) "of clothing the very stuff and substance of romance in the homely, direct, and every day terms of plain matter of fact."[75] Tales of dramatic adventure in strange and distant places provided that vicarious experience which is for many people one of the main purposes of reading, and the travel books had the advantage in Quaker eyes of being true narratives, written in an unadorned style not too alien from Quaker literary standards as exemplified in their journals. At least one Quaker merchant of Philadelphia made a notable contribution to the literature of travel. Jonathan Dickinson's *God's Protecting Providence*, the story of his shipwreck and capture by man-eating Florida Indians, ran true to type in being a thrilling narrative couched in unimpassioned, matter-of-fact language. Its popularity among Friends (it ran through no less than eight editions, mostly by Quaker printers, before 1775) was certainly owing as much to its exciting dramatic qualities as to its edifying nature.[76]

In 1699 we find Isaac Norris I writing to England for the recently published *Voyage Round the World* of the piratical

74. MS Diary, Vol. II (entry for 24 Jan. 1745/6); Isaac Foster to John Smith, 21 April 1763, Smith MSS, VI, 54; MS Diary, Vol. VIII (entry for 5 Oct. 1749).
75. John Livingston Lowes, *The Road to Xanadu* (Boston and New York, 1927), 313.
76. See Andrews and Andrews, eds., *Jonathan Dickinson's Journal*, especially bibliographical notes in Appendix B.

William Dampier, a book just then enjoying great popular success in London. Half a century later, his son Isaac II was writing to Susanna Wright, a Quaker bluestocking on the banks of the Susquehanna, requesting the loan of "Wrights travells"—probably Edward Wright's *Observations Made in Travelling through France, Italy, &c. in the Years 1720, 1721, 1722;* and within a few years his younger brother Charles was dispatching to the same pioneer settlement of Wright's Ferry the two volumes of Frederick Norden's *Travels in Egypt and Nubia,* recently translated from the Danish.[77]

Almost every Quaker library contained several travel books: Lloyd Zachary had Hakluyt's *Voyages* and Sir Humphrey Gilbert's *Discovery of a New Passage to Cataia;* John Smith's diary contains many such entries as "Read in the Evening as usual in the new Collection of Voyages"; and James Logan owned, in addition to Hakluyt and Purchas, a considerable list of titles such as Gilbert Burnet's *Travels into Switzerland, Italy, and Germany* and William Bosman's *Description of the Coast of Guinea.* In 1732 when Logan prepared his memorial on "The State of the British Plantations in America," calling attention in good imperialist fashion to the value of the American colonies to Great Britain and the menace of French expansion in the interior, he made use of Hennepin's and Lahontan's accounts of their travels in North America and of Delisle's map of Louisiana and the Mississippi. Books like these, supplementing the oral reports of traveling Quaker ministers and ship-captains, broadened the horizons of the Quaker merchants and helped to prevent their developing too provincial an outlook upon the world.

BELLES-LETTRES

In a delightful essay on the reading habits of early Americans, Louis B. Wright has pointed out what should by this time be abundantly clear with respect to the Quakers: that such books

---

77. Isaac Norris I to Thomas Lloyd, 13 June 1699, Copies of Letters, Norris Papers, I, 61; Isaac Norris II to Susanna Wright, 22 July 1746, Norris Family Letters, II, 44; Charles Norris to James Wright, 29 Oct. 1759, Miscellaneous MSS, Norris Papers, 27.

as were read in the colonies were read, by and large, with a purpose, whether edificatory or practical.[78] There is no question that so far as Friends were concerned, the "weight" of the meeting was thrown in favor of such purposeful and useful reading and against the moral dangers and waste of precious time involved in reading imaginative works. The advice of Philadelphia Yearly Meeting in 1721, often repeated in later years, was "that no friends suffer Romances, playbooks and other vain and idle pamphlets, in their houses or families, which tend to corrupt the minds of youth. But instead thereof that they excite them to the reading of the holy scriptures and other good and religious books."[79] In actual practice, however, many of the wealthier and more sophisticated merchants undoubtedly came to agree with Friend John Smith (even to the point of not being unduly disturbed by the order of his nouns) that "to read for *delight and profit*" was a rational and permissible way to employ one's leisure time.[80] Although the meeting continued officially to frown upon works of the imagination, the undeniable fact is that a good many of its leading members came to develop a discriminating taste for belles-lettres, both ancient and modern.

In the persistent quarrel between the ancients and moderns, James Logan, for one, aligned himself on the side of the ancients. "I confess," he wrote to his friend Josiah Martin, "as I advance in years the Ancients Still gain upon me and the Greeks particularly, the more for this reason, that as they give us the only old Accounts of time (besides the S[acred] S[criptures]) I am pleased to observe what the Notions of Men were at the greatest distance from me." Homer, Hesiod, and Herodotus he named as Greek authors who especially pleased him for this reason; "besides," he added, "I have a particular fancy for that Language."[81] It was no idle boast when Logan wrote in his will that his library contained "above 100 vols. of authors in folio, all

---

78. "The Purposeful Reading of Our Colonial Ancestors," *ELH: A Journal of English Literary History*, 4 (1937), 85-111.
79. Epistle to Quarterly and Monthly Meetings, MS Minutes of Phila. YM, I, 242.
80. *Pennsylvania Chronicle*, 24 Oct. 1768 (my italics).
81. Letter dated 26 Oct. 1718, Logan Letter Book, 1717-31, 39.

in *Greek,* with mostly their versions" and "all the *Roman* Classicks without exception." It is doubtful whether any library in the colonies excelled Logan's in Greek literature. One can hardly name a Greek author of any importance whose works were not on his bookshelves at Stenton. He had a low opinion of the drama (he complained to his London bookseller about the price of a volume of Aeschylus, declaring that his works consist "but of Seven crabbed Tragedys of no great Use"[82]); nevertheless he owned the works of Sophocles, Aeschylus, Euripides, Aristophanes, and Menander.

All the great Roman classics stood in serried ranks on his shelves, but of them all his favorite appears to have been Cicero, on whose career as statesman, orator, philosopher, and man of letters he may have consciously or unconsciously modeled his own. He rendered the *De senectute* into English for his own amusement and later allowed Benjamin Franklin to publish his version, giving that Philadelphia "booster" an opportunity to claim for it the honor of being the first translation of a classic both made and printed in the New World and to hail it as "a happy omen that Philadelphia shall become the seat of the American Muses."[83] With his impressive background in classical literature, Logan was able to correspond on equal terms with savants like Johann Albertus Fabricius of Hamburg, one of the most erudite classicists of the age, and with Colonel Robert Hunter, the scholarly governor of New York and New Jersey.[84] None of the other Quakers could match Logan's classical learning, al-

---

82. Letter to C. Bateman, 15 Nov. 1721, Logan Letter Book, 1717-31, 225.
83. Preface to *M. T. Cicero's Cato Major; or, His Discourse of Old-Age* (Philadelphia, 1744). Logan was also the translator of the *Moral Distichs* of Dionysius Cato, published by Franklin in 1735.
84. In 1723 the Philadelphia scholar (who was also a fur merchant) sent Fabricius a buffalo skin as a token of gratitude for the many classical texts the German had furnished him.—Letter to Fabricius, 8 April 1723, Logan Letter Book, 1717-31, 311. Logan's extensive correspondence with Hunter has been summarized by Joseph E. Johnson, who observes that it embraced "all manner of literary and scientific topics, ranging from Gay's Pastorals to the astronomical tables of Kepler and Tycho, from musical strings to an Italian translation of Cato's *Disticha de moribus,* from the peace negotiations of 1711 to the motion of a pendulum, from the poems of Lucan to the medical researches of Dr. Colden."—A Statesman of Colonial Pennsylvania, 492-93.

though Isaac Norris possessed the major Latin authors and some of the Greeks in his library at Fairhill, and most of the other merchants, who had attended the Latin school, could boast of a bowing acquaintance with Virgil, Horace, Ovid, and Cicero, thus meeting one of the primary requirements in the contemporary definition of the gentleman.

As for modern literature in the libraries of the Quakers, it was chiefly represented, as one would expect, by English works. Nevertheless, a scattering of French, Spanish, and Italian books and a few Latin works by Humanist writers of the Renaissance, suggests that the more literate Friends were not unaware of the literary currents that were flowing on the continent of Europe. Since James Logan's own tastes and sympathies were similar to those of the great Humanists, it is not odd that his library contained the *Colloquies* and the *Praise of Folly* of Erasmus (the latter with Holbein's illustrations), the *Colloquies* of Ludovico Vives, and the *Epistolae obscurorum virorum* attributed to Ulrich von Hutten. Italian literature was well represented at Stenton by the *Divina commedia* of Dante, the *Gerusalemme liberata* of Tasso, the *Emblemata* of the jurist and moralist Alciati, the *Epitalame e la sampogna* of the *concettist* Marini, and the glittering and artifical pastoral drama *Il pastor fido* of Guarini. The dramatic works of Racine, Corneille, and Molière were all on Logan's shelves, as were the essays of Montaigne, the works of Boileau, and the *Lettres philosophiques*, containing Voltaire's famous remarks on the Quakers. *Don Quixote* and (most surprising for a Quaker library) the licentious *Heptameron* of Marguerite of Navarre were the chief specimens of Spanish literature in Logan's collection.

Many of the eighteenth-century Friends shared their period's irrecoverable enthusiasm for the *Turkish Spy* of Giovanni Paolo Marana and its long-winded imitators, purporting to be critical observations upon Occidental manners and institutions by Oriental visitors. Logan, Isaac Norris I, and John Smith are all known to have possessed the eight volumes of the *Turkish Spy* and Smith also read the *Jewish Spy* and the *Chinese Letters* of the Marquis d'Argens. *The Travels of Cyrus*, a palpable imitation of the universally popular *Télémaque*, written by the Chevalier de Ramsay, Fénélon's friend and biographer, was another Quaker favorite: James Logan bought the French version for his daughters, and both John Smith and John Reynell had copies of the English translation.[85] In 1722 Isaac Norris I ordered a copy of the *Arabian Nights' Entertainment*, which had only recently become known to European readers; he soon countermanded his order (for what reason does not appear), but this famous collection of tales later turns up in the inventory of Lloyd Zachary's books.[86] Dr. Zachary also owned a copy of *Zaïde: Histoire Espagnole*, a romance of intrigue by Mme. de la Fayette.

Benjamin Franklin, who as a bookseller knew the literary tastes and habits of the Philadelphians, testified to the avidity and impartiality with which they read English writers: "We are a kind of Posterity in respect to them," he submitted, and went on to explain that Americans were at too great a distance to be affected by the factions and controversies which beset English letters and consequently read everything that came their way.[87] This generalization was as true of his Quaker customers as of any other group in colonial Philadelphia.

John Smith, in particular, read widely in English literature, both that of his own day and that of earlier periods. The oldest English work with which he is known to have been acquainted is the *Mirror for Magistrates;* in his "Atticus Papers" he cites one of the tragedies comprising this collection of stories of wickedness and misfortune in high places. We know that he read Shakespeare, for he tells us so in his diary. In 1746 and 1747, while courting Hannah Logan, he was reading *Paradise Lost;* and the words of Eve in Book IV, beginning "With thee conversing I forget all time" so struck his fancy ("being Apropos to my own Circumstances") that he committed them to memory,

85. James Logan to Josiah Martin, 5 Nov. 1733, Logan Letter Books, IV, 347; invoice dated 7 Feb. 1737/8, Coates-Reynell Papers, 1736-37.

86. Isaac Norris I to Isaac Norris II, 12 June 1722, Norris Letter Book, 1716-30, 312.

87. Franklin to William Strahan, 12 Feb. 1744, *Writings*, II, 242.

and later wrote them out in his diary, with only a few trifling errors. The only other seventeenth-century poets whom he is known to have read are Edmund Waller and John Oldham. While visiting the great library of his father-in-law at Stenton, he read Owen Felltham's *Resolves, Divine, Moral, and Political;* and the *Miscellanies* of the urbane Marquis of Halifax was among his books when he died.

It was in the literature of his own century, however, that Smith was most at home. He knew the writings of the great Augustans—Pope, Swift, Addison, and Steele—and had a surprisingly wide acquaintance among the major and minor writers of the mid-eighteenth century. He was conversant enough with Addison's popular *Cato* to quote, *à propos* of his recent marriage:

> When Love's well tim'd, 'tis not a fault to Love,
> The strong, the brave, the virtuous, and the wise,
> Sink in the soft Captivity together.

In view of the traditional Quaker attitude towards the theater, John Smith's approval of this and other plays calls for comment. The Quaker objection was directed not so much to the plays themselves (so long as they were not salacious or irreverent) as to the public performance of them. Smith's attitude towards theatrical productions is well illustrated by an incident which took place on the day in 1749 when the first professional American company opened in Philadelphia with a performance of *Cato*. Smith chanced to be at a tavern and the daughter of the tavern-keeper "being one of the Company who were going to hear the Tragedy of Cato Acted it occasioned some Conversation" in the course of which he felt called upon to express "sorrow that any thing of the kind was Encouraged &Ca."[88] Apparently little danger was to be apprehended from the mere reading of plays, however, for Smith's diary reveals that he scanned a good many. He appears to have enjoyed, for example, the comedies of Richard Steele—*The Conscious Lovers, The*

---

88. Smith to James Pemberton, 28 April 1749, Pemberton Papers, V, 67; MS Diary, Vol. VIII (entry for 22 Aug. 1749).

Funeral, and *The Lying Lover*—plays which represented an attempt to carry out the stage reforms of Jeremy Collier, and contained, in the words of Parson Adams, "some things almost solemn enough for a funeral."

Smith's acquaintance with contemporary British literature was extraordinarily wide. He was familiar not only with the more important figures like Thomson and Young, but also with many lesser men—poets and prose writers who have disappeared from the view of all but specialists. It is obvious that he took pains to keep abreast of the most recent developments in the English literary scene. His library included, in addition to Thomson's *Seasons* and Young's universally admired *Night Thoughts,* a minor book of Young's called *The Centaur Not Fabulous,* Thomson's neoclassical tragedy of *Sophonisba,* a curious didactic poem, *The Art of Preserving Health,* by the contemporary John Armstrong, and the works of John Banks, Henry Needler, Richard Glover (author of a turgid epic called *Leonidas*), and Elizabeth Rowe, a prolific writer of sacred and profane verse whom Smith called "a beautiful Author." Of the contemporary prose writers whom he read one may mention Charles Gildon, whose collection of essays entitled *The Post-Man Robb'd of His Mail; or, The Packet Broke Open* had been published under the pseudonym of Sir Roger de Whimsey; William Melmoth the younger, author of *Fitzosborne's Letters;* and Fulke Greville who, with his wife, published in 1756 a volume of *Maxims, Characters, and Reflections.*

On the question of novel-reading John Smith's attitude was surprisingly liberal. As a Quaker he was naturally concerned with the relation of reading to morality and he felt that many novels had a tendency to corrupt the minds of the young. He made, however, some significant exceptions: "Those of *Fenelon, Fielding,* and *Richardson,*" he admitted, "ought unquestionably to be considered as excellent in their kind, and cannot be read to any bad purpose, unless there are minds, like some sorts of spiders, which are supposed to increase their venom by sucking the sweetest flowers."[89] Acting upon this enlightened view, he endeavored to keep himself *au courant* with the latest novels published in the mother country. In 1748 he was reading Fielding's *Joseph Andrews,* and in the next year, *Tom Jones.* The latter book indeed he read only a few months after its publication, borrowing it from his cousin James Pemberton, who had just brought it from England; he sat up late reading it on the day it came into his hands, and subsequently acquired a copy of his own.[90] He secured Richardson's *Sir Charles Grandison* in 1760 and tried without success to locate a copy of *Clarissa* in the Philadelphia bookstores.[91] He often read "improving" stories like *The Adventures of David Simple* by Sarah Fielding, sister of the author of *Tom Jones,* and Dr. Samuel Johnson's *Rasselas,* but he also devoured Smollett's roistering *Peregrine Pickle* and no doubt followed with interest the correspondence which his younger brother Richard carried on with Smollett himself.[92]

None of Smith's contemporaries among the Quaker merchants displayed such a consuming passion for English literature, but there were few who were not acquainted with at least some of the classics and current "best sellers." Even the most consistent Friends often found edification in contemporary literature. In 1730, for example, Thomas Chalkley quoted Addison's "How are thy servants blest, O Lord!" which he had heard from the lips of Robert Jordan, another Quaker minister; he wrote the lines out in his journal, he records, "as well in Memory of that great Author, as also that they answered my State and Condition in my watery Travels, and the Extreams of Heat and Cold, and some poisonous Airs, I have often breathed in."[93] As a young man William Savery, another "public Friend," read Young's *Night Thoughts* and "by the assistance of the gracious

89. *Pennsylvania Chronicle,* 24 Oct. 1768.
90. MS Diary, Vol. VIII (entries for 26, 27 Sept. 1749).
91. James Logan, Jr. to John Smith, 5 Dec. 1760, Smith MSS, V, 137.
92. See Edward S. Noyes, ed., *The Letters of Tobias Smollett* (Cambridge, Mass., 1926), 80-82.
93. *Journal,* in *Works,* 237-38.

Helper" found that it spoke to his condition. "Friends' writings and even the holy scriptures," he confessed, "were irksome to me; but the energy, depth, and solemn subject of that book, roused me to more serious thought than ever before, and here I date my gradual progress from the brink of that precipice, which must otherwise inevitably have proved my ruin."[94]

The merchants turned to literature for delight as well as profit. Even from the fragmentary evidence at our command, it can be confidently said that the major English poets were known and appreciated for their intrinsic qualities. The first donation of books by an American to the Library Company of Philadelphia, for example, was William Rawle's gift in 1733 of a set of six volumes of Edmund Spenser.[95] One of the earliest copies of *Paradise Lost* in the colonies outside New England was that imported by Isaac Norris I in 1722.[96] This same Friend had imported a copy of Pope's *Essay on Criticism* in 1715, less than four years after publication.[97] His son Isaac Norris II was a subscriber in 1758 to the magnificent Baskerville edition of Milton.[98] Like his father, he was apparently a reader of Pope, for he owned Pope's translation of Homer and his *Letters*, first published in 1735.[99] Charles Norris, younger brother of Isaac II, was also a reader of the best contemporary literature; a list of books which he lent to Susanna Wright, the literary Quakeress of Wright's Ferry, included Young's *Night Thoughts*, Thomson's *Poems*, Dr. Benjamin Hoadly's comedy *The Suspicious*

---

94. *Friends Miscellany*, I, 146.
95. Abbott, *Short History*, 4.
96. Isaac Norris I to Isaac Norris II, 12 June 1722, Norris Letter Book, 1716-30, 312. The earliest known colonial copy of *Paradise Lost* outside of New England, according to Professor Leon Howard, was in the library of Godfrey Pole in Virginia in 1716.—"Early American Copies of Milton," Huntington Library, *Bulletin*, No. 7 (1935), 172. We have already seen, however, that William Penn ordered Milton's works in 1699 (above, p. 145); we do not, of course, know that they reached him in America.
97. Isaac Norris I to John Askew, 17 Aug. 1715, Norris Letter Book, 1709-16, 516. In the same letter he ordered "all Popes poems."
98. See Benjamin Franklin to Isaac Norris II, 16 Sept. 1758, *Writings*, III, 454; Isaac Norris II to Franklin, 23 Nov. 1758, Norris Letter Book, 1756-66, 95.
99. Isaac Norris II to Susanna Wright, 22 July 1746, Norris Family Letters, II, 44. Pope's *Homer* was one of the books which Elizabeth Sandwith (later the wife of Henry Drinker) read in her youth.—*Extracts from the Journal of Elizabeth Drinker*, 19 (entry for 4 Dec. 1759).

Husband, Pope's *Letters*, the *Essay on Man*, and the *Plan of Pope's Gardens*.[100]

Relatively little can be learned about the literary taste of the Pemberton family, although one can assume that it was more conservative than that of the Norrises or John Smith. James Pemberton, visiting London in 1748, gave some indication of his attitude towards imaginative literature when he observed that "tho' every shop is fill'd with books yet the generall taste of the Age now runs so much in romances and idle tales that [I] have not mett with any to please me." It is perhaps germane to point out that the estate of Israel Pemberton I, valued at over nine thousand pounds, contained a library appraised at only five pounds.[101]

James Logan's library, although not so rich in English literature as in the classics, did nevertheless contain works of Chaucer, Spenser, Shakespeare, Crashaw, Abraham Cowley (William Penn's favorite poet), Sir John Denham, John Gay, Sir Richard Blackmore, and Katherine Philips ("the matchless Orinda"). Upon reading Pope's *Essay on Man*, Logan was moved to set down his reactions in heroic couplets, commencing in eulogistic vein:

> Illustrious Pope! how Truth triumphant Shines
> In the Strong Periods of thy labour'd Lines!

but proceeding presently to sharp censure:

> ... thy Muse might in low rural layes
> Have but aspir'd to Some mean Songster's praise,
> Had not the feeble Cyon of thy Wit
> On th' energetic Stock of Malice hit.

---

100. Undated paper in Norris Papers, Miscellaneous, 38. A letter to Susanna Wright, dated 30 April 1761, mentions his loss of several volumes of Swift's works, and indicates that he has just acquired six volumes of Robert Dodsley's *Collection of Poems by Several Hands*, a popular anthology containing contributions by nearly every fashionable versifier of the day.—*Ibid.*, 31. His interest in Pope's highly formalized gardens at Twickenham may have been related to his preoccupation with the gardens at his own "plantation" outside Philadelphia.

101. James Pemberton to Israel Pemberton, Jr., 10 March 1748/9, Pemberton Papers, V, 43; inventory of Israel Pemberton's estate, Philadelphia Registry of Wills.

His conclusion was as caustic as Pope himself:

> ... and may you thus combin'd
> Patron and Poet, the just treatment find
> Due to the Foes of Freedom and Mankind.[102]

Of the classics of English prose Logan's library contained Sir Philip Sidney's *Arcadia*, Robert Burton's *Anatomy of Melancholy*, Sir Thomas Browne's *Pseudoxia Epidemica*, and Jonathan Swift's *Tale of a Tub*. As for his attitude towards the drama, one may note for what it is worth that William Prynne's *Histriomastix* was counterbalanced on his shelves by *The Stage Acquitted*, an anonymous reply to Jeremy Collier's strictures upon the theater; and the presence in his library of Dryden and Lee's *Oedipus*, Thomas Southerne's *The Spartan*, John Banks' *Unhappy Favorite*, Ambrose Philips' *Distressed Mother*, and Nahum Tate's adaptation of *King Lear* suggests that, like his son-in-law John Smith, he was not unwilling to read plays in his study, however thoroughly he may have agreed with his fellow Quakers that playhouses were "synagogues of Satan."

Most Quaker merchants kept up with the leading literary periodicals. James Logan on a visit to England in 1710 supplied his friend Isaac Norris I with copies of Addison and Steele's *Tatler* as they came off the press, and before he returned to Philadelphia he was able to send the first number of its successor, the *Spectator*. Norris remarked that his initial impulse on seeing the *Tatler* papers would have been to brush them aside as "Idle and Useless," had not Logan taught him "to find Instruction as well as delight" in them.[103] The omnivorous John Smith read, in addition to the *Tatler*, the *Spectator*, and the *Guardian*, the popular *Gentleman's Magazine*, its imitator and rival the *London Magazine*, the *Universal Magazine* with its antiquarian lore and popular science, Samuel Johnson's *Rambler* and *Idler*,

---

102. Gulielma M. Howland Collection, Haverford College Library.
103. Isaac Norris I to Logan, 29 Nov. 1711, Norris Letter Book, 1709-16, 225; 13 Oct. 1711, *ibid.*, 295.

and the *American Magazine,* published in Philadelphia by William Bradford.[104]

Other merchants were not such voracious consumers of periodical literature as John Smith, but there is evidence that one or another of the current English magazines was regularly received and read by Lloyd Zachary, John Reynell, Israel Pemberton, Jr., Thomas Wharton, James Logan, William Logan, Isaac Norris II, and Charles Norris. The subscription list for William Bradford's *American Magazine* included such Quaker names as those of Abel James, William Griffitts, Joseph Richardson, Benjamin Mifflin, and Joseph Wharton.[105] Since any literary periodical depends for its success upon the existence of an audience able both to buy and to appreciate it, the *American Magazine,* which was unquestionably the most brilliant and original literary magazine in colonial America, no doubt owed something to this group of wealthy and literate Quaker merchants whose tastes had been formed by the best of the British magazines.

In these periodicals the Quaker merchants found not only much of the best writing of the day, but also the latest accounts of significant events and trends of thought in the political, literary, scientific, and religious worlds. The busy merchant who read only the *Gentleman's Magazine,* for example, could ransack as he would an abundant "magazine" or storehouse of science, genealogy, biography, antiquities, topography, laws, criticism, poetry, parliamentary proceedings, and news summaries.[106] Had the merchants read only these magazines, they

---

104. After Smith retired to Burlington, Anthony Benezet acted as his agent in purchasing back numbers of magazines from Philadelphia and New York booksellers to complete his files. See Benezet's letters in Brookes, *Benezet,* 235-36, 256-62. William Logan in 1750 proposed to Smith a joint project of collecting complete files of the Philadelphia newspapers "from the Beginning of their Coming out."—Letter dated 27 April 1750, Smith MSS, V, 55. Smith's files of the *Pennsylvania Gazette* and the *American Weekly Mercury* are now in the American Antiquarian Society, Worcester, Massachusetts, having been purchased by a later and more famous collector of early American newspapers, Isaiah Thomas.

105. Bradford's subscription list is in the Bradford Papers, Hist. Soc. Pa.

106. See Walter Graham, *English Literary Periodicals* (New York, 1930), 145-60,

could have laid claim to being well-read in the general literature of their time. As we have seen, however, their interests carried most of them far beyond this level of reading, and gave a few of them title to be mentioned in the same breath with Virginia gentlemen, Charleston planter-aristocrats, or Boston merchants and lawyers among the best-read and most cultivated men in colonial America.

• *Chapter Nine* •

VOTARIES OF SCIENCE

L OVE of science was, in Thomas Paine's phrase, the "reign-
ing character" of the colonial Philadelphia mind, achieving its most complete embodiment in Benjamin Franklin.[1]
But obviously the phenomenon of a Franklin could not
have occurred in a vacuum. Recent scholarship has wisely emphasized the almost universal diffusion of the scientific spirit
among Philadelphians. Relatively little attention has been given,
however, to the role of the Friends, particularly in promoting
such undertakings as the American Philosophical Society and the
Pennsylvania Hospital.

QUAKERISM AND THE "NEW PHILOSOPHY"

The rise of experimental science in England was contem-
poraneous with the ascendency of the Puritan religious ethos,
of which Quakerism, as we have seen, was a variant expression.[2]
This fact was once regarded merely as an interesting coincidence
without much significance. More recently, however, it has come
to be recognized that there was a positive connection between
religion and the rise of the new science.[3] An effort will be made

1. Bridenbaugh, *Rebels and Gentlemen*, 357-58.
2. See above, p. 52.
3. G. N. Clark enumerates five channels by which science in the age of Newton
was activated from the outside: (1) economic life (e.g., mining, transport, etc.),
(2) war, (3) medicine, (4) the arts, and (5) religion.—*Science and Social
Welfare in the Age of Newton* (Oxford, 1937), 61-91. It may be pointed out

in the following pages to show that there was an intimate connection between the religious ethos characteristic of Quakerism and the demonstrable aptitude of Friends for scientific pursuits.[4] As in the earlier discussion of the relationship between religion and economic activity, the contention here is not that scientific activity was directly the product of Quakerism in the sense of being the second term in a cause-and-effect relationship, but rather, to quote a modern sociologist, "that the religious ethic, considered as a social force, so consecrated science as to make it a highly respected and laudable focus of attention."[5] The most significant area of agreement between the Quaker-Puritan position and that of modern science as it emerged at the end of the seventeenth century lay, as I shall attempt to show, in their combination of empiricism and rationalism.

Some of the generalizations employed in the earlier discussion of Quakerism and capitalism apply with equal force here. Practical, methodical activity in the world was considered an evidence that one was indeed living "in the Light"; the expenditure of physical energy and the handling of material objects was identified with industry, whereas abstract speculation and contemplation, when not directed towards purely religious ends, was equated with idleness. This distinction coincided in a remarkable way with that which was coming to be recognized between the new experimental science and the older deductive scholastic science. Experimentation was "the scientific expression of the practical, active and methodical bents" of the Puritan, and equally, as the sociologist would undoubtedly agree, of the

here that the second and fourth of these factors can be eliminated from a discussion of the relationship between Quakerism and the new science, and that the first and third must be accentuated. Attention will be focused here upon the fifth factor as being, in the author's opinion, the most fundamental, but this should not be taken to imply that it was the only factor operative.

4. E Hanbury Hankin has noted the striking fact that the number of Quaker Fellows of the Royal Society is many times larger in proportion to the size of the Society of Friends than the number of non-Quaker Fellows in proportion to the non-Quaker population of Great Britain. Quaker Fellows include such distinguished scientists as John Dalton, Lord Lister, Sylvanus Thompson, and Arthur S. Eddington.—*Common Sense and Its Cultivation* (London, 1928), 261-67.

5. Merton, *Science, Technology, and Society*, 465.

Quaker.[6] In this aspect of the Puritan-Quaker ethos the new science found one of its major sanctions.

The connection can be observed most clearly in education. Quaker schools established in the last third of the seventeenth century in England and the colonies were organized around a new educational theory introduced by the Puritans to replace the traditional classical curriculum. The new realistic concept, embodied in the curricula of the dissenting academies, emphasized the empirical and the utilitarian at the expense of the dialectical and the humanistic.[7] Things rather than words were the stuff of education, and Baconian science with its experimental, antischolastic basis naturally found a place in the reformed curriculum. There is no positive evidence that Quaker leaders or schoolmasters were influenced by the treatises of John Durie, Sir William Petty, Samuel Hartlib, and the other reformers, but there is abundant evidence that the Quaker theory of education was in essential harmony with their insistence upon "the importance of dealing sensibly with concrete and material things, of actually expending energy in the pursuit of truth . . . in contrast to the non-physical activity . . . of those who sought truth in books and the mind."[8]

William Penn was a friend of both Durie and Petty, and the similarity of his notions to theirs is too obvious to be overlooked.[9] Like them, he had no patience with "the vain Quiddities, idle and gross Terms, and most sophistical Ways of Syllogizing, with the rest of that useless and injurious Pedantry (to Mankind, brought into the Christian Religion by Popish School-Men, and so eminently in Vogue in *Oxford* and *Cambridge* . . .)." And like them, he would emphasize *realia:*

---

6. *Ibid.,* 452.
7. Irene Parker, *Dissenting Academies in England* (Cambridge, England, 1914).
8. Richard F. Jones, *Ancients and Moderns,* 112-13.
9. Penn met Sir William Petty before 1669 (Marquis of Lansdowne, ed., *Petty Papers,* [Oxford, 1928]), II, 95 and Durie in 1677 (Hull, *William Penn and the Dutch Quaker Migration,* 129). Penn described Durie as "a man . . . who had learned in good Measure to forget his Learning, School-Divinity, and Priest's Craft, and for his approach towards an inward Principle is reproachfully saluted by some with the honest Title of *Quaker.*" The church historian Mosheim likewise says of him: "*Quakerus ille fuit ante Quakeros.*"—Hull, 130.

The first Thing obvious to Children is what is *sensible;* and that we make no Part of their Rudiments.

We press their Memory too soon, and puzzle, strain and load them with Words and Rules: to know *Grammar* and *Rhetorick*, and a strange Tongue or two, that it is ten to one may never be useful to them; leaving their natural Genius to *Mechanical* and *Physical* or natural Knowledge uncultivated and neglected: which would be of exceeding Use and Pleasure to them through the whole Course of their Life.

To be sure, Languages are not to be despised or neglected. But Things are still to be preferred.[10]

Insistence on the priority of things over words was such a cardinal principle in Quaker thinking that Ralph Waldo Emerson could later describe George Fox succinctly and accurately as "a realist even putting a thing for a name."[11] William Penn described Fox as "a divine and a naturalist," adding that although he was "ignorant of useless and sophistical science," he had in him "the foundation of useful and commendable knowledge"; he confessed that he had often been surprised at Fox's "questions and answers in natural things."[12] That Fox's philosophy of education included the utilitarian and scientific emphases is clear from his proposals for the first Quaker schools at Waltham Abbey and Shacklewell, where the object, in his words, was to provide instruction "in whatsoever things were civil and useful in the creation."[13] The scientific impulse was closely allied with a humanitarian concern for the development of medicine; this motive is clearly apparent in Fox's later proposal for a school which would teach, besides languages, "the nature of herbs, roots, plants, and trees."[14] No doubt this projected school was the same one to which the Quaker botanist Thomas Lawson referred in 1690:

---

10. *A Serious Apology for the Principles and Practices of the People Call'd Quakers* (1671) in *Works*, II, 56; *Some Fruits of Solitude, ibid.,* I, 820.
11. Notes for a lecture on Fox, in James Elliot Cabot, *A Memoir of Ralph Waldo Emerson* (Boston, 1887), II, 713.
12. Preface to Fox's *Journal*, I, 1.
13. *Journal*, II, 89.
14. Minute of Six Weeks Meeting (11 May 1675), quoted in Braithwaite, *Second Period*, 528.

Now some years ago, George ffox, William Pen, and others, were concerned to purchase a piece of land near London for the use of a Garden Schoolhouse and a dwelling-house for the Master, in which garden, one or two or more of every sorte of our English plants were to be planted, as also many outlandish plants. My purpose was to write a book on these in Latin, so as a boy had the description of these in book-lessons, and their vertues, he might see these growing in the garden, or plantation, to gain the knowledge of them: but persecutions and troubles obstructed the prosecution hereof, which the Master of Christ's College in Cambridge hearing of, told me was a noble and honorable undertaking, and would fill the Nation with philosophers.[15]

If the theory of education underlying this scheme has a contemporary ring, it is because its assumptions are essentially the same as those of progressive education—the assumptions, namely, of the modern philosophy of science.

The arguments by which Puritans and Quakers vindicated the place of science in education were also used to recommend scientific study and experimentation as a form of recreation.[16] The high standard of personal morality which the Quakers set for themselves kept them away from the playhouse, the ball-room, the gambling den, and the bull pit. Scientific study as an avocation had the virtues of being useful, of exercising the mental powers, and, by revealing God's plan in the natural world, of promoting a reverent frame of mind. Hence Robert Barclay could recommend as "innocent Divertisements, which may sufficiently serve for Relaxation of the Mind. . . *To follow after Gardening, To use Geometrical and Mathematical Experiments,*

---

15. Letter to Sir John Rodes, 18 Jan. 1690, Locker-Lampson, ed., *A Quaker Post-Bag*, 21. This appears to have been a persistent concern of George Fox, for he bequeathed to the Friends' meeting in Philadelphia a plot of land to be used for a similar purpose: a schoolhouse and botanical garden, the latter to be planted "with all sorts of physical plants, for lads and lasses, to learn simples there, and the uses to convert them to,—distilled waters, oils, ointments, &c."—Thomas Lower to D. Lloyd, 13 Feb. 1716, Maria Webb, *The Fells of Swarthmoor Hall* (London, 1865), 367.
16. This point has been made by Dorothy Stimson, "Puritanism and the New Philosophy in Seventeenth-Century England," Institute of the History of Medicine, *Bulletin*, 3 (1935), 321-34.

and such other things of this Nature."[17] And William Penn, who submitted that "the *Best Recreation* is to do Good," allowed that to "*Study moderately such Commendable and Profitable Arts*, as Navigation, Arithmetick, Geometry, Husbandry, Gardening, Handicraft, Medicine, &c" was a form of recreation consistent with Truth.[18]

If the empirical bent of the Quakers tended to render the method of the "New Philosophy" congenial to them, a certain rational character inherent in the mental habits of at least some of them provided a frame of mind conducive to its prosecution. To speak of rationalism in connection with a religious group usually regarded as the most mystical of Protestant sects may seem paradoxical. It can be granted that there was little of the rational about George Fox and certain others of the first generation of Friends, but with Robert Barclay and William Penn of the second generation we come into a different intellectual atmosphere, one in which the eighteenth-century Philadelphia Friends breathed most easily. For Barclay man's natural reason was a sort of secondary light, subordinate to the divine light and incapable by itself of leading to a saving knowledge of God. Nevertheless, he hastened to add, "we do not hereby affirm, as if Man had received his Reason to no purpose, or to be of no service unto him, in no wise: We look upon Reason as fit to order and rule Man in things Natural."[19] In the realm of nature, therefore, which was the realm with which science concerned itself, reason was a trustworthy instrument and man was free to use it.

In William Penn's writings reason was given even broader scope. Ordinarily Penn maintained a clear distinction between the Inner Light and natural reason, but occasionally the lines blurred. In *The Sandy Foundation Shaken* and *The Christian Quaker*, Penn appealed frankly to right reason to establish his doctrine of the Inner Light, and in another controversial work he declared flatly that "God is the Fountain as well of Reason

17. *Apology*, Prop. XV, sec. ix, in *Writings*, II, 540-41.
18. *No Cross No Crown*, in *Works*, I, 355.
19. *Apology*, Props. V and VI, sec. xvi, in *Writings*, II, 144-45.

as Light: And we assert our Principle not to be without Reason, but most Reasonable." What could be more typical of the spirit of free rational inquiry associated with the "New Philosophy" than Penn's words written against ecclesiastical authoritarianism: "For a Man can never be certain of that, about which he has not the Liberty of Examining, Understanding or Judging"? [20]

Since man is endowed by God with natural reason in addition to the Inner Light, it behooves him to utilize it to God's glory and his own benefit: "It were happy if we studied Nature more in natural Things, and acted according to Nature: whose Rules are *few, plain, and most reasonable.*" By thus applying reason to the study of nature, man will the better understand "the *Heavens, Earth* and *Waters,* with their respective, various and numerous Inhabitants: Their Productions, Natures, Seasons, Sympathies and Antipathies: their Use, Benefit and Pleasure." Moreover (and in this conviction the religious ethos provided the most potent sanction for the furtherance of natural science), "an *Eternal Wisdom, Power, Majesty* and *Goodness* [becomes] very *conspicuous* to us: through those sensible and passing Forms: The World wearing the Mark of it's Maker, whose Stamp is every where visible, and the Characters very legible to the Children of Wisdom." [21] Although seldom articulated as such, the doctrine of Providence as the undergirding and sustaining presence of God in nature was one of the premises of Quaker thought, providing a basis for what in other religious traditions was to be called "natural theology." [22] If, as Whitehead has said, a living science requires "a widespread instinctive conviction in the existence of an *Order of Things,* and in particular, of an

20. *Wisdom Justified of Her Children* (1673), in *Works,* II, 473; *An Address to Protestants* (1679), *ibid.,* I, 778. This was a persistent theme with Penn. Compare this maxim from *Some Fruits of Solitude:* "Truth never lost Ground by Inquiry, because she is *most of all Reasonable.*"—*Ibid.,* I, 852.

21. *Some Fruits of Solitude, ibid.,* I, 820-21.

22. See, for example, the twenty-first maxim in Part I of *Some Fruits of Solitude,* where, in the manner that was to become classic with Paley, Penn cites examples of the cunning contrivance of the human body as so many reasons why man should "Admire and Adore his good and great God."—*Works,* I, 821-22. Compare the Puritan view of Providence as described by Miller, *New England Mind,* 208 ff., 225 ff.

Order of Nature," one can see how some of the basic assumptions of Quakerism promoted a habit of thinking congenial to the reception of the new science.[23]

In view of the community of assumptions and the parallelism of method in the Quaker ethos and the "New Philosophy," it is hardly surprising to discover that on 2 November 1681, less than a year before he set sail for Pennsylvania, William Penn was "propounded Candidate" of the Royal Society of London, the principal nursery of the new science.[24] Penn's activity in connection with the Royal Society appears to have been slight, although he is known to have been personally acquainted with a number of the more prominent Fellows, including Sir William Petty, Robert Hooke, Robert Wood, Edward Bernard, John Aubrey, Dr. John Wallis, Sir Isaac Newton, and John Locke.[25]

If any further evidence is needed of the scientific temper of Penn's mind, it is abundantly provided in a letter which he wrote to John Aubrey from Philadelphia, a few months after his arrival there:

I value my selfe much upon the good opinion of those Ingeneous Gentlemen I know of the Royall Society, and their kind wishes for me and my poor Provinces: all I can say is that I and it are votarys to the prosperity of their harmless and usefull inquierys. It is even one step to Heaven to returne to nature and Though

---

23. Alfred N. Whitehead, *Science and the Modern World* (New York, 1925), 5.
24. Henry J. Cadbury, "Penn, Collinson, and the Royal Society," Friends Hist. Assoc., *Bull.,* 36 (1947), 19-24. Penn's actual election as a Fellow took place on 9 Nov. 1681, at which time he presented to the Society a map of Pennsylvania.
25. Thomas Clarkson, *Memoirs of the Private and Public Life of William Penn,* I, 228, II, 313*n*; Hull, *William Penn,* 246, 276. Penn's familiarity with the Royal Society's procedures in its meetings at Gresham College is interestingly reflected in the manuscript versions of his first Frame of Government for Pennsylvania, where he specifies that, with a few exceptions, all questions shall be decided by the ballot-box "as it is used at Gresham College."—Penn MSS, VIII, 91, 101, Hist. Soc. Pa. On the Royal Society's use of the ballot, see Thomas Sprat, *History of the Royal Society* (London, 1702), 93. Since the use of the ballot was relatively unusual in the seventeenth century, students of electoral procedures have exercised their ingenuity to discover the source of Penn's knowledge of it, suggesting, for example, that he might have acquired it during a sojourn in Emden in Friesland or from the pages of Harrington's *Oceana.*—Charles Seymour and Donald P. Frary, *How the World Votes* (Springfield, Mass., 1918), I, 218. In all this discussion Penn's familiarity with the procedure at Gresham College seems to have gone unnoticed.

I love that proportion should be observed in all things, yett a naturall Knowledge, or the Science of things from sence and a carefull observation and argumentation thereon, reinstates men, and gives them some possession of themselves againe: a thing they have long wanted by an ill Tradition, too closely followed and the foolish Credulity so Incident to men.

Penn then put his finger upon the basic identity between the method of the new science and the appeal to immediate experience which was the core of Quakerism. Making a frank avowal of his loyalty to the experimental method in both the natural and the supernatural spheres he wrote: "I am a Greshamist throughout; I Love Inquiry, not for inquiry's sake, but care not to trust my share in either world to other men's Judgments, at Least without having a finger in the Pye for myself." [26]

QUAKER VIRTUOSI

The intellectual climate of Quaker Philadelphia was never hostile to the spirit of scientific inquiry. One index of the prevailing temper of mind lies in the fact that early Pennsylvania had no law against witchcraft. Furthermore, in the colony's only witchcraft trial—which took place almost ten years before the more famous trials in Salem—the accused woman was found guilty merely of "having the Comon Fame of a Witch," and the case was promptly dismissed.[27] Further evidence of the degree to which the rational and scientific spirit permeated the thought of even the less intellectual Friends appears in the reaction of Hannah Pemberton, wife of James Pemberton, to news of the disastrous earthquake in Lisbon in 1755. Questioning the prevalent interpretation of it as a divine judgment upon the sinful inhabitants, she maintained that it was inconsistent with the

---

26. Letter dated 13 June 1683, *Pa. Mag. of Hist.*, 13 (1889), 460, corrected to the original in the Bodleian Library, Oxford.—Cadbury, "Penn, Collinson, and the Royal Society," 24.

27. *Minutes of the Provincial Council*, I, 94-96; Amelia Mott Gummere, *Witchcraft and Quakerism* (Philadelphia, 1908), 39. I do not wish to make too much of this point, for I realize that many contemporaries like Cotton Mather shared the widely prevalent belief in witchcraft and yet were scientifically minded. It is merely submitted as evidence of a tendency among Friends to delimit the area of supernatural action and thus to widen the realm in which natural causes operated.

justice and goodness of God to involve innocent residents such as the English merchants and their families in the punishment of the "Bloodthirsty Inquisitors." "In the Philosophical Translations [*sic;* undoubtedly the *Philosophical Transactions* of the Royal Society are meant] are many Histories of Earthquakes," she pointed out, adding that scientists could advance wholly natural explanations for them. "Rational beings," she concluded, must recognize that such phenomena as earthquakes cannot be "repugnant to the nature of things, or what we call the Attributes of the divine Being."[28] Such an attitude, closely akin to that of her enlightened contemporary, Professor John Winthrop of Harvard, clearly bespoke a habit of mind receptive to scientific ideas.

Of the many Quaker amateurs of science in Philadelphia, the earliest and most distinguished was James Logan. Patron of colonial investigators like John Bartram and Thomas Godfrey, he was also a speculator and experimenter in his own right; he corresponded with the leading European savants of the day and saw his scientific writings published and quoted abroad. Logan was largely self-taught in mathematics and natural philosophy. Having in his sixteenth year, as he put it, "happily met with a book of the Leyborns on the Mathematics," he made himself master of it "without any manner of Instruction."[29] It is the judgment of a recent writer that, had he been able to give more attention to research and study, he would undoubtedly have "ranked as our first able mathematical scholar."[30] In spite of an enforced preoccupation with trade and his duties as secretary of the province, President of the Council, and Chief Justice, he found time to ponder and annotate copiously his copy of the *Principia mathematica* and other works of Newton. He mastered Newton's abstruse method of fluxions and gave particular attention to the theory of the moon's motion, to which he sug-

---

28. Pemberton Papers, XI, 34.
29. Autobiographical fragment, quoted in Myers, *Immigration*, 239.
30. Frederick E. Brasch, "The Newtonian Epoch in the American Colonies, 1680-1783," American Antiquarian Society, *Proceedings*, New Ser., 49 (1939), 329.

gested a number of additions and emendations.[31] Few Americans, it is safe to say, had gone as far into higher mathematics as this self-taught Quaker fur merchant and politician.

Dissatisfied with what he conceived to be the tediousness and obscurity of Huygens's determinations of the foci of lenses, he invented his own system, demonstrating it both analytically and geometrically, and writing it out in English and Latin. The Latin version was published at Leyden in 1739 under the title *Canonum pro inveniendis refractionum, tum simplicium, tum in lentibus duplicium focis, demonstrationes geometricae.*[32] The range of Logan's interests in the fields of optics and astronomy is shown by the papers which he communicated to the Royal Society and which were published in the *Philosophical Transactions:* "An Account of Mr. T. Godfrey's Improvement of Davis's Quadrant" (a vindication of the claims of his Philadelphia protégé over those of John Hadley, the English inventor); "Concerning the Crooked or Angular Appearance of the Streaks or Darts of Lightning in Thunderstorms" (a discussion of a problem which also exercised the minds of such other Americans as Jonathan Edwards, James Bowdoin, and Benjamin Franklin[33]); and "Some Thoughts on the Sun and Moon, When Near the Horizon Appearing Larger than When Near the Zenith." Early in 1717 he ordered from Joseph Williamson, a clock- and instrument-maker in England, some lenses for a telescope: "if I had one of 25 or 30 foot [focus]," he observed, "I could easily mount it." In the same letter he announced a plan to build a small observatory. His enthusiasm for astronomy persisted for many years: at the age of seventy-four he was making observations of a comet.[34]

Strong as his interest was in the physical sciences, Logan was

---

31. See his letters to William Jones in Rigaud, ed., *Correspondence;* also Brasch, "Newtonian Epoch," 328-29.
32. Logan to William Jones, 16 Oct. 1738, Rigaud, ed., *Correspondence*, I, 336. The English manuscript of this treatise is in Logan Papers, II, 115-16.
33. Sereno E. Dwight, *The Life of President Edwards* (New York, 1830), 742-44; I. Bernard Cohen, *Benjamin Franklin's Experiments*, 311-15.
34. Letter dated 1 March 1716/17, Logan Letter Book, 1702-26, 155-56; Logan Papers, II, 114.

even more powerfully drawn to biology, a field in which he made his most substantial contribution. His research in the pollination of Indian corn formed an important link in the chain of experiments leading up to the magistral work of Koelreuter on plant hybridization. Indeed it is not too far-fetched to suggest a relationship between Logan's experiments and the modern development of hybrid corn upon which much of the wealth of the American Corn Belt is based. Taking his departure from a passage in Wollaston's *Religion of Nature Delineated,* and building upon the earlier work of Millington and Grew, Logan carried out a series of carefully controlled experiments, commencing at least as early as 1727, in an effort to discover the function of pollen in fertilizing ears of maize. From these experiments he concluded that "the pollen evolved from the anthers, is the true masculine semen, and is most clearly entirely necessary to the fecundation of the uterus and seeds, which fact nevertheless all the centuries concealed up to ours."[35] There had been earlier efforts to obtain data about the sexuality of plants: Camerarius in 1694 had used *Zea mays* in his experiments, and in 1716 Cotton Mather had made records of wind pollination and hybridization.[36] Logan, however, was the first to develop a technique of preventing the pollen from reaching the stigmas by wrapping the ears in light muslin and the first to test by properly controlled experiments the many conjectures regarding the sexuality of plants current in the early eighteenth century.

After satisfying himself that his conclusions were sound, he sent a detailed description of the experiments to Peter Collinson, who submitted it to the Royal Society for publication. The full account, written in Latin and printed at Leyden in 1739, was a remarkable example of careful and minute observation. Dr. John Fothergill translated it and had it printed in England in 1747. Within a few years it had come to be widely cited in botanical literature as authoritative on the sexual reproduction of plants.

35. *Experimenta et meletemata de plantarum generatione* (1739), quoted in H. F. Roberts, *Plant Hybridization before Mendel,* 70.
36. Conway Zirkle, "Some Forgotten Records of Hybridization and Sex in Plants, 1716-1739," *Journal of Heredity,* 23 (1932), 446.

John Mitchell, the Virginia botanist, referred to it in 1748 in the *Ephemerides Leopoldina;* it was also cited in academic dissertations published in Tübingen and Upsala.[37] The great Linnaeus paid its author the compliment of naming a family of trees and shrubs *Loganaceae*. The traffic in scientific ideas between Europe and Philadelphia thus became a two-way exchange, as the findings of a Quaker merchant-*virtuoso* in the little town on the Delaware had their faint but perceptible reverberations in the ancient academic halls of Europe.

Astronomy was a favorite study of eighteenth-century Philadelphians. David Rittenhouse, foremost among American astronomers, was not a Friend, although his mother and his two successive wives were. More important than any Quaker influence which his womenfolk may have exerted upon him was the impetus given to his scientific interests by his maternal uncle, who bequeathed him a copy of Newton's *Principia* when he was only thirteen. The fact that this uncle, a humble Quaker artisan, should have possessed such a book is only an additional evidence of the degree to which the scientific spirit permeated American Quaker thinking.[38] Two of Rittenhouse's colleagues in the observation of the transit of Venus in 1769 were birthright Friends: John Lukens, Surveyor-General of Pennsylvania, and Owen Biddle, a clockmaker who later became an importing and exporting merchant in Philadelphia.[39] One of the earliest colonial hydrographic cartographers was Joshua Fisher (1707-1783), a Philadelphia merchant, whose chart of Delaware Bay, published in 1756, remained standard for nearly a century.[40]

The versatile Quaker scrivener and merchant Joseph Breintnall, described by Benjamin Franklin as "a good natur'd, friendly middleag'd man . . . very ingenious in many little Nicknackeries," submitted to the Royal Society two scientific papers which were

37. Conway Zirkle, *Beginnings of Plant Hybridization*, 142-55; John Fothergill to James Logan, 4 May 1750, Maria Dickinson Logan Family Papers, Hist. Soc. Pa.
38. Edward Ford, *David Rittenhouse* (Philadelphia, 1946), 11.
39. Henry D. Biddle, "Owen Biddle," *Pa. Mag. of Hist.*, 16 (1892), 229-329.
40. Hazel S. Garrison, "The Cartography of Pennsylvania before 1800," *ibid.*, 59 (1935), 281.

published in the *Philosophical Transactions:* one on the aurora borealis, and the other on the effects of a rattlesnake bite. His most interesting experiments, however, demonstrated that absorption and conduction of heat are functions of color. Around the year 1730 he carried out a carefully controlled experiment, placing several pieces of cloth of different colors on the snow and observing which pieces sank most quickly into the snow as they absorbed the sun's heat. Benjamin Franklin is known to have performed a similar experiment, and it is possible that he implanted the original idea in the mind of his Quaker associate.[41]

Some of the merchants devoted leisure hours at their "plantations" to the application of scientific procedures to agriculture in an effort to improve the lax practices which had been encouraged around Philadelphia as elsewhere in the American colonies by the existence of cheap and plentiful lands. Friend Hugh Roberts, an "ingenious acquaintance" of Benjamin Franklin and a fellow member of the Junto, was one of these; he welcomed the appearance of Jared Eliot's *Essays upon Field Husbandry* and ventured, on Franklin's urging, to send some observations on the draining of swamps and meadows to the Connecticut agriculturalist.[42] Another correspondent of Eliot was William Logan, son of James Logan. Less erudite and of a more practical turn of mind than his father, he retired, after a dozen years or so as a merchant, to his fifty acres at Stenton, resolving to spend the rest of his life in making improvements in agriculture. He congratulated Jared Eliot for experimenting under American conditions instead of merely accepting the conclusions of English agriculturists. Always on the lookout for new methods, he acquired one of Eliot's improved drill plows, forerunner of the modern grain drill. He co-operated with his cousin Charles Read of New Jersey in testing Eliot's seeds, and made interesting observations of

---

41. Frederick B. Tolles, "A Note on Joseph Breintnall, Franklin's Collaborator," *Philological Quarterly*, 21 (1942), 247-49. Breintnall's manuscript account of his experiment is in Logan Papers, X, 100. The document is dated 3 Aug. 1737, but the experiment had first been performed seven years earlier. See Stephen Bloore, "Joseph Breintnall," *Pa. Mag. of Hist.*, 59 (1935), 42-56; I. Bernard Cohen, "Franklin's Experiments on Heat Absorption as a Function of Color," *Isis*, 34 (1943), 404-7.
42. Franklin to Eliot, 12 Sept. 1751, *Writings*, III, 53.

his own upon fruit culture and newly developed meadow grasses. His memoranda on husbandry showed him to be one of the most progressive farmers of his time. Both Logan and Roberts contributed ideas and observations to Charles Read's "Notes on Agriculture," which have recently come to light.[43] Thomas Gilpin (1727-1778), a Quaker zoologist, made studies of the wheat fly, the scourge of Pennsylvania's staple crop, and recommended effective measures for its control. He also investigated the American locust, establishing seventeen years as the period of its reappearance, and later made useful observations of the migration of herring from European shores to America. The results of his work he communicated to the local philosophical societies which had been established as the American counterparts of the Royal Society of London.[44]

The eagerness of Quaker merchants to absorb scientific knowledge can be judged from the copious notes which John Smith took on the scientific lectures of Dr. Adam Spencer in 1744. This was the same Dr. Spencer who had first introduced Benjamin Franklin to the study of electricity. The lecturer ranged over the whole domain of natural philosophy, paying his respects to the laws of gravitation and optics, to magnetism and electricity, meteorology and physiology, and performed experiments to illustrate his observations. Smith, an absorbed spectator, jotted down the oracular remarks of the omniscient doctor and preserved his notes among his papers, where they can be consulted today as an index of the kind of science that was being discussed in Quaker circles in colonial Philadelphia.[45]

43. Logan's letters to Eliot are reprinted in Eliot's *Essays upon Field Husbandry in New England*, H. J. Carman and R. G. Tugwell, eds., 226-34. See also Rodney H. True, "Some Pre-Revolutionary Agricultural Correspondence," *Agricultural History*, 12 (1938), 107-17. Logan's "Memoranda on Husbandry," containing his observations on the growing of turnips, sainfoin, and fowl meadow grass, as well as some elaborate "Observations on Drained Meadows" (perhaps Hugh Roberts'), are in the Library of the United States Department of Agriculture, Washington, D. C. On Logan's and Roberts' relations with Read, see Carl R. Woodward, *Ploughs and Politicks*, 286, 303, 314, 364.

44. Thomas Gilpin, Jr., "Memoir of Thomas Gilpin," *Pa. Mag. of Hist.*, 49 (1925), 289-328; Bridenbaugh, *Rebels and Gentlemen*, 345-49.

45. Smith's notes are in Smith MSS, V, 254-55. They have been reprinted in full in I. Bernard Cohen, "Benjamin Franklin and the Mysterious 'Dr. Spence,'" Franklin Institute, *Journal*, 235 (1943), 7-10.

In the light of all this evidence of scientific interest and activity, one can hardly share the surprise expressed by the Anglican writer of *Caspipina's Letters* on the eve of the Revolution at learning from a Friend, himself a Fellow of the American Philosophical Society, that the Quakers had "stepped forth and joined the votaries of Science."[46] Johann David Schoepf, writing a few years after the Revolution, showed a sounder grasp of the facts, erring only in making too sweeping a generalization, when he noted that the sciences were much indebted to the Quakers and that "the American Philosophical Society was founded by them."[47] The genealogy of the American Philosophical Society is exceedingly complicated, but the indisputable fact of interest to us is that Quakers took a leading part in each of the organizations which prepared the way for its final emergence and they accounted for nearly half the membership of the Society itself in the early years. There was hardly a prominent Quaker merchant of the 1760's who was not enrolled in one or more of these early organizations dedicated to scientific advancement, a fact which testifies unequivocally to their genuine interest.

At least two of the original participants in Franklin's Junto of 1727, sometimes considered the remote parent of the American Philosophical Society, were nominal members of the Society of Friends; namely, Joseph Breintnall and William Coleman. Francis Rawle, Samuel Rhoads, Hugh Roberts, Samuel Powel, Joseph Wharton, and Owen Biddle were members of the reorganized Junto which became known in the early 1760's as "The Society Meeting Weekly for Their Mutual Improvement in Useful Knowledge." Later in the decade this group changed its name to "The American Society Held at Philadelphia for Pro-

---

46. Duché, 68. Elsewhere in the same letter Duché observes that the American Philosophical Society "numbers many of the most sensible of this denomination among its Fellows."—63-64.

47. *Travels in the Confederation*, trans. Alfred J. Morrison (Philadelphia, 1911), I, 63. A recent President of the American Philosophical Society makes the similarly categorical statement that the Society was "started by a group of Quaker scholars and investigators." He mentions particularly Israel and James Pemberton, for their interest in the study of Indian civilization and antiquities. —Roland S. Morris, "The Contribution of Friends to American Adult Education," *The Friend*, 113 (1939), 172.

moting Useful Knowledge," announcing as its purpose "to order, take account, consider and discourse of philosophical experiments and observations." Of the fifty-nine subscribers to the "Obligation" of the Society, approximately a third were Friends, including such well-known merchants as Richard Wells, Henry Drinker, and Edward Penington, the lawyer Nicholas Waln, and the physician Dr. Charles Moore. The aims of the "American Society" were in harmony with the practical bent of the Quakers, as can be seen from its avowed concern with new methods of distilling and brewing, of draining meadows and restoring the fertility of soils, of assaying mineral ores and improving inland navigation. At the same time, it did not exclude pure science from its purview; "all newly discovered fossils in different countries," for example, were objects of interest to the Society.[48]

The first American Philosophical Society, founded by Franklin in 1743, included among its nine founders at least five who were or had been members of the Society of Friends.[49] When the Society was reconstituted in 1768, it could boast as trophies in its race for membership against the rival American Society a number of highly respectable Quakers, such as Israel and James Pemberton, John Smith, John Reynell, Joseph Richardson, Joseph Fox, and Richard Hockley.[50] At the end of 1768, the two societies united to form one agency for coordinating "philosophical" and practical inquiries throughout the American colonies. The Quaker merchants, who constituted a large frac-

---

48. Peter S. DuPonceau, *An Historical Account of the Origin and Formation of the American Philosophical Society*, 17, 24, 34; "Rules of the American Society Held at Philadelphia for Promoting Useful Knowledge," *Pa. Mag. of Hist.*, 24 (1900), 6-16.

49. Franklin to Cadwallader Colden, 5 April 1744, *Writings*, II, 276-77. Samuel Rhoads was a Friend in good standing; Dr. Thomas Bond had recently been disowned for disunity, and Dr. Phineas Bond, John Bartram, and William Coleman were also to be read out of meeting within a few years. The religious background of Thomas Godfrey, Logan's protégé, is, like the rest of his biography, obscure, but it is probable that he came from Quaker stock. Bartram and Godfrey, two of Philadelphia's most important scientists, are omitted from detailed consideration here because although they looked to the merchants for patronage, they actually stood outside the circle of mercantile aristocrats with whom we are primarily concerned.

50. See list of members in *Early Proceedings of the American Philosophical Society*, 3-6.

tion (close to half) of its 146 resident members, contributed financial support, social prestige, and, not least, an intelligent and informed curiosity about natural science and a genuine interest in its advancement. Other colonies may have had as many individuals, particularly among the clergy, who were actively engaged in scientific pursuits, but few, it is safe to say, could point to as many laymen, men of business, sufficiently interested in the promotion of knowledge to act as patrons of an organization dedicated solely to scientific ends. It was as much owing to the presence of this group of wealthy and intelligent Quaker laymen as to the efforts of the great Franklin that Philadelphia should have been the scene of the first American scientific society.

"THE IMPROVEMENT OF PHYSICK"

On the threshold of his career, George Fox had an experience wherein, as he said, the Creation was opened to him and he was shown "how all things had their name given them, according to their nature and virtue." He was "at a stand" in his mind whether or not in the light of this divinely given knowledge he should "practise physic for the good of mankind,"[51] but decided finally to devote his life to ministering to the souls rather than to the bodies of men. A large number of his followers, similarly concerned for the "good of mankind" in the physical as well as the spiritual sense, took up the study of medicine and became leaders in the profession. To mention the names of Quaker doctors such as Fothergill, Lettsom, and Dimsdale is to enumerate some of the chief medical luminaries of eighteenth-century England. The fact that Friends were excluded from most other professions was no doubt partly responsible for their prominence in the medical

---

51. *Journal*, I, 28. That Fox's interest in medicine persisted is seen in the fact that in 1657 he drew up some queries "concerning the ground of all diseases, and the natures and virtues of medicinal things," which he propounded to some "mountebanks."—*Ibid.*, I, 359. The context shows that this incident was related to his interest in the "Hermetic philosophy," which included, along with elements of magic and quackery, the early phases of modern astronomy, chemistry, botany, and medicine. See Geoffrey F. Nuttall, " 'Unity with the Creation': George Fox and the Hermetic Philosophy," *Friends Quarterly*, I (1947), 134-43.

field, but the humanitarian (and we may now add the scientific) motive can never be overlooked.

The association of humanitarian concern with zeal for the advancement of science was notably displayed by John Bellers, an English Friend who was a pioneer in social reforms as well as a Fellow of the Royal Society. In 1714 he addressed to Parliament a comprehensive and far-seeing set of proposals for state action looking towards "the Improvement of Physick." His plan was premised upon two indisputable facts: that more than three-quarters of the English population were unable to afford medical advice and treatment, and that medical knowledge was neither sufficiently advanced nor widely enough diffused to be very helpful even to those who could afford to pay a physician's fee. A brief review of the salient features of his extraordinary plan will establish the general framework of idea and concern within which Quakers approached the practice of medicine.

Conceiving "the Improvement of Physick" to be a "Necessary . . . Branch of the *Politicks*," Bellers called upon Parliament to establish hospitals for the poor and to require that clinical data be carefully recorded. At the hospital for incurables, therapeutic experimentation (lack of opportunity for which had greatly impeded medical progress) was to be permitted with the patients' consent. Autopsies (against which there was strong popular sentiment) should regularly be performed and the findings made available "for the Universal spreading of *Knowledge* among the *Faculty*." In order that the benefits of medical care might be extended into the provinces, a "Doctor and Chirurgeon" should be appointed to attend the sick poor in each hundred and parish. A "Public Laboratory, and a Physical Observatory" should be maintained, not only for the preparation of known medicines, "But also, to make a general Search among the *Vegitables* and *Minerals* &c. What further Discoveries can be made, for to help the Sick."

Hospitals should be established at the Universities (where medical teaching was still essentially scholastic) so that students could receive more adequate training "by adding *Practice* to their *Aphorisms* and *Theory*." The College of Physicians and the Company of Surgeons should be stirred out of their torpor and required to set up and enforce standards of medical practice and to see that provincial practitioners received the benefits of the latest medical knowledge; in these provisions Bellers was anticipating the functions of modern medical societies and journals. Finally, the Royal Society should be subsidized so that it could "carry on that Useful and Great Design of improving Men in the Knowledge of NATURE (and the MECHANICKS) of which MEDICINE is a principal Branch." In this remarkable scheme the good Quaker set forth a program of public health and medical research, the full potentialities of which were not to be realized in the two centuries and a half to come.[52]

Since the practice of medicine received both social and religious approval in Quaker circles, it is not surprising to find that there were several physicians among the earliest settlers of Philadelphia. Quaker merchants, moreover, frequently encouraged their sons to prepare themselves for the profession: indeed the expense of medical training tended to limit candidates to those who had considerable means.

One of the first permanent settlers in Philadelphia, arriving before Penn himself, was John Goodson, "chirurgeon" to the Free Society of Traders. For at least ten years before his emigration, this Friend had been practicing in Bartholomew Close in London. In 1671, when the Six Weeks Meeting, an executive body of London Quakers, directed that a suitable place be found "In or about the Citty" for Friends who might be "distracted or troubled in minde, that soe they may not be put amongst the world's people or Run about the Streets," it was Dr. John Goodson who had provided a large house for their reception and care.

---

52. *An Essay Towards the Improvement of Physick* (London, 1714). The revolutionary nature of Bellers' proposals can only be appreciated in the light of the backward state of medical science and practice in the early eighteenth century. See Richard H. Shryock, *The Development of Modern Medicine*, Ch. 3. Bellers' ideas on science, like his radical social views, were somewhat akin to those of Gerrard Winstanley, the seventeenth-century Digger.— George Rosen, "Left-Wing Puritanism and Science," *Bulletin of the History of Medicine*, 15 (1944), 375-80.

In a day when insanity was still generally regarded as evidence of demoniacal possession, it is significant that it should have been a medical man who offered to care for these unfortunates. This pioneer Philadelphia doctor was clearly in the vanguard of his profession in recognizing mental disorder as a form of disease.[53] His successors among the Philadelphia Quakers were to keep alive this concern for the mentally ill; one may note that provision of medical care for the insane was one of the primary reasons for the founding of the Pennsylvania Hospital, in which, as we shall see, Friends played a leading part. From his earliest days in Philadelphia, when he lived in a cave on the banks of the Delaware, to his death in 1727, Goodson was a prominent citizen, serving as a Commissioner of Property and later acting with Samuel Carpenter as "Assistant" to Deputy-Governor Markham. In both its professional and civic aspects, his career set the pattern for the Quaker doctors of colonial Philadelphia.

For the most part, medical practice in Philadelphia's first quarter-century was in the hands of Welsh Quakers. One of the passengers on the ship *Welcome*, which brought William Penn to Pennsylvania, was Dr. Thomas Wynne, a Welshman who had studied anatomy and surgery in Shropshire, becoming, in his own words, an expert "in the use of the Plaister Box and Salvatory, the Trafine and Head Saw, the Amputation Saw, and the Catling, the Cautery, Sirring and Catheter."[54] Neither he nor Dr. Edward Jones, another early Welsh immigrant, appears, however, to have devoted his major attention to the profession while in Pennsylvania. Dr. Jones made his chief contribution to the medical history of the colony by training his son Evan Jones as a doctor. Dr. Griffith Owen, a Friend of great weight in the Society, was the most active practicing physician in the early years; his sons Edward and Griffith also became "practitioners of physic."

---

53. Bedford Pierce, "The Treatment of the Insane," *Friends Quarterly Examiner*, 36 (1902), 74; Braithwaite, *Second Period*, 571n.
54. *An Anti-Christian Conspiracy Detected, and Satan's Champion Defeated* (1679), quoted in Charles H. Browning, *The Welsh Settlement of Pensylvania*, 182.

The chief link between the first generation of Welsh Quaker physicians and the later native-born Philadelphia doctors was provided by Dr. Evan Jones, who gave his nephew, Dr. Thomas Cadwalader (1707-1779), the first rudiments of medical training. Cadwalader later studied anatomy in London under the celebrated Cheselden and attended courses at the University of Rheims. Soon after his return to Philadelphia, he was prevailed upon by his medical colleagues to conduct a series of anatomical dissections which have been hailed as "the first formal course in medical science" in the American colonies.[55] Within a few years, he had acquired a large practice, part of which he appears to have retained after moving to Trenton, New Jersey. It was there that Dr. Alexander Hamilton met him in 1744 and, describing him as "a fallen-off Quaker," recorded his vehement views on the evils of superstition, idle ceremonies, and priestcraft, views which could have been rooted in his Quakerism, but which may have been sharpened and intensified by his association with scientists and medical men in Europe. Cadwalader's medical fame rests chiefly upon his *Essay on the West-India Dry-Gripes*, a monograph on lead-poisoning published by Franklin in 1745. Appended to the essay was a remarkable clinical report on a case of osteomalacia or softening of the bones, based upon an autopsy; it has been claimed that this was the first autopsy to be performed for scientific purposes in the American colonies.[56]

Dr. Lloyd Zachary, another American-born descendant of Welsh Quaker stock, also sat at the feet of Dr. William Cheselden and attended lectures on surgery at St. Thomas's Hospital in London.[57] During the quarter-century following his return from

55. Eileen R. Cunningham, "A Short Review of the Development of Medical Education and Schools of Medicine," *Annals of Medical History*, New Ser., 7 (1935), 234. Dr. Caspar Wistar advances the interesting conjecture that the dissections were conducted under the auspices of James Logan.—"State of Medicine in Philadelphia, from the First Settlement of Pennsylvania to the year 1762," *Eclectic Repertory and Analytical Review*, 8 (1818), 276.

56. William S. Middleton, "Thomas Cadwalader and His Essay," *Annals of Medical History*, 3d Ser., 3 (1941), 101-13; Charles W. Dulles, "Sketch of the Life of Dr. Thomas Cadwalader," *Pa. Mag. of Hist.*, 27 (1903), 266-78; Bridenbaugh, *Gentleman's Progress*, 31.

57. See certificate signed by Dr. William Cheselden and Joshua Symonds, 15 June 1725, Charles Morton Smith MSS, I, 56, Hist. Soc. Pa.

England in 1725, Dr. Zachary developed a large and profitable practice in Philadelphia, and participated fully in the social and humanitarian life of the Quaker aristocracy. His cousins Charles and Samuel Preston Moore also became doctors: the former was the second American to receive an M.D. from the University of Edinburgh.[58] Like the Moore brothers, Drs. Phineas Bond (1717-1773) and Thomas Bond (1712-1784) came to Philadelphia from Maryland, bringing with them certificates of good conduct from their home meetings and high professional qualifications acquired in the medical centers of Europe, Thomas having attended the practice of the Hôtel Dieu in Paris and Phineas having studied at Leyden, Paris, Edinburgh, and London. They too played active parts in the civic, social, and intellectual life of the town, but in the process they sloughed off their Quakerism. Thomas was testified against in 1742 for "disorderly conduct" involving the taking of an oath, and Phineas was disowned in 1748 for neglecting attendance at meeting and joining in military preparations.[59] Dr. Benjamin Morris, son of an affluent merchant and brewer acquired his professional training and his excellent medical library at Leyden.[60]

In enumerating the leading Quaker doctors, one should not overlook Dr. John Morgan, a birthright Philadelphia Friend, who studied at Edinburgh and Paris and later founded the first medical school in the colonies, or Dr. John Jones, great-grandson of Dr. Thomas Wynne, grandson of Dr. Edward Jones, and cousin of Dr. Thomas Cadwalader, who obtained his M.D. at Rheims and became Professor of Surgery at King's College in New York, where he wrote the first American textbook on surgery. As these instances show, the fact that Quakers were barred from attendance at the English universities was far from being a serious handicap, for by going to other centers of study, particularly

---

58. Samuel Lewis, "List of the American Graduates in Medicine in the University of Edinburgh," *New England Historical and Genealogical Register,* 42 (1888), 159.
59. MS Minutes of Phila. MM, II, 258, 305, 343; III, 60, 62; Wistar, "State of Medicine," 275.
60. William G. Malin, MS Sketch of the History of the Medical Library of the Pennsylvania Hospital, Hist. Soc. Pa.

Edinburgh and Leyden, they received the best training that the eighteenth century could offer.[61]

Thus Quaker humanitarianism coupled with an interest in science helped bring it about that Philadelphia was better supplied with competent medical practitioners than any other American town. John Reynell commented upon the plethora of physicians in 1755, observing that "we have Such great Plenty of 'em, that I wonder how they do to live, indeed some of 'em [I] believe are hard set for a Livelyhood while others who have an Establish'd Reputation get beforehand fast...."[62]

The humanitarian and scientific motives which the Quaker merchants shared with the doctors led to the founding of the first general hospital in the colonies. As early as 1709 Philadelphia Friends had been interested in such a project, commissioning James Logan to seek financial assistance and a charter while he was on a visit to the mother country.[63] Nothing came of this proposal immediately, but forty years later, when Dr. Thomas Bond, full of enthusiasm about the "hospital movement" in England, enlisted the support of Benjamin Franklin in his campaign for a hospital in Philadelphia, the Quaker merchants rallied around and made themselves responsible for raising the greater part of the sum of £4750 with which construction was commenced. The two Israel Pembertons, Isaac Norris, George Emlen, and Joshua Crosby each contributed £100; Anthony Morris, Sr., gave his bond for £75; William Attwood, Joseph Wharton, Caspar Wistar, Samuel Powel, Anthony Morris, Jr., and John Smith all subscribed £50; and other Quakers contributed lesser amounts.[64] When the first petition for aid to the hospital was submitted to the Assembly, over two-thirds of the signers were Friends, and the majority of the Assemblymen who voted the charter were, of course, also members of the meeting.

---

61. Francis R. Packard, "How London and Edinburgh Influenced Medicine in Philadelphia in the Eighteenth Century," *Annals of Medical History*, new ser., 4 (1932), 225.
62. Letter to Thomas Sanders, 17 Dec. 1755, Reynell Letter Book, 1754-56.
63. MS Minutes of Phila. MM, I, 268 (25 Nov. 1709).
64. Subscription list, printed in [Benjamin Franklin], *Some Account of the Pennsylvania Hospital*, 39-40.

The first board of managers elected under the charter was dominated by Friends and control of the institution remained in Quaker hands throughout the colonial period and for many years thereafter.[65] In fact, the hospital became a sort of headquarters and rallying-point for the Quakers, as the College of Philadelphia did for the Anglicans.[66]

That the hospital was directly contributory to the "good of mankind" hardly needs to be underlined. That it promoted the advancement of scientific knowledge is equally clear, for it brought into being not only the first dispensary, and the first real medical library (built around the collections of the Quaker doctors Lloyd Zachary and Benjamin Morris), but the first opportunity in British America for the systematic clinical observation necessary for genuine medical research. Thus did the Quakers—merchants as well as professional physicians—contribute to the furtherance of medical science in Philadelphia.

---

65. Of the twelve original Managers the following were Friends: Joshua Crosby, President, Israel Pemberton, Jr., Samuel Rhoads (designer of the first building), Hugh Roberts, Joseph Morris, John Smith, and Charles Norris. John Reynell was the first Treasurer.—Thomas G. Morton, *History of the Pennsylvania Hospital*, 12.

66. This Quaker activity in establishing the Pennsylvania Hospital was not unrelated to current political events. In 1750 Governor Hamilton and the anti-Quaker party were actively entreating the Assembly to appropriate funds for the military defense of the frontier. The Quaker majority in the legislature steadfastly refused to vote moneys for military purposes. There is reason to believe that the generosity of Friends in relation to the hospital was calculated, as Governor Hamilton intimated to Thomas Penn, to demonstrate that "when they are not restrained by principle they can be as liberal as others."—Penn MSS, Official Correspondence, I, 157.

Chapter Ten

THE INNER PLANTATION
AND THE OUTER

T HE founding of the Pennsylvania Hospital in 1751
foreshadowed a new era in Philadelphia Quakerism.
Within five years, as we noted earlier, tensions arose
over the military defense of the frontier, causing the
Quakers to retire from active political life. Thus after seventy-
five years of preoccupation with the outward plantation, they
turned their attention once again to cultivating the plantation
within. Great Quaker merchant princes who had once controlled
the political and economic destinies of the commonwealth came
to be numbered among "the quiet in the land." Their outward
energies, hitherto devoted to affairs of state, were channeled into
humanitarian concerns; the Hospital replaced the State House
as the center of their activities.

A new spirit settled down over the life of the Society of
Friends in Philadelphia. Quaker tribalism—the sense of being a
"peculiar people" called by God to be separate from the "world"
—had been appreciably modified and in some areas had all but
disappeared during the years of political and economic dominion;
now it returned with renewed strength, and Philadelphia Friends
came at length to resemble their co-religionists in Ireland, Great
Britain, and the rural districts of the Middle Colonies in their
extreme group-consciousness with its social corollaries of co-
hesiveness and exclusivism. This change represented more than
merely a belated settling into the normal eighteenth-century

Quaker patterns of quietism and inwardness; it was a conscious reaction from the life that had characterized Philadelphia Quakerdom during the preceding three-quarters of a century, and an implied criticism of the inconsistencies and concessions to the "world" which had accompanied it.

"NON-CONDUCTORS AMONG THE WIRES"

The notion of being a "peculiar people" had never been completely foreign to the Philadelphia Quaker mind. In the earliest years, to be sure, there had been little occasion for a conscious policy of self-segregation, for virtually all the first Philadelphians, if not actually Quakers, were willing to submit themselves to the discipline of the meeting. An early settler recalled that in the 1680's "there was no difference in forms of worship; for the Quakers, having built a·large Meeting house about the centre of the city, all came there. . . ."[1] Furthermore, Friends at that period were full of evangelical optimism. "Dear friends," they wrote exultantly to London Yearly Meeting, "the majesty of truth is great here, and does prevail, and grow, and reign, and is become dreadful to the workers of iniquity. Yea, it will increase more and more, to the ends of America."[2] Two events of the 1690's—the Keithian schism and the establishment of Christ Church—brought an end to the unity; the optimism did not long survive the coming of multitudes of immigrants eager to accept Quaker hospitality but in no wise disposed to accept the Quaker faith and discipline.

As early as 1702, when the town was but twenty years old, James Logan estimated that only one-third of its denizens were Quakers; his estimate may have been too low, but it is quite clear that even at this early date Friends no longer constituted a majority in Philadelphia. Within a few years, a great tide of immigration set in, first from Germany and later from Ireland, and the Quakers found themselves engulfed. We find Logan in 1726 deploring the presence in the Quaker city of an unassimilable

1. William Fishbourne, "Some Few and Short Hints," Miscellaneous MSS, Etting Collection, I, 56.
2. MS Minutes of Phila. YM, I, 7 (1684).

mass of foreigners over whom the Monthly Meeting could exercise little control: good order and discipline prevailed "among the better sort," he wrote, but "we have vast numbers of the loose and profligate as must be expected when the profession is in a manner National." Symptomatic of the change taking place in the character of Philadelphia's population as the hordes from Ireland poured in is the fact that in 1730 the Monthly Meeting was obliged to take notice of disturbances caused by "firing Guns and Revellings occasioned by the Classing together Nationally Numbers of People under Pretence of Keeping a day to their Saint called Saint Patrick." A committee of weighty Friends waited upon the Governor, begging him to "Discountenance such doings for the future."[3]

As the eighteenth century wore on, the Quakers came to form a smaller and smaller proportion of the town's population. It is not possible to gauge their relative (and probably absolute) decline with accuracy, but contemporary estimates shed some light upon what was happening. In 1750 the eight hundred Quaker families represented only a little more than a quarter of the total population of Philadelphia. Ten years later, when two ministers visited all the Quaker homes in the city under a religious concern, they found that there were only about six hundred families; if we reckon six persons to a family and accept the figure of twenty thousand for Philadelphia's population in 1760, we discover that the proportion of Friends had declined to a little more than one-fifth. By 1770, Robert Proud, the Quaker historian, set the Quaker component at one-seventh of the total. The fractions are only approximate but the general drift is (and was) unmistakable.[4]

3. Logan to Penn, 11 May 1702, *Penn and Logan Correspondence*, I, 102; Logan to John Hoop, 7 Feb. 1726/27, Logan Letter Books, III, 68; MS Minutes of Phila. MM, II, 185 (27 March 1730).
4. Bridenbaugh, *Rebels and Gentlemen*, 16-17; "An Account of Friends Families belonging to Philadelphia Monthly Meeting and Some Few Families not Altogether in Unity, Visited by Daniel Stanton and John Pemberton. Began in 1757 and Finished in 1760," *Pa. Mag. of Hist.*, 16 (1892), 219-38; Evarts B. Greene and Virginia Harrington, *American Population Before the Federal Census of 1790* (New York, 1932), 117-18; Proud, *History*, II, 339. Proud's manuscript "Memoranda" in the Friends Historical Library of Swarthmore

As the Quakers saw themselves becoming outnumbered, and their control even over their own members threatened, by other denominations, they began to perceive a need to strengthen their solidarity by emphasizing the religious peculiarities which differentiated them from their fellow Philadelphians of other persuasions. An evidence of incipient group-consciousness can perhaps be detected in the complaint laid before the Monthly Meeting in 1688 that "the burying place is made too Common," and the accompanying proposal that Friends have one to themselves. No action was taken immediately, but fourteen years later instructions were given that the Quaker dead should be segregated in a special burying ground. In that year also the question was raised "how far friends may be concerned in the burials of such of their relations as are not friends." This issue likewise was not settled at once, but nine years later the Yearly Meeting concluded that Friends should "be careful to keep themselves and their Children from going, with the dead, into any of their worship houses. And avoid as much as may be to hear any of their sermons."[5] At about this time too, the meeting adopted a stricter policy with respect to "outgoings in marriage"; the number of Friends disowned for marrying "in the world's way" increased markedly after about 1720. Here, as in the case of attendance at funeral services, the apprehension appears to have been lest Friends be contaminated or misled by the ministrations of "hireling priests."

When the spectacular revival of religion known as the Great Awakening burst upon Philadelphia in the 1740's, bringing with it a mighty renewal of pious fervor among members of other denominations, only a handful of Quakers were swept from their moorings. The majority were by this time so thoroughly insulated from contact with other religious bodies that the waves of religious enthusiasm that boiled all about them scarcely touched

College contain some ingenious calculations based upon the numbers of interments in the burying grounds of the various denominations; these findings tend to set the Quaker component during the period 1750-70 at still lower fractions.

5. MS Minutes of Phila. MM, I, 52 (22 Feb. 1688/9, 29 March 1689); 162 (29 May 1702), 169 (27 Nov. 1702); MS Minutes of Phila. YM, I, 138 (1711).

the hems of their garments. Whittier's poetic description of the Philadelphia Friend of this period is historically accurate:

> The Quaker kept the way of his own,—
> A non-conductor among the wires,
> With coat of asbestos proof to fires.[6]

Thus at the same time that their commercial and civic activities were bringing them more and more into the society of "the world's people," breaking down the cultural barriers that separated them from their fellow Philadelphians, the Quakers were painstakingly building up in the strictly religious area of their lives a series of sectarian hedges and walls. When the pendulum should have swung back to an emphasis upon the spiritual life, these could provide the necessary conditions for a culturally insulated and autonomous existence.

"REFORMATION IN THE SOCIETY"

Within a few years it was borne in upon Friends that, if the traditional Quaker way of life were to be preserved intact, they must take more drastic measures than simply prohibiting their members from attending the religious services of other denominations. They came presently to the realization that in their zeal to transfigure and, as it were, irradiate the "world," to make it over in the image of the Kingdom of God, they had themselves become involved in compromises—compromises which were not only proving fatal to the "holy experiment" but were threatening the spiritual integrity of the Society of Friends itself. The spirit of compromise and concession was seen to have overtaken Philadelphia Quakerism in almost every phase of life—in business, in politics, in intellectual pursuits, in social intercourse, most insidiously and thoroughly perhaps in the very manner of living—the houses, furniture, and clothing—of the weightiest Friends. It was the political crisis of 1756 that hastened this recog-

---

6. "The Preacher," *The Complete Poetical Works of John Greenleaf Whittier*, (Cambridge Edition: Boston and New York, 1894), 73. For a fuller discussion of this subject, see Frederick B. Tolles, "Quietism Versus Enthusiasm: The Philadelphia Quakers and the Great Awakening," *Pa. Mag. of Hist.*, 69 (1945), 26-49.

nition. In April, 1756, as we have seen,[7] war was declared against the Delaware Indians, and many Friends felt conscientiously bound to abdicate their political offices. Indeed, as William Logan remarked with satisfaction to John Smith, "very few of the Sober Sort" even cast ballots in the fall election of 1756.[8] The emissaries despatched by London Yearly Meeting to counsel the Philadelphians in this crisis brought their weight to bear against officeholding, and two years later the Yearly Meeting put its seal on the new position by cautioning members against holding any civil office "by which they may in any respect be engaged in or think themselves subjected to the necessity of enjoining or enforcing the Compliance of their Brethren or others with any Act which they conscientiously scruple to perform."[9] With this action the "holy experiment" came to an end.

But the years 1756-1758 marked more than the end of an era in the political history of Pennsylvania; they witnessed the beginning of a thoroughgoing "reformation" in the Society of Friends. Not alone the inconsistencies involved in political action, but the subtle accommodation to the spirit of the "world" that had become evident in every phase of life were brought to light, and the reverberations of this radical reformation did not cease until the whole fabric of Philadelphia Quaker life had been profoundly altered. Hints of what was coming preceded the actual crisis. The General Spring Meeting of Ministers and Elders in March, 1755, took notice of the "Commotions and Stirrings of the Powers of the Earth at this Time near us," and drew from thence the moral that Friends must endeavour to have their minds "sufficiently disentangled from the surfeiting Cares of this Life, and redeemed from the Love of the World, that no earthly Possessions nor Enjoyments may bias our Judgments, or turn us

---

7. Above, pp. 26-28.
8. Letter dated 1 Oct. 1756, John Smith Correspondence, Hist. Soc. Pa.
9. MS Minutes of Phila. YM, II, 120 (1758). Hershberger, it may be noted, goes too far in interpreting this action as a categorical prohibition of all officeholding by Friends. See his "Pennsylvania Quaker Experiment in Politics," 217-18. James Pemberton, for example, who had led the movement for withdrawal in 1756, allowed himself to be re-elected to the Assembly nine years later, after peace had returned. See in this connection Theodore Thayer, "The Quaker Party of Pennsylvania, 1755-1765," Pa. Mag. of Hist., 71 (1947), 19-43.

from that Resignation, and entire Trust in God, to which his Blessing is most surely annexed."[10] Philadelphia Monthly Meeting's answers to the Queries early in 1756 reflected growing uneasiness among Friends. In response to the Query: "Are Friends careful to bring up those under their Direction in Plainness of Speech and Apparel, in frequent reading the holy Scriptures, to restrain them from reading pernicious Books and the Corrupt Conversation of the World?" the meeting felt obliged to answer: "It is too obvious to be unobserved by those who are honestly concern'd to maintain the Testimony of Truth, that there's a great declension in many professing among us from the primitive Simplicity of our Forefathers in the Particulars mention'd in the Query. . . ."[11]

Signs of a new spiritual sensitivity began to be apparent in the spring of 1756: "Many of our Friends," wrote one interested observer, "begin to rouse from that Lethargy in which they have too long been plunged, thro' a love of this World, an endeavor to reconcile those two contrarities the World and Heaven."[12] Party feeling ran high for a season between those who advocated a root-and-branch reformation, involving complete separation from the "world," and those who saw the need for change but were loath to give up the comfortable manner of living to which they had become accustomed. John Hunt and Christopher Wilson, the two Friends sent to Philadelphia by London Yearly Meeting, played an important irenic role in preventing an actual schism. There were some, reported William Logan's wife, who were "so hot in their own Zeal in carrying on the Reformation that they are in Danger of Judgeing all who don't think as they do." No one was more zealous, she added, than the affluent Israel Pemberton, "who gives friends daily uneasiness by his froward Conduct."[13]

---

10. *An Epistle from Our General Spring Meeting of Ministers and Elders for Pennsylvania and New-Jersey, Held at Philadelphia, from the 29th of the Third Month, to the 1st of the Fourth Month, Inclusive,* 1755, 2-3.
11. MS Minutes of Phila. MM, IV, 199 (30 Jan. 1756).
12. Anthony Benezet to Jonah Thompson, 24 April 1756, Brookes, *Benezet,* 220.
13. Hannah Logan to Jonah Thompson, 9 Jan. 1759, Friends Historical Library of Swarthmore College.

There were others in Philadelphia who could call for a divorce from the spirit of the "world" with better grace than Israel Pemberton, for they had preached and practiced simplicity all their lives. Among these was Anthony Benezet, whose plain speaking had galled the spirits of the more opulent merchant princes for many years. As time passed, he confided to his friend John Smith, he became more deeply convinced of the truth of Solomon's animadversions upon "Huckstering and Merchandizing" and the difficulties and dangers attendant upon them.[14] He cautioned Smith, now living in retirement at Burlington, against accepting membership in the Governor's Council lest it marry him too much to the "world." His words of advice are eloquent of the new atmosphere of Philadelphia Quakerism in these years:

dear John, remember, human nature is apt to deceive itself, especially when her propensities are flattered. I fear the snares consequent upon such a station will exceed the good thou canst do in it. The common conversation and very breath of most politicians is earthly and sensual, and too often devilish, not to mention the weakness of flesh and blood, which in spite of all our good resolution, if too much exposed to danger, will, like some combustible matter, catch fire, when only approached near the flame. Our Saviour's Kingdom was not of this world. One thing is necessary, which I am more and more convinced is most likely to strike the deepest root, in as much as possible withdrawing from the spirit of the world.[15]

This blunt Quaker schoolteacher never spared the feelings of his wealthier co-religionists. Eighteen years later, when many of the leading Philadelphia Friends were in exile in Virginia for supposed seditious activities during the Revolution, he assumed the role of a pitiless Ezekiel expostulating with the children of Israel in their Babylonian captivity. His castigation of their sins was thorough and sweeping:

We have professed to be called and redeemed from the spirit of the world, from that prevalent pride and indulgence so contrary to the low, humble, self-denying life of Christ and his immediate

14. Letter dated 8 May 1765, Brookes, 262.
15. Letter dated 1 Aug. 1760, *ibid.*, 242.

followers; but have we indeed been such, has not our conformity to the world, our engagements of life, in order to please ourselves and gain wealth, with little regard to the danger to the better part, been productive to all the evils pointed out in the Gospel, has it not naturally led us and begot a desire in our children to live in conformity to other people; hence the sumptuousness of our dwellings, our equipage, our dress; furniture and the luxury of our tables have become a snare to us and a matter of offence to the thinking part of mankind . . . and the meek humble and poor self-denying life of Christ is become of no repute, or rather as a Shepherd was to the Egyptians.[16]

The major impetus towards "reformation" and separation from the "world," however, came from the younger generation. An English Quaker, William Reckitt, visiting Philadelphia in 1758, found the elders of the meeting "too much in the outward court, which is only trodden by the Gentiles, or such as are in the spirit of the world; yet a young and rising generation is here . . . whom the Lord hath visited by his power and good spirits in their hearts."[17] Attendance at meetings for worship and discipline increased markedly in the years before the Revolution, and it was noticeable that younger Friends were much in evidence.[18] The dramatic act of Nicholas Waln, one of these younger Friends, in giving up the "world" in which he had made a notable place for himself, and dedicating his life wholly to the service of God may be taken to mark the beginning of the end of the period of transition. This young Friend, a brilliant and popular lawyer, fond of fine clothes and choice wines, and owner of a gaudy yellow carriage, surprised Friends in the Market Street meeting house one morning in February, 1772, by kneeling in prayer and committing himself unreservedly to a life of devotion to God

---

16. Letter to James Pemberton, 28 Jan. 1778, *ibid.*, 326-27.
17. *Some Account of the Life and Gospel Labours of William Reckitt* (London, 1776), 138.
18. See Israel Pemberton to Samuel Spavold, 13 Oct. 1762, Parrish Collection, Pemberton Papers. Joseph Oxley, who attended Philadelphia Yearly Meeting in 1770 found it "a very large, awful, and solemn gathering, such as I had not seen before, so consistent in appearance of dress and uniformity throughout, agreeable to our holy profession, as greatly affected my mind."—*Some Account of the Life of Joseph Pike . . . also A Journal of the Life and Gospel Labours of Joseph Oxley* (London, 1837), 317.

and service to his fellow men. "Teach me," he implored, "to despise the shame, and the opinions of the people of the world. Thou knowest, O Lord! my deep baptisms. I acknowledge my manifold sins and transgressions. I know my unworthiness of the many favours I have received; and I thank Thee, O Father! that Thou has hid Thy mysteries from the wise and prudent and revealed them to babes and sucklings. Amen."[19] Abandoning his lucrative law practice and his gay attire, Nicholas Waln was to become one of the leaders in the period of evangelical piety and humanitarian effort that followed the American Revolution. The great figures of that period in Philadelphia Quakerism were to be ministers rather than political leaders; most of them—Friends like Thomas Scattergood, George Dillwyn, Rebecca Jones, and William Savery—had come of age in the years following the withdrawal from political life.[20]

In 1777, in the midst of momentous civil "Commotions" which subjected the peaceable Friends to a severe testing, the finishing touches were put on the "reformation." Each local meeting "within the verge" of Philadelphia Yearly Meeting appointed committees to visit the membership and impress upon them the importance of plainness of speech, behavior, personal apparel, and household furniture, a "religiously guarded" education, temperance in the use of alcoholic liquors, the manumission of any remaining slaves, and finally, withdrawal, insofar as possible, from the baneful influences of the "world."[21] The first four reforms were aimed at specific evils recognized to be prevalent in the Society, and the last was proposed as the means of preventing backslidings in the future. In erecting barriers against the "world," thus strengthening their group solidarity and isolating themselves from the main currents of American life, the Quakers of the early Republic adopted a pattern of behavior characteristic of sects like the Mennonites, whom in many particulars they now came more and more to resemble. In less than a century Philadelphia Quakerism had come full circle.

19. Jones, *Later Periods*, I, 203-4.
20. Francis R. Taylor, *The Life of William Savery* (New York, 1925), 2-3.
21. Jones *et al.*, *Quakers in the American Colonies*, 571-79.

"IF THE SALT HAVE LOST HIS SAVOR..."

The experience of the Philadelphia Quakers illustrates in a striking way the dilemma of the religious community in the world. How are spiritual values to be communicated to a secular society? The *church,* as sociologists following Troeltsch and Weber have defined it, recognizes the strength of the unregenerate world and, rather than abandon the attempt to influence it directly or risk the loss of its position by contradicting it, accepts the main elements in the existing situation and attempts to remain in a position where it can get a hearing. The church therefore lives on compromise. As Troeltsch has said, "it dominates the world and is therefore dominated by the world." The *sect,* on the other hand, rejects compromise and insists upon perfection. It demands of its members literal obedience to the ethical imperatives of the Sermon on the Mount and either renounces the "world," leaving it to its own evil devices, or attacks it in a radical spirit, thus courting persecution and suppression. In either case the sect, in insisting upon its ideal of perfection, is in danger of being ineffectual.[22]

The Society of Friends in Pennsylvania, and especially in Philadelphia, while retaining many of the outward marks of its sectarian origin, came increasingly between 1682 and 1756 to display the characteristics of the church-type, including the generic trait of compromise. Perhaps it was its residual Calvinism that drove it, when opportunity offered, to an effort to dominate and transform the "world" instead of withdrawing from it. At any rate, the attempt was made, and its positive achievements in the realms of civil liberties, race relations, humanitarianism, and public welfare can never be gainsaid. Where else, outside of Utopian fiction, has a government founded upon such idealistic principles survived for as long a period as three-quarters of a century?

From the beginning, however, there were contradictions inherent in the position of the merchant-kings of this Quaker Uto-

---

22. See J. Milton Yinger, *Religion in the Struggle for Power,* 16-28.

pia. Committed as they were to perpetuating William Penn's "holy experiment" in a society rapidly becoming (by virtue of the Founder's own liberality) largely non-Quaker in composition, they found themselves perforce more and more deeply involved in the "world"—inextricably involved if they were to continue to play out the roles assigned them in the Founder's original conception: "to promote good Discipline and just Government among a plain and well intending people." The people were no longer "plain" in the Quaker sense and some question could be raised whether they were "well intending" with respect to such matters as the use of military force on the frontiers, yet the Quaker merchants felt impelled to continue in power as long as a shadow of the "holy experiment" could be maintained.

The fact is that by 1756 the "holy experiment" had become attenuated until it was in truth little more than a shadow. Having cast their lot in the world, the Quaker merchants found that, despite their resolution not to be of the world, they made concessions to it at many points. In economic life the ideal of intramundane asceticism led inevitably, as it did with other groups, to the acquisition of great wealth. True, the Quakers considered themselves only as stewards of that wealth and attended to the claims of "the Lord's poor" with a sensitivity and generosity matched, perhaps, by no other Protestant group. Granting this sincere humanitarianism which, in its remarkable persistence through three centuries, stands eternally to their credit, it yet remains true that many Quakers developed an attachment to their property which sometimes, as Anthony Benezet was never slow to point out, blinded them to the real nature of their obligation to their neighbors. It is also clear that along with the acquisition of great wealth came a fondness for luxury and ostentatious living which, however masked by a superficial plainness, was wholly out of harmony with "the simplicity of Truth" as preached by the primitive Friends. In the intellectual and cultural realm it is more difficult to pronounce judgment. One would not want to suggest that intellectual curiosity and familiarity with the best achievements of the human spirit in art and literature are inconsistent with true religion; one can nevertheless submit that the wide reading and scholarly preoccupations of a Logan or a Norris betoken a certain spiritual restlessness and a disposition to seek in the satisfactions of secular learning something to fill the void created by an inadequate religious life. And finally, in the political realm, one cannot overlook the compromises with principle into which the Quaker politicians were betrayed in their efforts to remain in power—for example, the money appropriated "for the King's use" when it was obviously to be used for purposes inconsistent with the Quaker peace testimony. These compromises led a perspicacious English Friend to declare in 1756 that Friends' connection with the government

hath been of great disservice . . . to the real end of our being raised up as a peculiar people to bear our testimony to Him whose kingdom is in peace and righteousness. The love of power, the ambition of superiority, the desire of exemption from suffering, strongly operate with many under our name, to continue in stations wherein they sacrifice their testimony, and are as salt which hath lost its savour.[23]

In view of what our study has shown, it is difficult not to agree with Samuel Fothergill that, after seventy-five years of thoroughgoing immersion in the "world" of provincial Pennsylvania, the salt had indeed lost its savor. Or, to recur to George Fox's metaphor with which this book began, the inward plantation had been suffered to fall into decay, the tender vines and lilies of the spiritual life choked out by the coarser and hardier weeds of material wealth and power. Some years after the Revolution, a Quaker poet, looking back over the course of the "holy experiment," was led unconsciously to take up Fox's figure of speech and develop it. His prosody was shaky, but his simple theology gave him a clue to the interpretation of this chapter in the history of Quakerism which *mutatis mutandis* is not essentially different from our own:

Grievous to see and painful to relate
So great a Change in Pennsylvania's State

23. Samuel Fothergill to Ann Fothergill, 28 April 1756, Crosfield, *Memoir of Samuel Fothergill*, 255-56.

That threescore Years, unhappy! should produce
Weeds so destructive, and in common use.
Should any Query how it happen'd here?
The answer's ready, and the reason Clear:
While men securely Slept, then Satan found
His time to sow with Tares the fertile Ground.
But in her early State, while yet but new,
Fruit of a different kind, and better grew,
If we believe report, and that say true.[24]

The "holy experiment" ended in 1756 not because of anything so simple as a difference of policy respecting the defense of the frontier; it ended because in their whole way of living the Philadelphia Quaker merchants who bore leading parts in the government, had departed from that simplicity and spirituality which were of the essence of Quakerism and of William Penn's vision of a holy community on the banks of the Delaware. Realizing this, they abandoned the outer plantation and turned again to the cultivation of the plantation within. For the increased spirituality and humanitarian zeal which followed upon this decision they paid a price: the loss of immediate influence upon the world, the development of a narrowly sectarian mentality, and a liability to internal strife and schism. Weighing the gains and losses against those of the earlier period, one reaches no clear resolution of what remains a perpetual dilemma. One must content oneself with the recognition that in both periods the Quakers made distinctive, indeed unique, contributions to the developing life of the American people.

---

24. Joseph White, "The Little Looking Glass New Fram'd and Enlarg'd," MS in Friends Historical Library of Swarthmore College.

APPENDICES

BENJAMIN FRANKLIN AND
THE QUAKERS

I T is often assumed, especially in Europe, that Benjamin Franklin was a Quaker. It is no mere coincidence that Franklin is
also regarded, more particularly again in Europe, as the arch-
exemplar of the spirit of American capitalism. The poet John
Keats, for example, once referred to Franklin as "a philosophical
Quaker full of mean and thrifty maxims"; and Ernst Troeltsch,
the great German sociologist who followed Max Weber in
exploring the relationship between Protestantism and the capitalist spirit, made the same significant blunder of calling Franklin a Quaker.[1] Franklin, of course, for his part, did not neglect to foster this confusion when he shrewdly conceived it to
be to his advantage. At the end of the eighteenth century, French-
men were full of enthusiasm for the ideal figure of *le bon Quaker*
which the *philosophes* had constructed; Franklin, arriving in
France in 1776 and finding that he was popularly identified with
this semi-mythical figure, took pains to dress the part. Soon after
his arrival, the police, whose business it was to be accurate in their
observations, duly reported that "this Quaker wears the full
costume of his sect."[2]

---

1. M. B. Forman, ed., *The Letters of John Keats* (New York, 1935), 235;
Troeltsch, *Social Teaching*, II, 239.
2. Edith Philips, *The Good Quaker in French Legend* (Philadelphia, 1932),
92; Carl Van Doren, *Benjamin Franklin*, 569-70; Edward E. Hale and Edward
E. Hale, Jr., eds., *Franklin in France* (Boston, 1887), 90.

Franklin was not, of course, an active member of any church, although he was careful for business reasons to remain on good terms with all religious groups. Nevertheless, from the time of his first arrival in Philadelphia, he was intimately associated in his political and business life with the Quaker merchants. As clerk of the Assembly for fifteen years, he came to know all the great Quaker politicians; as an elected member of the Assembly, although dissenting from the Quaker position on military defense, he took his place after 1751 along with Isaac Norris and Israel Pemberton as one of the powers in the so-called "Quaker party"; and upon the withdrawal of the more prominent Friends from the Assembly in 1756 he became the acknowledged leader of the anti-Proprietary forces, which were still known as the "Quaker party."

It is clear from his correspondence that he maintained close personal relations with such Friends as James Logan, Isaac Norris, Israel Pemberton, Abel James, Samuel Rhoads, and Hugh Roberts. His manifold civic projects—the fire companies, the Philadelphia Contributionship, the Pennsylvania Hospital, and the American Philosophical Society—inevitably brought him into constant association with public-spirited Quaker merchants. He shared many intellectual interests with them: we find him, for example, at James Logan's country seat, discussing "magic squares" and other mathematical curiosities with the most learned man in the province, who reciprocated by submitting his botanical and philosophical writings to the younger man for criticism.[3]

The most significant association, however, was in the area of economic life. It is impossible to prove that the ideas which have caused Franklin to be identified forever as the classic American *bourgeois* were derived from his Quaker connections; but some circumstantial evidence, so Thoreau once observed, is very strong, as when one finds a trout in the milk. Most suggestive is the fact that Franklin received his first business training from Thomas Denham, a Quaker merchant who came to his rescue in

---

3. Franklin to Peter Collinson, n.d., *Writings*, II, 456-60; Franklin to James Logan, 30 Oct. 1748, *ibid.*, II, 367; Franklin to Logan, n.d., Sparks MSS.

London and employed him as a clerk in his store upon their return to Philadelphia. Franklin's later recollections supply ground for believing that Denham's influence upon him at this period was strong: "I attended the business diligently," he wrote, "studied accounts, and grew, in a little time, expert at selling. We lodg'd and boarded together; he counsell'd me as a father, having a sincere regard for me. I respected and loved him. . . ."[4] It is unfortunate that our knowledge of Denham is so scanty. His account book at the Historical Society of Pennsylvania tells us little about him but there is no reason to doubt that his economic outlook and practice were essentially those of the other Quaker merchants in Philadelphia.

We have seen that one Friend—Abel James—recognized a familiar Quaker theme in Franklin's praise of the economic virtues. There is a tantalizing bit of evidence which hints that Franklin reciprocated by identifying the Quakers as the exponents *par excellence* of these very virtues. His friend Richard Jackson, commenting on the *Observations Concerning the Increase of Mankind* which Franklin sent him in manuscript, wrote that "The powerful efficacy of manners in increasing a people, is manifest from the instance you mention, the Quakers; among them industry and frugality multiplies and extends the use of the necessaries of life."[5] One looks in vain in the various editions of the *Observations* for a reference to the Quakers. One can only

---

4. *Autobiography*, in *Writings*, I, 289. Denham had removed from Bristol, England *ca.* 1715 under a cloud. The records of Bristol Men's Two-Weeks Meeting explain that "by Falling into bad Company he Spent his Substance and thereby became insolvent under which circumstance he was when he left this nation." —III, 227 (21 March, 1714/15). Neither the Philadelphia nor the Bristol records vouchsafe much additional information about him. The Bristol records tend to bear out the substance of Franklin's interesting story (*Writings*, I, 286) about Denham's returning to England to repay his creditors in full, but they make it clear that this took place in 1721 or 1722 rather than four years later when he was in England with Franklin. According to the records of Philadelphia Monthly Meeting, Denham died on 4 July 1728; this coincides with Franklin's recollection that they both fell ill in February of that year and that Denham succumbed after "a long time," leaving him "a small legacy."—*Ibid.*, I, 289. The records of Bristol Men's Two Weeks Meeting were kindly searched for me by Russell S. Mortimer, Assistant Librarian, British Library of Political and Economic Science.

5. Carl Van Doren, ed., *Letters and Papers of Benjamin Franklin and Richard Jackson, 1753-1785*, (Philadelphia, 1947), 60.

conjecture that before publication Franklin deleted some specific identifying words from the following sentence: "If there be a Sect, therefore, in our Nation, that regard Frugality and Industry as religious Duties, and educate their Children therein, more than others commonly do; such Sect must consequently increase more by natural Generation, than any other Sect in Britain."[6] His first clause describes the Quakers accurately, in any event, and Franklin certainly knew them well enough to have had them in mind in writing the words.

---

6. *Writings*, III, 70.

"GOSPEL ORDER":
THE QUAKER METHOD OF
SETTLING DISPUTES

WHENEVER a difference arose between two Friends, the aggrieved party was instructed to speak or write to the person by whom he felt he was injured and endeavor "by Gentle means in a brotherly and loving manner" to obtain satisfaction. If this failed, he was to choose one or two judicious Friends to accompany him and assist him in settling the claim. "But if there doth appear in the matter, to be either unsettled differences in Accompts, or Reason of Debate," the parties to the dispute were to choose referees or arbitrators, engaging themselves to abide by their decision.

Any Friend who refused to accept this impartial arbitrament could be complained of to the Monthly Meeting. The meeting then summoned the parties before it and "to avoid . . . the Contention and indecent noise which some in those Cases are too apt to fall into," directed a further hearing outside the meeting, appointing several Friends to assist. If the parties refused to attend such a hearing, the meeting appointed a number of Friends to listen to all the evidence and, acting as umpires, make a final decision, which should be reported to the next Monthly Meeting. If, after all these steps had been duly taken, either party refused to accept the final award, "such Person must be dealt with as one disorderly, and that regards not peace either in himself, or in the church and that slights the Love, order, and unity of the Brethren: and after due admonition, if he or she persists therein, let such be disowned and testified against by the Meeting, after which the other Friend may seek his Remedy against him or her (so disowned) at the Law."

There was a provision for rehearing by the Monthly Meeting and for appeal to the Quarterly Meeting. Only under certain extraordinary circumstances ("as the Partys absconding or leaving the Country with design to defraud their Creditors;—or that the going through the Meeting [on account of the time it would take up] be a manifest and apparent Damage to the Creditors," *etc.*) did the meeting ever give Friends permission to go to law without first giving "Gospel Order."[1]

---

1. This account is drawn from the manuscript Book of Discipline of 1719.

BIBLIOGRAPHICAL ESSAY

GENERAL

MANUSCRIPTS

THIS book is based largely upon original sources. Its foundations were quarried in the first instance from the magnificent manuscript collections of the Historical Society of Pennsylvania. The Logan Papers, *ca.* 12,000 items, 1664-1871; the Norris Papers, 70 vols. and 16 boxes, 1742-1860; the Pemberton Papers, 70 vols., 1641-1880; and the Coates-Reynell Papers, 70 vols. and 48 boxes, 1702-1843, provided the richest yields. These are four amazingly extensive, well-preserved, and splendidly arranged bodies of source materials, covering the history of four leading Quaker mercantile families. Out of the plethora of letter books; incoming correspondence, and miscellaneous documents of all kinds it was possible to reconstruct a great part of the mercantile, civic, and cultural life of the great Quaker merchant princes of colonial Philadelphia. Some additional Pemberton Papers are in the Etting Collection, 1558-1917, also in the Historical Society of Pennsylvania. Supplementary Logan Papers are found in the Maria Dickinson Logan Family Papers, 1671-1890. Other collections at the Historical Society of Pennsylvania which furnished valuable material were the Cox-Wharton-Parrish Papers, 1600-1900; the Penn Manuscripts, 1629-1834; the Dreer Collection, 1492-

1917; the Clifford Papers, 1722-1832; the Charles Morton Smith Collection, 1685-1843; the Taylor Papers, 1672-1775; the Wharton Papers, 1679-1834; the Day Book of Joseph Richardson, 1744; and the Letter Books of Samuel Powel, Jr., 1724-1747.

Almost equal in importance to the four major collections mentioned in the first paragraph are the Smith Manuscripts, 1678-1808, in the Library Company of Philadelphia, which include the manuscript diary of John Smith in eleven volumes. This fascinating day-by-day record of Philadelphia Quaker life in the 1740's and 1750's has been edited in part by Albert Cook Myers under the title of *Hannah Logan's Courtship* (Philadelphia, 1904). Some extracts were also printed by R. Morris Smith in *The Burlington Smiths* (Philadelphia, 1877). Second in value only to the diary of John Smith is that of Elizabeth Drinker, the early years of which overlap the period covered in this study. I had the privilege of consulting a typewritten copy in the possession of Dr. Cecil Drinker of Boston. Dr. Drinker has published parts of this diary, dealing chiefly with medical matters, under the title of *Not So Long Ago: A Chronicle of Medicine and Doctors in Colonial Philadelphia* (New York, 1937). Henry D. Biddle edited *Extracts from the Journal of Elizabeth Drinker, 1759-1807* (Philadelphia, 1889). A letter-book, 1715-21, of Jonathan Dickinson at the Library Company of Philadelphia supplements an earlier one, 1698-1701, at the Historical Society of Pennsylvania. The Gulielma M. Howland Collection in the Haverford College Library contains some valuable Logan family material. The Howell Manuscripts, 1753-64, the Woolman Manuscripts, and letters in the Charles F. Jenkins Autograph Collection at the Friends Historical Library of Swarthmore College furnished significant details. The Sparks Manuscripts in the Harvard University Library supplied an important bit of evidence concerning James Logan.

Absolutely indispensable in providing the background of the corporate religious life of the Philadelphia Quaker community are the manuscript minutes and other records of Philadelphia Monthly Meeting and Philadelphia Yearly Meeting, housed at the Department of Records, Philadelphia Yearly Meeting, 302 Arch Street, Philadelphia. Extracts from the minutes of Philadelphia Monthly Meeting have been printed in the Genealogical Society of Pennsylvania, *Publications*, 1-15. The second volume of William Wade Hinshaw's monumental *Encyclopedia of American Quaker Genealogy* (Richmond, Ind., 1936-) indexes the data of genealogical interest in the Philadelphia Monthly Meeting records. This volume is useful in determining whether a given individual was a member of the meeting; it also supplies vital statistics, helps in unraveling family relationships, and records disciplinary actions, including disownments. There are many manuscript copies of the 1719 Book of Discipline of Philadelphia Yearly Meeting in existence, since every meeting once had one for its own use; I have used a copy at the Friends Historical Library of Swarthmore College.

PRINTED SOURCES

Some valuable original accounts of the early settlements in Pennsylvania are collected and helpfully edited by Albert Cook Myers in *Narratives of Early Pennsylvania, West New Jersey, and Delaware, 1630-1707*, in J. Franklin Jameson, ed., *Original Narratives of Early American History* (New York, 1912). Several of the Quaker merchants, including Isaac Norris I, David Lloyd, James Logan, John Kinsey, and John Smith, had a hand in the collection of material for an early history of Pennsylvania. Samuel Smith finally assumed responsibility for these materials and, assisted by his brother John Smith, prepared an historical narrative in two parts. The first part has been edited from the original MSS by William M. Mervine and published by the Colonial Society of Pennsylvania as *The History of the Province of Pennsylvania* (Philadelphia, 1913). The second part, devoted to the progress of Quakerism in Pennsylvania, was printed in part by Samuel Hazard in his *Register of Pennsylvania*, 6-7 (1830-31). Much of the material in Robert Proud's *History of Pennsylvania* (2 vols., Philadelphia, 1797) was drawn from Smith's narrative.

The correspondence between James Logan and William Penn, together with a number of letters of Isaac Norris, copied by Deborah Norris Logan and edited by Edward Armstrong, was published in the Historical Society of Pennsylvania, *Memoirs*, IX-X (1870-1872); Mrs. Logan's transcriptions, it should be noted, were not always accurate. The valuable correspondence of James Logan with Thomas Story, the originals of which are at the Library of the Society of Friends, London, was edited by Norman Penney as a supplement to the Friends Historical Association, *Bulletin*, in 1927.

The published journals of the Quaker ministers reveal more about the spiritual condition of the writers than about the outward life of the Quaker community; nevertheless, they provide a valuable insight into the Quaker piety of the period and occasionally drop revealing hints about external matters. Their full titles (invariably lengthy) may be found in Joseph Smith's *Descriptive Catalogue of Friends Books* (2 vols., London, 1867). I have made use of the journals of the following: Thomas Chalkley, John Churchman, James Dickinson, Jonathan Dickinson (in the recent edition of Evangeline W. and Charles M. Andrews), William Edmundson, Thomas Ellwood, John Fothergill, George Fox (the Bi-Centenary Edition), Joseph Oxley, Catherine Philips, William Reckitt, Daniel Stanton, Thomas Story, and John Woolman (Amelia Mott Gummere's definitive edition). Similar in nature, being based chiefly upon journals and letters, are George Crosfield's *Memoirs of the Life and Gospel Labours of Samuel Fothergill* (New York, 1844) and *The Life and Travels of John Pemberton*, edited by W[illiam] H[odgson], Jr. (London, 1844).

Some of the more impressionable travelers who visited Philadelphia left engaging, though not always accurate, descriptions of the "curious customs" of the Quakers; others, less impressed by the novelty of Quaker ways, made caustic comments on what seemed to them the hypocritical manners of the wealthy Friends. Professor Peter Kalm, the Swedish botanist, made some interesting observations on the *Quakerus philadelphianus* in his *Travels in North America;* I have used Adolph B. Benson's edition in two volumes (New York, 1937). Jean Pierre Brissot de Warville in his *Nouveau voyage dans les Etats-Unis de l'Amérique septentrionale* (3 vols., Paris, 1791) and the Marquis de Barbé-Marbois in his letters, edited by Eugene P. Chase as *Our Revolutionary Forefathers* (New York, 1929) shared their countrymen's interest in *le bon Quaker*. *Gentleman's Progress; the Itinerarium of Dr. Alexander Hamilton, 1744,* ed. by Carl Bridenbaugh (Chapel Hill, N. C., 1948), presents a less flattering picture.

Benjamin Franklin's writings are of course full of revealing glimpses of the Quakers; I have used Albert H. Smyth's edition (10 vols., New York, 1907), supplementing it with Carl Van Doren's magisterial *Benjamin Franklin* (New York, 1938). The references to Friends in *Caspipina's Letters* (Bath, 1777) by the Reverend Jacob Duché are surprisingly sympathetic considering that the author was an Anglican clergyman. The diary of Jacob Hiltzheimer, extracts from which have been edited by Jacob Cox Parsons (Philadelphia, 1893), reflects the activities of a circle composed partly of "wet Quakers." The New Englander's view of Philadelphia Quaker society can be found in John Adams' diary in the second volume of his *Works* (Boston, 1856), edited by Charles Francis Adams, and in Josiah Quincy's journal in Massachusetts Historical Society, *Proceedings,* 49 (1916).

PERIODICALS

The *Pennsylvania Magazine of History and Biography* is a rich mine of source materials. The multitude of diaries, letters, and other personal documents, together with articles and brief notes which fill the seventy-odd volumes of this periodical have provided a substantial portion of the material out of which this study was constructed. Individual references would extend this bibliographical essay unduly; my footnotes, however, testify to the extent of my reliance upon this magazine. Almost equally productive were the files of the Friends Historical Association *Bulletin* and the Friends Historical Society *Journal.* Since these journals are well indexed, references to individual articles are not given here except in a few special instances.

SECONDARY WORKS: HISTORY.

Thompson Westcott's encyclopedic "History of Philadelphia," printed in the *Philadelphia Sunday Dispatch* between 1867 and 1884, is a virtually inexhaustible resource; especially is this true of the unique form in which it exists at the Historical Society of Pennsylvania in 32 bound volumes, illustrated with original documents and pictures assembled and mounted by D. McNeely Stauffer. More convenient for reference purposes is the three-volume *History of Philadelphia* (Philadelphia, 1884) by J. Thomas Scharf and Thompson Westcott, based on Westcott's fuller text. John Fanning Watson's *Annals of Philadelphia and Pennsylvania in the Olden Time* (3 vols., Philadelphia, 1881) is full of curious and useful lore collected by an indefatigable antiquarian who was not always sufficiently critical of the sources of his information. *Rebels and Gentlemen: Philadelphia in the Age of Franklin* (New York, 1942) by Carl and Jessica Bridenbaugh is a brilliant picture of social and cultural life in colonial Philadelphia; my account of one segment of that life owes much to this broader panorama. Horace Mather Lippincott's *Early Philadelphia: Its People, Life, and Progress* (Philadelphia, 1917) and Agnes Repplier's *Philadelphia: The Place and the People* (New York, 1898) capture something of the flavor of life in provincial Philadelphia.

Carl Bridenbaugh's *Cities in the Wilderness: The First Century of Urban Life in America, 1625-1742* (New York, 1938) is indispensable: the pioneer study of the early towns, it is so prodigal of factual information and so conveniently arranged as to be virtually an encyclopedia of colonial urbanism. *The Founding of American Civilization: The Middle Colonies* (New York, 1938) and *The Golden Age of Colonial Culture* (New York, 1942), both by Thomas J. Wertenbaker, are suggestive studies in colonial cultural history. James Truslow Adams' *Provincial Society, 1690-1763* in Arthur M. Schlesinger and Dixon Ryan Fox, eds., *A History of American Life*, III (New York, 1927) provides a general social and cultural backdrop for the story of the colonial Philadelphia Quakers.

SECONDARY WORKS: BIOGRAPHY.

Two convenient sources of biographical data about colonial Philadelphians are John W. Jordan's *Colonial and Revolutionary Families of Pennsylvania* (3 vols., New York, 1911) and Charles P. Keith's *Provincial Councillors of Pennsylvania* (Philadelphia, 1883); although the emphasis in both these works is genealogical, they supply a good deal of information, some of which is not available elsewhere. Isaac Sharpless's *Political Leaders of Provincial Pennsylvania* (New York, 1919) contains essays on James Logan, Thomas Lloyd, David Lloyd, Isaac Norris II, John Kinsey, and James Pemberton. *The Dictionary of American Biography* includes excellent biographical sketches of Anthony Benezet, Thomas Cadwalader, Thomas Chalkley, Richard Hill, John Kinsey, David Lloyd, Thomas Lloyd, James Logan, Anthony Morris I, Isaac Norris I, Isaac Norris II, Griffith Owen, Israel Pemberton II, James Pemberton, John Pemberton, Francis Rawle, Joseph Richardson, William Savery, Edward Shippen, Nicholas Waln, Samuel Wharton, Thomas Wharton, Caspar Wistar, and John Woolman.

There is a deplorable shortage of sound full-length biographies of colonial Philadelphians. There is not even an adequate biographical study of William Penn, although William I. Hull's *William Penn: A Topical Biography* (New York, 1937) is helpful, and the older books by Thomas Clarkson (*Memoirs of the Private and Public Life of William Penn* [Philadelphia, 1814]) and Samuel M. Janney (*The Life of William Penn* [Philadelphia, 1852]) contain much important material. Edward C. O. Beatty's *William Penn as Social Philosopher* (New York, 1939) is a thorough and enlightening monograph. Joseph E. Johnson's unpublished dissertation, *A Statesman of Colonial Pennsylvania: A Study of the Private Life and Public Career of James Logan to the Year 1726* (Doctoral Thesis, Harvard University, 1943) covers the earlier part of James Logan's career with exhaustive scholarship. The older books by Wilson Armistead (*Memoirs of James Logan* [London, 1851]) and Irma Jane Cooper (*The Life and Public Services of James Logan* [New

York, 1921]) are inadequate. Ethyn W. Kirby's *George Keith* (New York, 1942), Marion D. Learned's *Life of Francis Daniel Pastorius* (Philadelphia, 1908), and Burton A. Konkle's unpublished David Lloyd and the First Half-Century of Pennsylvania (MS copy in Friends Historical Library of Swarthmore College) are the only other full-dress studies of Pennsylvania Quakers of the first generation.

George S. Brookes's *Friend Anthony Benezet* (Philadelphia, 1937), which supersedes the older *Memoirs of the Life of Anthony Benezet* (Philadelphia, 1817) by Roberts Vaux, is especially valuable on account of the many letters of Benezet which it reprints in full. Theodore Thayer's *Israel Pemberton: King of the Quakers* (Philadelphia, 1943) is particularly good on the political activities of the younger Israel Pemberton. Studies of the two Isaac Norrises and of John Kinsey are greatly needed. Three family histories containing useful material are Josiah G. Leach's *History of the Bringhurst Family* (Philadelphia, 1901), John Jay Smith's *Letters of Doctor Richard Hill and His Children; or, The History of a Family as Told by Themselves* (Philadelphia, 1854), and *The Morris Family of Philadelphia* (5 vols., Philadelphia, 1898-1909) by Robert C. Moon.

BY CHAPTERS

CHAPTER I. THE TWO PLANTATIONS

Insight into the nature of early Quakerism can best be gained from *The Works of George Fox* (8 vols., Philadelphia, 1831) and the writings of Robert Barclay and William Penn. There have been many editions of Barclay's *Apology for the True Christian Divinity* (1678), the major intellectual monument of seventeenth-century Quakerism; I have used the text which appears in *Truth Triumphant, through the Spiritual Warfare, Christian Labours, and Writings, of that Able and Faithful Servant of Jesus Christ, Robert Barclay* (3 vols., London, 1718). The writings of William Penn, which are of central importance in revealing the ideological framework of Quaker social development, are also available in many editions; my references, with a few exceptions, are to *A Collection of the Works of William Penn* (2 vols., London, 1726). Two important interpretative studies, throwing new light on primitive Quakerism are Rachel H. King, *George Fox and the Light Within* (Philadelphia, 1940) and Geoffrey F. Nuttall, *The Holy Spirit in Puritan Faith and Experience* (Oxford, 1946). There is a brief discussion of the relationship of prophetic Quakerism to Puritanism in the author's "Desiderata in Quaker History," Friends Hist. Assoc., *Bull.*, 36 (1947), 3-11.

The most convenient narrative of Quaker development is Elbert Russell's *History of Quakerism* (New York, 1943). For a more extended account, in which sound scholarship is blended with deep and genuine insight into Quakerism, see the volumes in the "Rowntree Series," especially William C. Braithwaite's *Beginnings of Quakerism* (London, 1912), the same author's *Second Period of Quakerism* (London, 1919), Rufus M. Jones's *Later Periods of Quakerism* (2 vols., London, 1921), and *The Quakers in the American Colonies* (London, 1911), in which Rufus M. Jones was assisted by Amelia M. Gummere and Isaac Sharpless. Ezra Michener's *Retrospect of Early Quakerism* (Philadelphia, 1860) is helpful on the institutional aspect of early Philadelphia Quakerism. James Bowden's *History of the Society of Friends in America* (2 vols., London, 1854) contains material not readily found elsewhere, and Pierre Brodin's *Les Quakers en Amérique au dix-septième siècle et au début du dix-huitième* (Paris, 1935) is a judicious study by a modern French writer.

Indispensable source materials on Quaker government in Pennsylvania are to be found in the *Minutes of the Provincial Council of Pennsylvania*, in *Colonial Records of Pennsylvania* (Philadelphia and Harrisburg, 1851-52), I-IX, and the *Votes and Proceedings of the House of Representatives of the Province of Pennsylvania*, in *Pennsylvania Archives*, 8th ser. (Harrisburg, 1931-35), I-VIII. Among modern treatments of the political history of colonial Pennsylvania, perhaps the most useful are Charles P. Keith's *Chronicles of Pennsylvania . . . 1688-1748* (2 vols., Philadelphia, 1917) and the relevant chapters in Herbert L. Osgood's *The American Colonies in the Seventeenth Century* (3 vols., New York, 1904-1907) and *The American Colonies in the Eighteenth Century* (4 vols., New York, 1924). The third volume of Charles M. Andrews' *The Colonial Period of American History* (4 vols., New Haven, 1934-38) contains a good account of the early years. William R. Shepherd's *History of Propietary Government in Pennsylvania*, in *Columbia University Studies in History, Economics, and Public Law*, VI (New York, 1896) is helpful on the institutional development of the province, and Winfred T. Root's *Relations of Pennsylvania with the British Government, 1696-1765* (Philadelphia, 1912) has an especially full and reliable treatment of the problem of imperial defense. Julian P. Boyd's discussion of the Indian policy of colonial Pennsylvania in his historical introduction to *Indian Treaties Printed by Benjamin Franklin, 1736-1762* (Philadelphia, 1938) is one of the most penetrating of recent contributions to colonial history.

Special attention is given to the role of the Friends in provincial politics in Isaac Sharpless's *Quaker Experiment in Government* (Philadelphia, 1898). Two articles by Guy F. Hershberger, "The Pennsylvania Quaker Experiment in Politics, 1682-1756," *Mennonite Quarterly Review*, 10 (1936), 187-221, and "Pacifism and the State in Colonial Pennsylvania," *Church History*, 8 (1939), 54-74, present thoughtful criticisms of Quaker policy from the Mennonite non-resistant point of view. The aftermath of the Quaker ascendancy is discussed by Charles H. Lincoln in *The Revolutionary Movement in Pennsylvania* (Philadelphia, 1901) and by J. Paul Selsam in *The Pennsylvania Constitution of 1776: A Study in Revolutionary Democracy* (Philadelphia, 1936); their interpretation should be checked by the findings of Theodore Thayer in his article on "The Quaker Party of Pennsylvania, 1755-1765," *Pa. Mag. of Hist.*, 71 (1947) 19-43. Thayer's essay on "The Friendly Association," *ibid.*, 67 (1943), 356-76, should also be consulted in this connection.

Chapter II. A Door of Mercy

The best sources of information on the geographical distribution and social status of the Quakers in Restoration England are the episcopal returns of 1669, edited by G. Lyon Turner as *Original Records of Early Nonconformity under Persecution and Indulgence* (3 vols., London, 1911-14). The certificates of removal which Quaker settlers brought from their home meetings are printed by Albert Cook Myers in *Quaker Arrivals at Philadelphia, 1682-1750* (Philadelphia, 1902). The same author's *Immigration of the Irish Quakers into Pennsylvania, 1682-1750* (Swarthmore, Pa., 1902) and William I. Hull's *William Penn and the Dutch Quaker Migration to Pennsylvania, Swarthmore College Monographs on Quaker History*, 2 (Swarthmore, Pa., 1935) cover the migration of two national groups of Quakers with admirable thoroughness. The story of the Welsh Quaker migration and settlement can be followed in T. Mardy Rees's *History of the Quakers in Wales and Their Emigration to North America* (Carmarthen, Wales, 1925) and Charles S. Browning's *Welsh Settlement of Pensylvania* (Philadelphia, 1912). No detailed studies of the social background of the English Friends or of their migration to Pennsylvania have been made, but light is thrown on these subjects by certain books dealing with the major Quaker centers in England: see especially Ernest E. Taylor's *The Valiant Sixty* (London, 1947); William Beck and T. Frederick Ball's *London Friends Meetings* (London, 1869); and William Tanner's *Three Lectures on Friends in Bristol and Somerset* (London, 1858). Joseph Besse's *Collection of the Sufferings of the People Called Quakers* (2 vols., London, 1753) contains an extraordinary amount of detailed information about the persecution of Friends.

Chapter III. The Way To Wealth

All discussions of the economic ethics of Protestantism owe something to Max Weber's great seminal essay *The Protestant*

Ethic and the Spirit of Capitalism, trans. by Talcott Parsons (New York, 1930); Weber's observations on Quakerism, like many other portions of his essay, are based mainly upon shrewd and fruitful insights rather than upon wide reading in Quaker sources. After Weber, my chief debt in this field is to Ernst Troeltsch's *Social Teaching of the Christian Churches*, trans. by Olive Wyon (2 vols., New York, 1931); Troeltsch adds some suggestive details, amplifying Weber's hints, but his treatment is not based upon a thorough study of Quaker sources and his conception of Quakerism as simply a form of the Anabaptist movement leads him to neglect the residual Puritanism. Helpful and stimulating applications and modifications of the Weber thesis are found in H. Richard Niebuhr's *Social Sources of Denominationalism* (New York, 1929), R. H. Tawney's *Religion and the Rise of Capitalism* (New York, 1926), and J. Milton Yinger's *Religion in the Struggle for Power* (Durham, N.C., 1946). The only available study of Quaker economic ethics is Isabel Grubb's *Quakerism and Industry before 1800* (London, 1930); this is a fairly comprehensive survey of the formal pronouncements by Quaker writers, but these are not checked by the actual practice of Quaker businessmen.

CHAPTER IV. THE HOLY COMMUNITY

It is surprising that there is no adequate historical treatment of Quaker humanitarianism, taking account of its sources and its varied manifestations; nor, except in isolated studies of particular meetings, have we any analysis of the nature and extent of the control which the meetings exerted over the life of the individual Friend. Auguste Jorns' *The Quakers as Pioneers in Social Work*, trans. by T. K. Brown (New York, 1931), the only general treatment of Quaker philanthropy, leaves many questions unanswered. Eduard Bernstein's *Cromwell and Communism: Socialism and Democracy in the Great English Revolution* (London, 1930) contains some suggestive observations on the transmutation of primitive Quaker radicalism into philanthropy; and A. Ruth Fry's *John Bellers, 1654-1725: Quaker, Economist, and Social Reformer* (London, 1935) reprints the major writings of an important social critic. The background of social thinking among religious groups in England can be studied in Margaret James's *Social Problems and Policy during the Puritan Revolution, 1640-1660* (London, 1930) and in Richard B. Schlatter's *Social Ideas of Religious Leaders, 1660-1688* (London, 1940); the latter work contains a useful appendix summarizing the existing secondary material on Quaker social ethics.

Chapter V. In The Counting House

Mary A. Hanna's *Trade of the Delaware District before the Revolution*, in Smith College *Studies in History*, 2 (1917), 239-348 is a competent survey of the commerce of the entire area contributory to Philadelphia. An excellent analysis of the structure of colonial Philadelphia business is "The Organization of Business in Colonial Philadelphia" by Harry D. Berg in *Pennsylvania History*, 10 (1943), 157-77. "The Economic Relations of Boston, Philadelphia, and New York, 1680-1715," by Curtis Nettels in the *Journal of Economic and Business History*, 3 (1930-31), 185-215 is an important study of one phase of Philadelphia's commerce. Wilbur C. Plummer's "Consumer Credit in Colonial Philadelphia," *Pa. Mag. of Hist.*, 66 (1942), 385-409, documents the statement that credit rather than cash was the rule in retail transactions, but the evidence upon which he bases his findings apparently includes no Quaker business records. The fact that one can cite only short articles on particular aspects of the economic life of colonial Philadelphia reveals the need for a full-length study. A mass of useful data for such a study is found in *Prices in Colonial Philadelphia* (Philadelphia, 1935) by Anne Bezanson, Robert D. Gray, and Miriam Hussey.

There is an extensive literature on the early iron industry. The most authoritative book is Arthur C. Bining's *Pennsylvania Iron Manufacture in the Eighteenth Century* (Harrisburg, 1938), but *Forges and Furnaces in the Province of Pennsylvania*, in Pennsylvania Society of the Colonial Dames of America, *Publications*, 3 (Philadelphia, 1914) yields much useful information not readily accessible elsewhere. Two older books—J. B. Pearse's *Concise History of the Iron Manufacture of the American Colonies* (Philadelphia, 1876) and James M. Swank's *History of the Manufacture of Iron in All Ages* (Philadelphia, 1892)—are still valuable. The English iron industry, in which Quakers were prominent, is well described in Thomas S. Ashton's *Iron and Steel in the Industrial Revolution* (Manchester and London, 1924).

The paper-money controversy and its sequel are best followed in the contemporary literature to which it gave rise: Francis Rawle's *Some Remedies Proposed for Restoring the Sunk Credit of the Province of Pennsylvania; with Some Remarks on Its Trade* (Philadelphia, 1721); the address of "several gentlemen and merchants," together with the reply of the paper-money exponents and the merchants' rebuttal, all printed in Proud's *History of Pennsylvania*, II, 152-62; James Logan's *obiter dicta* on the depression of 1721-23 in his *Charge Delivered from the Bench to the Grand-Jury* (Philadelphia, 1723); Rawle's *Ways and Means for the Inhabitants of Delaware to Become Rich* (Philadelphia, 1725); the anonymous *Dialogue Shewing What's Therein to Be Found* (Philadelphia, 1725), perhaps attributable to Isaac Norris; and Rawle's rejoinder, *A Just Rebuke to a Dialogue Betwixt Simon and Timothy, Shewing What's Therein to Be Found* (Philadelphia, 1726). An adequate discussion of the paper-money question in Pennsylvania is found in Richard A. Lester's *Monetary Experiments: Early American and Recent Scandinavian* (Princeton, 1939); and a brief comment on Rawle's *Ways and Means* appears in Frank A. Fetter's "Early History of Political Economy in the United States," American Philosophical Society, *Proceedings*, 87 (1944), 51-60.

CHAPTER VI. QUAKER GRANDEES

Little has been written on either the social theory or the manner of life of the upper-class Quakers. Information regarding Quaker dress in the eighteenth century can be found in Amelia M. Gummere's rather unsystematic treatise *The Quaker: A Study in Costume* (Philadelphia, 1901). Clara L. Avery's *Early American Silver* (New York, 1930) contains a useful commentary on the output of Joseph Richardson and other Philadelphia Quaker silversmiths. *The Colonial Architecture of Philadelphia* (Boston, 1920) by Frank Cousins and Phil M. Riley is a helpful study, which can be supplemented by the photographs and text in Harold Eberlein and Cortlandt Hubbard's *Portrait of a Colonial City: Philadelphia, 1670-1838* (Philadelphia, 1939). The social life of the American colonial aristocracy is engagingly surveyed by Dixon Wecter in *The Saga of American Society* (New York, 1937).

CHAPTER VII. THE TASTE FOR BOOKS

The most compendious and understanding account of Quaker educational ideals and practices is to be found in Howard H. Brinton's little study entitled *Quaker Education in Theory and Practice* (Wallingford, Pa., n.d.). Thomas Woody's *Early Quaker Education in Pennsylvania*, in Teacher's College, Columbia University, *Contributions to Education*, 105 (New York, 1920) reprints some valuable source materials with commentary. Chapter 2 of James Mulhern's *History of Secondary Education in Pennsylvania* (Philadelphia, 1933), based upon the MS minutes of Philadelphia Monthly Meeting and of the Overseers of the William Penn Charter School, is a nearly definitive account of the Quaker school system in colonial Philadelphia. James P. Wickersham's *History of Education in Pennsylvania* (Lancaster, Pa., 1886) is still useful.

On book publishing in colonial Philadelphia, the second volume of Douglas C. McMurtrie's *History of Printing in the*

United States (New York, 1936) is standard; it may be supplemented by Charles R. Hildeburn's *Issues of the Pennsylvania Press, 1685-1784* (2 vols., Philadelphia, 1885). Two especially valuable articles are Carl Bridenbaugh's "The Press and the Book in Eighteenth Century Philadelphia," *Pa. Mag. of Hist.*, 65 (1941), 1-30 and Howard M. Jones's "The Importation of French Books in Philadelphia: 1750-1800," *Modern Philology*, 32 (1934), 157-77. "The Passing of Friends Library" by Henry J. Cadbury in *The Friend*, 103 (1930), 459-61, recalls some facts about the early collection of books belonging to Philadelphia Monthly Meeting. The history of the Library Company of Philadelphia, which had the enthusiastic support of Friends, can be read in *A Short History of the Library Company of Philadelphia* (Philadelphia, 1913) by George M. Abbott, and in *Benjamin Franklin's Library: A Short Account of the Library Company of Philadelphia* (New York, 1937) by Austin K. Gray. In preparing this study I have also consulted the manuscript records of the Library Company at the Ridgway Library, Philadelphia. E. V. Lamberton's "Colonial Libraries of Pennsylvania," *Pa. Mag. of Hist.*, 42 (1918), 193-234, should have special mention in this connection as a superior study.

Chapter VIII. Reading for Delight and Profit

The study of the reading of the Philadelphia Quaker merchants is beset with all the difficulties and vexations common to such inquiries. In general, the sources of information are of three sorts: (1) correspondence of the merchants, especially with their London agents; (2) actual volumes still in existence bearing the owner's signature or bookplate; and (3) a few inventories in the manuscript collections mentioned above and in the Philadelphia Registry of Wills (photostats of wills and inventories to 1719 are available at the Genealogical Society of Pennsylvania). This last type of source would normally be the most fruitful; unfortunately, diligent search has revealed not more than two or three complete itemized inventories of the larger libraries. In this respect, the source materials would appear to be less extensive than those which have been available to students of literary culture in other colonial regions. Compare especially Louis B. Wright, *The First Gentlemen of Virginia* (San Marino, Cal., 1940); George K. Smart, "Private Libraries in Colonial Virginia," *American Literature*, 10 (1938), 24-52; Thomas G. Wright, *Literary Culture in Colonial New England* (New Haven, 1920); Frederick P. Bowes, *The Culture of Early Charleston* (Chapel Hill, 1942); and Joseph Towne Wheeler's series of articles on the reading interests of colonial Marylanders in *The Maryland Historical Magazine*, 35-38 (1940-43).

For James Logan's library—the largest in the colony—we have, to be sure, an early manuscript catalogue, listing approximately 1625 titles, and the printed *Catalogus bibliothecae Loganianae* (Philadelphia, 1760) which lists approximately 2600 titles (it may be noted that in some cases one title may cover as many as 52 volumes). The manuscript catalogue dates from 1740 and therefore does not comprehend all his books; the printed catalogue, which appeared some nine years after Logan's death, does not include the books left to his sons and does contain the titles of some books subsequently added to the collection. Thus there is no complete and accurate record of the great library which Logan built up over the years at Stenton. Nevertheless we know more about this impressive collection than we do about any of its lesser rivals.

There is no inventory of the Norris library at Fairhill. Part of the collection (about 1500 volumes, according to a contemporary account) was given to Dickinson College after the Revolution by John Dickinson, son-in-law of Isaac Norris II. Some 632 volumes bearing a Norris autograph can be identified now. These are chiefly on medical, scientific, and theological subjects, and interestingly enough, almost none are in English. Some interesting comments on these books appear in James W. Phillips, "The Sources of the Original Dickinson College Library,"

Pennsylvania History, 14 (1947), 108-17. A few additional books containing a Norris signature have been located elsewhere, notably in the Historical Society of Pennsylvania.

A "List of John Smith's Books," comprising 116 titles, was found in the Smith Manuscripts (VIII, 60). From Smith's diary, in which he often commented upon the books he was reading, 74 additional titles have been gleaned. Other titles come from his correspondence and from his "Atticus" papers. For a detailed analysis of Smith's reading, consult Frederick B. Tolles, "A Literary Quaker: John Smith of Burlington and Philadelphia," *Pa. Mag. of Hist.*, 65 (1941), 300-33. Dr. Lloyd Zachary's library can be reconstructed from the inventory of his estate in the Logan Papers (XIX, 62); a list of his medical books drawn from this source has been printed by Samuel X. Radbill in his article on Dr. Zachary in the *Annals of Medical History*, third ser., 1 (1939), 517-18. A few titles from William Rawle's library were recovered from a list of books bought at a vendue in 1736, found in William Rawle's Waste Book at the Historical Society of Pennsylvania; the inventory of his estate in the Philadelphia Registry of Wills lists only "a Large Parsel of Books . . . £20." Twenty-six books which once belonged to Thomas Chalkley are now in the Haverford College Library, and a few of John Pemberton's are in the Friends Historical Library of Swarthmore College. Anthony Benezet's books are listed by Henry J. Cadbury in Friends Hist. Assoc., *Bull.*, 23 (1934), 63-75; 25 (1936), 83-85.

For the rest we are obliged to rely upon scraps of evidence found chiefly in the correspondence of the merchants. Charles Norris's letters to Susanna and James Wright, for example, often contain references to reading; one can only wish that the inventory of his estate (Norris Family Letters, I, 89), which mentions "30 Books" appraised at £40 in his office and "171 Volumes of Books" valued at £16 in "the back Room on the Third floor" were itemized in detail. One feels similarly frustrated when one comes upon the item of "A Parcell of Books Historys &c £28.8.6" in the inventory of Jonathan Dickinson's estate (printed in *Pa. Mag. of Hist.*, 59 [1935], 429) or the "3 ffolios and 43 Small books . . . £4.15.0" in the inventory of Thomas Denham's estate, Philadelphia Registry of Wills. This latter item is especially tantalizing because of the likelihood that Denham's *protégé* Benjamin Franklin was accustomed to browse in this small collection. But so it is, for the most part: we are left again and again with nothing more definite than "Sundry books," "A parcel of old books," and similar expressions. Executors of estates in eighteenth-century Philadelphia had other things to think about than the needs of future historians of literary culture!

CHAPTER IX. VOTARIES OF SCIENCE

A number of scholars, working independently, have recently explored the relationship between Puritanism and the rise of the new experimental science. Three studies pertinent to our inquiry are Robert K. Merton, "Science, Technology, and Society in Seventeenth Century England," *Osiris*, 4 (1938), 360-632; Richard F. Jones, *Ancients and Moderns: A Study of the Background of the Battle of the Books* (St. Louis, 1936); and Dorothy Stimson, "Puritanism and the New Philosophy in Seventeenth-Century England," Institute of the History of Medicine, *Bulletin*, 3 (1935), 321-34. A definitive presentation of the evidence relating to William Penn's membership in the Royal Society is Henry J. Cadbury's "Penn, Collinson, and the Royal Society," Friends Hist. Assoc., *Bull.*, 36 (1947), 19-24. Irvin Goldman discusses Penn's tendency to blur the distinction between the Inner Light and the light of reason in "Deviation toward Ideas of Natural Ethics in the Thought of William Penn," *Philological Quarterly*, 18 (1939), 337-52.

Useful in default of any full-scale treatment of science in the American colonies are three articles by Frederick E. Brasch: "The Royal Society of London and Its Influence upon Scientific Thought in the American Colonies," *Scientific Monthly*, 33 (1931), 336-55, 448-69; "The Newtonian Epoch in the American Colonies (1680-1783)," American Antiquarian Society, *Pro-*

ceedings, New Ser., 49 (1939), 314-32; and "James Logan, a Colonial Mathematical Scholar, and the First Copy of Newton's *Principia* to Arrive in the Colonies," American Phil. Soc., *Proceedings,* 86 (1943), 3-12. A number of important letters of James Logan on scientific subjects appear in Stephen J. Rigaud, ed., *Correspondence of Scientific Men of the Seventeenth Century* (2 vols., Oxford, 1841). Two biographies of scientifically-minded English Quakers shed valuable light upon the place of science in colonial Quaker life: R. Hingston Fox's *Dr. John Fothergill and His Friends* (London, 1919) and Norman Brett-James's *Life of Peter Collinson* (London, n.d.). The researches of I. Bernard Cohen into Franklin's contributions to science have incidentally illuminated the scientific interests of his Quaker contemporaries; see "Benjamin Franklin and the Mysterious 'Dr. Spence,'" Franklin Institute, *Journal,* 235 (1943), 1-25; "Franklin's Experiments on Heat Absorption as a Function of Color," *Isis,* 34 (1943), 404-7; and *Benjamin Franklin's Experiments* (Cambridge, Mass., 1941).

On Logan's experiments with Indian corn and their place in the history of plant hybridization, consult H. F. Roberts, *Plant Hybridization before Mendel* (Princeton, 1929) and Conway Zirkle, *The Beginnings of Plant Hybridization* (Philadelphia, 1935). For the efforts of William Logan and Hugh Roberts to improve the local agriculture, see Rodney H. True, "Some Pre-Revolutionary Agricultural Correspondence," *Agricultural History,* 12 (1938), 107-17; Jared Eliot's *Essays upon Field Husbandry in New England* in the edition of Harry J. Carman and Rexford G. Tugwell (New York, 1934); and Carl R. Woodward, *Ploughs and Politicks: Charles Read of New Jersey and His Notes on Agriculture* (New Brunswick, N. J., 1941). William Logan's manuscript "Memoranda on Husbandry" are in the Library of the United States Department of Agriculture, Washington, D. C. The complicated early history of the American Philosophical Society can be worked out from Peter S. DuPonceau's *Historical Account of the Origin and Formation of the American Philosophical Society* (Philadelphia, 1914), supplemented by the *Early Proceedings of the American Philosophical Society* (Philadelphia, 1884) and especially by Carl Van Doren, "The Beginnings of the American Philosophical Society" in *Proceedings*, 87 (1944), 277-89.

Biographical data concerning early Quaker doctors in Philadelphia can be found in George W. Norris's *Early History of Medicine in Philadelphia* (Philadelphia, 1886) and F. P. Henry, ed., *Standard History of the Medical Profession in Philadelphia* (Chicago, 1897). Dr. Caspar Wistar's "State of Medicine in Philadelphia, from the First Settlement of Pennsylvania to the Year 1762," *Eclectic Repertory and Analytical Review*, 8 (1818), 273-77 has a special value, having been written by a distinguished Philadelphia Quaker doctor only one generation removed from the colonial physicians. William S. Middleton's "Thomas Cadwalader and His Essay," *Annals of Medical History*, third ser., 3 (1941), 101-13 and Samuel X. Radbill's "Lloyd Zachary, 1701-1756," *ibid.*, 1 (1939), 507-18, are excellent sketches of two of the more important Quaker doctors. David J. Davis's "The Quakers and Medicine," Society of Medical History of Chicago, *Bulletin*, 4 (1928), 77-93 fails to throw much light on the problem of why so many Quakers became notable physicians, but Francis R. Packard's "How London and Edinburgh Influenced Medicine in Philadelphia in the Eighteenth Century," *Annals of Medical History*, New Ser., 4 (1932), 219-44, incidentally reveals one of the basic reasons in pointing out that the objection to oaths sent young Quakers out of England to the superior schools at Edinburgh and Leyden for their medical education.

There are three important books on the beginnings of the Pennsylvania Hospital: Benjamin Franklin's *Some Account of the Pennsylvania Hospital: from Its First Rise to the Beginning of the Fifth Month, Called May, 1754* (Philadelphia, 1754); Thomas G. Morton's *History of the Pennsylvania Hospital* (Philadelphia, 1895), containing some exceptionally valuable biographical appendices; and Francis R. Packard's *Some Account of the Pennsylvania Hospital of Philadelphia* (Philadelphia, 1938). William G. Malin's manuscript Sketch of the History of the Medical Library of the Pennsylvania Hospital at the Historical Society of Pennsylvania treats of a collection of books which, like the hospital in which it was housed, owed much to Quaker benefactions. Richard H. Shryock's admirable *Development of Modern Medicine* (Philadelphia, 1936) is essential for an understanding of the interrelationships of medicine and society in our period.

INDEX

COLONIAL AND REVOLUTIONARY AMERICAN HISTORY IN NORTON PAPERBACK

Stephen G. Kurtz and James Hutson (Eds.) *Essays on the American Revolution* 9419

Stanley I. Kutler (Ed.) *Looking for America: The People's History* (2nd Ed.) (Vol. I) 95007

Benjamin W. Labaree *America's Nation-Time: 1607–1789* N821

Benjamin W. Labaree *Patriots and Partisans: The Merchants of Newburyport 1764–1915* N786

James T. Lemon *The Best Poor Man's Country: A Geographical Study of Early Southeastern Pennsylvania* N804

Seymour Martin Lipset *The First New Nation: The United States in Historical and Comparative Perspective* 911

Kenneth Lockridge *Literacy in Colonial New England* 9263

Kenneth Lockridge *A New England Town: The First 100 Years* (2nd Ed.) 95459

John McCardell *The Idea of a Southern Nation: Southern Nationalists and Southern Nationalism, 1830–1860* 95203

Drew R. McCoy *The Elusive Republic: Political Economy in Jeffersonian America* 95239

Forrest McDonald *Alexander Hamilton* 30048

Forrest McDonald *The Presidency of George Washington* N773

Alan Macfarlane *The Family Life of Ralph Josselin, a Seventeenth-Century Clergyman: An Essay in Historical Anthropology* N849

Jackson Turner Main *The Antifederalists: Critics of the Constitution, 1781–1788* N760

Jackson Turner Main *Political Parties Before the Constitution* N718

Edmund S. Morgan *American Slavery—American Freedom: The Ordeal of Colonial Virginia* 9156

Edmund S. Morgan *The Challenge of the American Revolution* 876

Edmund S. Morgan *The Genius of George Washington* N060

Edmund S. Morgan *The Gentle Puritan: A Life of Ezra Stiles, 1727–1795* 30126

Edmund S. Morgan *The Meaning of Independence: John Adams, George Washington, and Thomas Jefferson* 896

Edmund S. Morgan (Ed.) *Prologue to Revolution* 9424

Benjamin Quarles *The Negro in the American Revolution* N674

Charles R. Ritcheson *Aftermath of Revolution: British Policy Toward the United States, 1783–1795* N553

Eric Robson *The American Revolution. In Its Political and Military Aspects, 1763–1783* N382

Charles Royster *A Revolutionary People at War: The Continental Army and American Character, 1775–1782* 95173

Darrett B. Rutman *Winthrop's Boston* N627

Darrett B. Rutman and Anita H. Rutman *A Place in Time: Middlesex County, Virginia, 1650-1750* 30318

Peter Shaw   *The Character of John Adams*   N856

R.C. Simmons   *The American Colonies from Settlement to Independence*   998

Julia Cherry Spruill   *Women's Life and Work in the Southern Colonies*   N662

Thad W. Tate and David L. Ammerman   *The Chesapeake in the Seventeenth Century: Essays on Anglo-American Society and Politics*   956

George B. Tindall   *America: A Narrative History*   Two Vols. 95356/95358

Frederick B. Tolles   *Meeting House and Counting House*   N211

Arthur B. Tourtellot   *Lexington and Concord*   N194

Alden T. Vaughan   *New England Frontier: Puritans and Indians, 1620–1675*   (Rev. Ed.) 950

Wilcomb E. Washburn   *The Governor and the Rebel: A History of Bacon's Rebellion in Virginia*   N645

Gordon S. Wood   *The Creation of the American Republic, 1776–1787*   N644

Peter H. Wood   *Black Majority: Negroes in Colonial South Carolina from 1670 Through the Stono Rebellion*   N777

Hiller B. Zobel   *The Boston Massacre*   N606